THE OUTER BANKS

THE
OUTER
BANKS

ANTHONY
BAILEY

Michael di Capua Books

Farrar, Straus and Giroux

New York

A portion of this book first appeared in The New Yorker

In memory of Peter Tripp

CAPTAIN SCAPETHRIFT:

And is it a pleasant country withal?

CAPTAIN SEAGULL:

As ever the sun shined on; temperate and full of all sorts of excellent viands: wild boar is as common there as our tamest bacon is here; venison as mutton. And then you shall live freely there, without sargeants, or courtiers, or lawyers, or intelligencers.

EASTWARD HO, *Act III, scene II, by George Chapman, Ben Jonson, and John Marston, 1605*

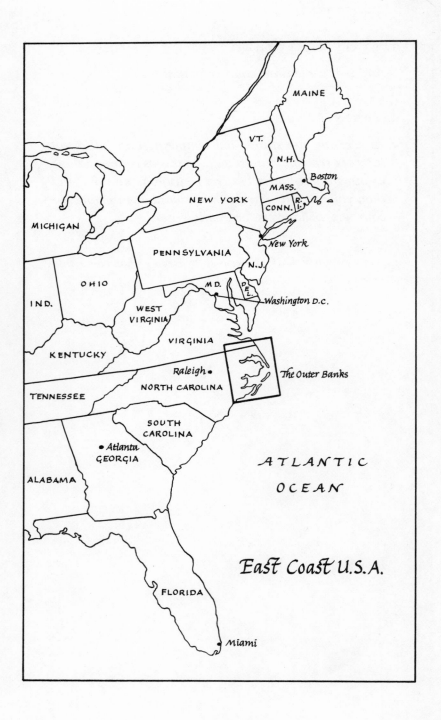

MAINE

VT.

N.H.

MASS.

Boston

NEW YORK

CONN.

R.I.

MICHIGAN

New York

PENNSYLVANIA

N.J.

OHIO

M.D.

DEL.

IND.

WEST VIRGINIA

Washington D.C.

KENTUCKY

VIRGINIA

Raleigh

The Outer Banks

NORTH CAROLINA

TENNESSEE

SOUTH CAROLINA

Atlanta

GEORGIA

ATLANTIC

ALABAMA

OCEAN

East Coast U.S.A.

FLORIDA

Miami

THE OUTER BANKS

What set me going were none of the impulses that traditionally bestir men—at least in books—and cause them to shake off their sedentary lives. No telegram arrived for me, as it did for Carruthers in *The Riddle of the Sands*, asking him to come yachting and duck-shooting in the Baltic. There was no accumulation of angst, ennui, and mal de siècle, of the sort that affected George, Harris, and the narrator of *Three Men in a Boat*, and made them plunge recklessly forth on a Thames camping voyage, together with Montmorency, the dog. Neither a religious urge to go on pilgrimage nor an anti-domestic desire to escape home and family sent me on my way. The hope of fame, fortune, or salvation had little to do with it. Later on, indeed, as I thought about Roder and Robin, Wayne and Nancy Gray, Dave McNaught and David Stick, and a few other men and women I met in the course of this trip and whom—despite the brevity of our acquaintance— I felt I had known for a long time, I wondered whether any motive of mine had a bearing on the matter: perhaps the journey had been predetermined, and these were people I had to meet, living in a place where I had to be. And when, at one moment, the venture became something of an adventure, I felt as if, in my **(4)** modest odyssey, I had put myself in the way of being pummeled and pushed about by more than natural forces—as if the guardians and guides of our fate were deciding that it was time to shake things and me up a bit.

And yet I did get myself to the North Carolina coast, and the term "the Outer Banks" had a part in this. Some names have that sort of effect on me. Valparaiso is one, Montana another—a city and a state to which I have never been, but to which my imagination is drawn. For a long time I have rolled the words "Outer Banks" around in my mind, anticipating what the place to which they were attached might actually turn out to be. "Banks," by itself, is a fairly straightforward way of describing skinny fragments of ocean-battered sand. It is the "Outer"—as in Outer Mongolia—that gives the mystery of the remote and beyond. Together, moreover, the two words imply the existence of a natural rampart protecting something worthwhile. Now and then I opened an atlas and examined what looked like a bent human arm, the hand on hip and elbow stuck out, halfway down the Eastern Seaboard of the United States. When I read that North Carolina was celebrating the four hundredth anniversary of the first English settlement on those shores—in a celebration smartly spread out over three years, from 1984 to 1987—I thought the time had come for an expedition to the Outer Banks. Autumn would surely be a good time for walking the beaches and breathing the salt air.

So one late September morning I found myself at a car rental desk in the airport of Norfolk, Virginia, listening to an unsmiling young woman tell me that my advance request for a smallest size, lowest cost, manual-gearshift car was being met by a thirty-dollar-a-day, air-conditioned, automatic Renault Alliance. For **(5)** a month I had been in New England. In the suitcase I had brought from my home in London I had my walking boots and lightweight rain jacket. In Connecticut I had been offered at a bargain price a rusting yellow four-wheel-drive Subaru station wagon which the owner, an old friend, had been trying to sell without success, despite tempting ads (like, for example, one starting "Looks Terrible, Runs Good," which had appeared every evening for a week in the New London *Day*.) Although the Sube, as it was familiarly called, would have been practical for Banks driving once I got there, I wasn't convinced that it would in fact get there; it had an alarming amount of wheel wobble when it reached 52 mph, and the notion of being tailgated by giant trucks on the Interstates at 50 mph did not appeal. A purchase might also mean a day spent impatiently in the seedy inspection chambers of the Connecticut Motor Vehicle bureaucracy, as the transfer of ownership was made legal. Looking even farther ahead, the Sube might not be the sort of vehicle to create a top-notch impression on the proprietors of hostelries where I wished to stay. Taking note of my means of getting there, they might decide that they were, after all, full up, or that they needed several nights' payment up front. Had I but known it, the Sube would have been at home on the Outer Banks. And had it died there, it would not have been out of place in several rusting-away places on those barrier islands.

The Avis girl—named Modestine, perhaps—would

have been pretty if only she smiled. I described to her my last, unwilling drive in a rental car with automatic shift, and how I had come into JFK closely pursued by a Carey bus and put my foot on the clutch pedal, only there was no clutch pedal but instead an extra-wide brake pedal, and the car came to a sudden, seat-belt-jerking halt, and the Carey bus stopped with a great clamor and shriek an inch behind me, the bus driver ashy white, then fiery red, cursing. But this anecdote didn't amuse her, or move her. "If you want a manual, check in again tomorrow or the next day and we'll see if we've got one," she said, and turned to the next customer, a naval officer. (*He* was smiling.)

(6)

But none of this dampened my starting spirits. The Alliance, moreover, proved to be an unexceptional but reliable vehicle, its French and American characteristics merging in somewhat bland *amitié*; and the only occasion on which it was involved in exciting motoring matters was the fault of its British driver reverting to Anglo-Saxon form and what was, on these shores, the wrong side of the road. (No harm done.) The car was new, and sufficiently uncommon for several people to ask, "How do you like your Renault?"—which led to conversations. This was the case on the Currituck Sound ferry the morning after my arrival in Norfolk, though the man putting the question was the driver of a pickup truck with an attached camper body, the only other vehicle apart from mine on the ferry, the *Governor J. B. Hunt Jr.*, as it sailed from Knotts Island to the village of Currituck. And if he hadn't first talked to me, as I stood at the bulwarks looking out at the calm sound, the low, wooded shores, and the pilings (on which seagulls and cormorants sat) marking the channel through the shallow waters of the sound, I would have struck up a conversation with him and his wife. Their truck had Ohio license plates. Having given him the benefit of my brief Renault renting experience, I asked where they came from in Ohio. "Dayton," he said. This gave us something else in common. I spent four childhood years during World War II, evacuated from England, in Dayton, and still think of that city **(7)** as a distant home. To reinforce the bond, the driver's wife told me that she came from London. Her family had run a pub, the Devereux Arms, near the Temple, just off Fleet Street, and as a child during the Blitz she had been sent out of town to stay with Sussex relatives—though this spot proved to be under the incoming flight path of German raiders.

The camper couple were also heading for the Outer Banks, and we stood together for a while looking out over Currituck Sound, comfortable with our coincidences. They and I had taken the slower, apparently less popular, and slightly more roundabout of two possible routes from Norfolk. A road to the west of Currituck Sound avoids the need to take the ferry—but we agreed we liked ferries, and the view of water. Getting to the Banks was a subject I had pondered at home in London in previous months. I'd looked at maps. I'd written to the tourist bureau in Manteo, the seat of Dare County, which includes a good deal of the Banks. (They stretch for 180 miles, about ten of these in Virginia and the rest extending roughly halfway down the North Carolina coast.) I wanted to start my journey at the top of the Banks and work south to where they end without having to retread my path. The problem was that although the upper Banks seemed to begin quite close to Virginia Beach, adjacent to Norfolk, no road was shown on the map as leading directly to them. Rather, the only continuous road made a sweeping detour westward, then southward, then eastward. The ferry we were on presented an alternative only to the first part of this journey. From the ferry's western terminus one had to drive for an hour to a long causeway and bridge, which would take one, finally, to the Banks at a point about forty-five miles south of where they begin. On North Carolina highway maps, no roads were shown as existing on the top twenty-five miles of the Banks in North Carolina. On Virginia maps, it was the same story, with no roads displayed on the ten miles or so above the Virginia/ North Carolina state line. Did this mean that no roads had been built there?

The Dare County tourist office evaded a simple answer to my written question as to whether I could drive directly from Virginia Beach to the beginning of the Banks by replying that I could get down via Knotts Landing to Currituck—the way I was now taking. Friends of friends with whom I had just spent the night in Virginia Beach had told me that there was indeed a road running south, close to the shore, almost to the North Carolina line, but that much of it went through refuges and state parkland and had been closed to public traffic at the bottom end for several years. Armed guards were mentioned. I might have hiked down along the beach, but I now had the rented car and there would have been problems in getting back to recover it except by walking back, and then driving around, as I was right now. A little later I discovered more about this almost-but-not-quite highway connection along the shore. I realized that the answer to my question to the tourist office couldn't have been made shortly and simply; any evasion, like this detour, was meaningful.

My hosts in Virginia Beach, the Harrisons, had lent me a backpack of a serious kind, suitable for mountaineering and trekking, together with two water bottles, a flashlight, and several Band-Aids left over from a recent camping trip. This would be the foundation of an outfit I thought I would need for camping during my journey, particularly when I reached the less frequented sections of the Banks. Bill Harrison, an energetic young lawyer, also gave me the benefit of his knowledge of the Banks, and of Banks mosquitoes. He quoted an acquaintance, an avid surf fisherman, as saying that you often needed two anchors, one tied to each ankle and planted in the sand, to stop the mosquitoes from carrying you away. Bill's pretty wife, Brien, gave me a big spray can of insect repellent called Deep Woods Off, which she put in the backpack. "I guarantee you'll use all of that," she said. The Harrisons owned a cottage in south Nags Head, a resort spot about halfway down the upper part of the Banks. There, if the cottage wasn't rented out, they spent vacations and long weekends. The cottage was set well back from the beach; another cottage stood between them and the sea. But that waterfront cottage was in danger of being washed away. Eventually the Harrisons would have oceanfront property and a clear view of the beach and the sea. "Even that won't be forever," said Bill. "The ocean keeps on coming. Sooner or later our cottage will go, too."

Before getting here, I have tried to keep my mind clear of any too definite thoughts of what I expect of the Banks. I'm superstitious in that respect, concerned that preconceptions of a detailed kind will have a fatal effect on how things will turn out—and that though, as I have said, I have often let my imagination wander in the direction of the Banks, I've also felt that the very act of imagining a specific landscape may ensure that the landscape, when I get there, is not like that at all. Thinking a place may be beautiful may counterproductively warp it into quite another appearance in reality. Nonsense, but perhaps brought about by the instinct not to cross one's bridges before one gets to them. In any event, driving out on a long, low bridge—named after the Wright Brothers—that spans the shallow waters where Currituck Sound meets Albemarle Sound, I feel the way one does in an aircraft at takeoff: any preconceptions that have insinuated themselves about the trip ahead are about to be abruptly shouldered aside by experience, by observations and perceptions. The land ahead, seen from the west, is like the bridge long and low, little more than an embankment. Several water towers and the undulating crests of trees form the skyline. I know from the maps that the arm shape of the Banks is that of a fairly thin, even wasted limb, but that here, at my point of arrival, is one of the places where the arm shows a little muscle, and there is a distance of several miles from sound to ocean. The bridge comes ashore; the road runs through an apparent suburb with school, bank, real-estate office, chamber of commerce, and visitors' center, all set back from the road and apart from each other by grass and trees.

Only when I stop at the visitors' center to ask about places to stay do I notice that the grass is sparse, the ground sandy; a snake slithers away across the concrete path into the waving grass. From the eastward slope of the sandy hill on which the center stands I can see the blue and shimmering sea, the Atlantic Ocean, for the first time, but it is visible across a junction of several roads, with traffic signals and large directional signs. And when, back in the Alliance, I reach this intersection, I'm presented with an almost urban choice of two roads heading south in parallel about a quarter of a mile apart, one named 158 Bypass, the other 158 Business. I take the first for a few miles before switching to the second. Mild shock and irritated disbelief attend my movements. There is a lot of traffic. The driver of a car behind me honks its horn in annoyance—bemused, I was going too slowly—and pulls out to overtake. I look out at sign after sign, billboard after billboard; utility poles, supermarkets, parking lots, restaurants, motels, housing developments. The Outer Banks! This is Kitty Hawk, then Kill Devil Hills, then

Nags Head—evocative names! Here have been super-imposed mostly grid-patterned developments called Sea Scape, Kitty Dunes Heights, Orville Beach, Virginia Dare Shores, First Flight Village, and Whispering Pines. Along here I see that dogs can be groomed, carpets cleaned, T-shirts printed, crises counseled, helium-filled balloon displays arranged, baby-sitters booked, stocks bought and sold, and hot tubs taken in solitude or company. All consumer life seems to be here. Indeed, 158 Bypass appears little different from the tawdry ribbon development on main roads outside any American city—little different, but in this case, for me, worse for being unexpected. Too late, I think; too late by maybe twenty or thirty years. The Outer Banks! And when I turn left off the Bypass and drive over to 158 Business, to continue south on it, I find the scene similar, though generally older and more ramshackle, to my eye not improved by recent infill of large ocean-front motels, condominiums, and time-share dwellings. Here the speed limit is 35 rather than 45, as it was on the Bypass. The road is narrower. I see my surroundings with less of a blur, though on this warm late-September afternoon a haze of heat and seaside ozone hangs in the air. Sand spills out of house yards and driveways onto the road. My eyes follow the scrappy in-and-out jumble of cottages and motels, signs saying VACANCY or FOR RENT. The sea is to be seen now and then between buildings which crowd upon low, disheveled dunes. The sea is also audible from time to time, the thud of surf on sand breaking through the constant whir and hum of traffic.

And yet should I be this shocked by my first sight of the Banks? The Harrisons had suggested that there had been an explosion in vacation house ownership here in the last decade. I remember now that a friend in New York who had taken his second honeymoon in these parts had used the words "Some of it is a bit honky-tonk." I am acquainted with stretches of the New Hampshire, Rhode Island, and New Jersey coasts, and it is surely obstinate romanticism that has let me maintain to the last moment my illusions about the Outer Banks, my dreams of unspoiled strands. Even a quick browse through the tourist literature handed to me by the visitors' center should have done the awakening trick. A young woman at the center told me that I would be able to work out where I was on the strip going south by mileposts, numbered consecutively by distance from the Wright Memorial Bridge. Not far past milepost 12 I pull into the small, scruffy parking area beside the Old Nags Head Café, whose roadside sign in smaller print also advertises bed and breakfast. As I climb out of the car, my feet descend on cracked concrete, my head rises into the exhaust of a fan from the bar next door. Well, if there's a room available, I'll stay the night before heading north again. Two or three days with friends in Washington may help me over my disappointment.

What a difference a night makes, at least when it has been spent at the Old Nags Head Café Bed and Breakfast. Roder says, pushing his fork into his scrambled eggs, "I'll tell you, some of us around here are waiting for the Big Storm. You know they call this coast the Graveyard of the Atlantic. Well, it may turn out to be the vacation cottage and condo graveyard, too." Robin says to me, "More coffee? More blueberry muffins?" Roder, whose full name is Robert Roderer, Jr., is in his late thirties, stocky, with lank fair hair; he hails—some twelve years back—from Dayton, Ohio (which I take for a cheerful omen), and looks as if he would have been at home on the quarterdeck of an eighteenth-century privateer. Robin Hubbard is a little younger than Roder, courteous, and gently spoken. Robin and Roder live together and are looking after the bed-and-breakfast while the owner, a Mrs. Winslow, is away in Mexico. Robin comes from Currituck County and works as a waitress in a restaurant, curiously or archly called the Tale of a Whale, situated on the causeway that connects the Outer Banks, near milepost 16, with Roanoke Island in the sound behind. Roder is a carpenter and cabinetmaker by trade. Our breakfast is agreeable; after my third blueberry muffin and third cup of coffee, Robin asks if I've made up my mind how long I'll stay. Last evening I told her that I was probably just staying the night. At present I am the establishment's only guest. Today is Thursday. I reply, "I'll stay till Monday, if that's okay." (15)

From the window of my bedroom upstairs, above the café, the scene is still as unkempt as it seemed yesterday, but in the salty morning light, with the surf noise continuous, there is something unintimidatory, almost friendly, about the mess. The Old Nags Head Café is on the west or inshore side of 158 Business, also called the Virginia Dare Trail or, most commonly, the Beach Road, on a plot of sandy ground which extends a hundred yards to 158 Bypass, whose official appellation is the Croatan Highway but is rarely called anything other than the Bypass. The café plus B & B is a two-story structure sided with red-painted asbestos-cement shingles, and much of its ground floor is taken up by the café and delicatessen, which are separately managed. Mrs. Winslow also owns a beach cottage, on the east side of the Beach Road; in this older part of Nags Head the ocean side of the road is almost entirely cottages, sometimes two or three deep. Mrs. Winslow's is alone on its lot, with its front porch nosed against a low dune, and a path alongside providing access to the beach for guests at the B & B. (Most beachfront cottages have signs at the road saying PRIVATE, KEEP OUT, or NO PUBLIC ACCESS.) South of the café is a vacant lot, then some dilapidated houses. West of it, across the Bypass, is a huge sand dune called Jockey's Ridge; with a height of 120 feet, it is the tallest dune on the Banks, or indeed on the Atlantic or Gulf Coast. So immense a pile of gleaming sand, it appears unreal, sloping ponderously down to the Bypass, looking as if it is just about to overwhelm a seedy little amusement park whose centerpiece is a miniature galleon, just to the south of the dune. On the ridge, though the morning is young, many people are flying brightly colored kites and learning how to manage hang gliders. North of the café an outfit called Kitty Hawk Sports sells clothes and equipment for outdoor activities and runs a hang-gliding school called Kitty Hawk Kites. Next door, a bar-and-grill called the Updraft is well placed to catch those who need sustenance of one sort or another after the strains of leisure.

Another factor in my morning mood is the beach. I walk through Mrs. Winslow's sandy yard, around the porch that extends from three sides of the cottage, and through a narrow gap in the dunes—here barely ten feet high and twenty feet from front to back. Then I turn left along the beach, northward. The tide is at half-ebb, so I am able to stride along on firm, damp sand at the water's edge; higher on the beach the sand is dry and loose, too soft for easy walking. Some people are sitting on porches or in beach chairs in front of their cottages. A few fishermen are casting into the surf, and several youths on surfboards are floating some way out, waiting for the right wave. Toward the horizon, a small white blob is a solitary sportfishing boat. I pass at the water's edge a child swimming and being watched by his father, who gives me an affable nod. I make my turnaround point a structure called the Nags Head Fishing Pier—battered-looking, spindly-legged, and wobbly-kneed, though a number of customers obviously feel secure enough to be angling from it. On its landward end the pier has a bar, lunch-eonette, and fishing-tackle store. As I walk back, I observe driftwood, the black egg cases of skate, like dark pouches of ravioli or wonton, sealed as if with a twist at each end, all sorts of shells, and a plastic fork or two. Occasionally in the sand there are deep, cleanly cylindrical holes, where fishermen have planted their rod holders and sat to wait for a fish to bite. The little dunes give the impression of being on the move back from the sea, exposing the cottages like chipped and stained teeth in old gums. **(17)**

The cottages form the majority of the beach build-ings, though there are also some tatty motels and a rather distinguished-looking, large, shingled inn. Some of the cottages are in the very front line, with the dunes or what is left of them drawn back around the cottages; some have no sand protection at all. One or two of the cottages are about to lose their front steps or front porches. A few have recently been set on new pilings, and many look as if they need such a remedy. Bill Harrison had told me that cottage owners who possessed a deep enough lot were able to have their cottages moved back as the sea advanced, but that if they lacked such depth of land, there was nothing they could do. Even some of the newer structures seem perilously close to dunes and sea. Mrs. Winslow's is one of an older group that don't strike me at first as wonderful but that—as I sit on the sand in front of them—seem to have a weathered breeding. It may be that on dampish, hazy mornings they look their best, with their gray-brown shingles, steep roofs with dor-mer windows, wide porches, each building darkly dis-tinct against the sand and brown-green beach grass, without highlights on any of its defects or wrinkles.

Robin has lent me a pamphlet on the Old Nags Head

cottages by Catherine V. Bishir, a North Carolina state archivist and historian. From this I learn that Nags Head became a popular summer resort for the families of merchants, planters, and professional men early in the nineteenth century, when the place's isolation and climate were found to provide a healthy escape from the malaria-prone mainland. The first development was on the Banks next to the sound. People arrived by schooner, transshipped to smaller boats, and landed at little piers from which oxcarts carried the passengers' trunks and boxes of provisions. Daytime amusements were ocean bathing, bowling, riding, and fishing, and in the evenings there were music and dancing at the hotel. The Civil War interrupted these pleasures; a number of buildings were destroyed; and afterward a new hotel and many new cottages were built. The ocean side now became attractive. The first to build there is thought to be Dr. W. G. Pool of Elizabeth City. Finding himself alone on the beach, he bought fifty neighboring acres of oceanfront land from the Midgett family for thirty dollars, and sold lots for a dollar each to his friends; in this way, he soon had the company of thirteen other families. (It was Dr. Pool who achieved a footnote fame by attending in 1869 an old Banker woman who paid him for his services with the portrait of a young lady. The painting, allegedly salvaged from a wreck, was identified by Dr. Pool as a likeness of Theodosia, Aaron Burr's daughter, who had sailed from South Carolina for New York in a small pilot boat and had never been seen again. The painting, according to the old lady, had come from an empty pilot boat which had washed ashore at Kitty Hawk and had been stripped by the Bankers—who believed that pirates must have disposed of the craft's crew and passengers, but had been frightened off before they could plunder the ship.)

(18)

Summer life in Nags Head in the late nineteenth century brought people together in convivial pleasures. The editor of the Elizabeth City *Economist* wrote in 1900 that the resort "intertwined our children in the happy days of childhood. It established new and dear social relations . . . [The children] grew up together and marital relations followed." Although bands played on the voyage out to the Banks, life was simple once there: informal clothes; no running water; no gaslights; no boardwalks; no motorcars until the mid-1920s. The Old Nags Head cottages reflected a desire for holiday simplicity. Many still standing were built by an Elizabeth City contractor, S. J. Twine. The Twine style was for full dormers in a one-and-a-half-story house, and wooden shutters, hinged at the top, that could be propped up to keep out the sun but let in the sea breeze. The railings of the porches provided the backs for what were called "lean-out benches." Kitchens were generally in a separate shed at the rear. Under the cottages, latticework screens were fixed between the foundation pilings to keep out wandering cows and pigs, seeking shade but "attended by fleas and flies." Parts of the region between sea and sound were wooded; other parts had been cleared for farming. In 1931, two brothers recalled that as boys they had helped their father cultivate "several acres of corn, potatoes, and garden vegetables at a point which is now underneath Jockey's Ridge."

In the afternoon, dodging the traffic on the Bypass, I walk over to the great dune. Jockey's Ridge like most dunes has its least precipitous flank facing the prevailing winds, which here blow from offshore, and most strongly from the northeast; but the ascent is steep nevertheless. The sand is warm and my shoes are soon full of it. I duck under the lines of kites that are being

(19)

flown. Lifting my knees high, I make it to the top. Several other ridges or rows of dunes, almost as high as this, Saharan in their sun-baked grandeur, rise immediately to the west and northwest. I scrunch across the summit of Jockey's Ridge toward a group of people having a hang-gliding lesson. The view from up here is all-around: to the west the sound, and to the east, over roads and businesses and cottages, the sea. And the Banks stretching north and south, a long thin strand. All is linear here; the mileposts make sense. I sit down close enough to the six students and their instructor to catch the drift of what passes between them. Three women and two men in their twenties and thirties sit wearing crash helmets, while a few yards beneath them another man, also helmeted, holds up a hang glider. The instructor, a young man, is showing him where to grip the frame below the nylon-covered wing, which is particolored like the spinnaker of a yacht. The instructor kicks up some sand, apparently so that he can judge the strength and direction of the breeze—it seems fairly light. Then he gives the student a downhill shove, and the man runs down the slope and hurls himself courageously forward, assuming a prone position in the harness under the wing. His track shoes are four or five feet off the ground; his arms are stretched out in front of him, hands gripping the frame. The bright glider glides. Then, suddenly, it seems to stall; it sinks. There is a flurry of sand as the student pilot hits the downward slope—a hard belly flop. He has flown about twenty yards. Pretty disappointing, I think, having worried that he might glide high and then down into the Bypass traffic. (I remember my first run on skis down the nursery slopes at St. Anton, in Austria, where the Arlberg Orient Express daily passed along the tracks at the foot of the

hill, causing me considerable anxiety as to how I would
avoid colliding with it, only to find that in practice I
arely got a quarter of the way down the slope without
ng head over heels or collapsing spread-eagled.)
ever, the other members of the class are by no
unimpressed; they give the trainee pilot a little
f applause. When I ask them whether the pro-
oyable and not terrifying, they unanimously
d it. One points out to me the door in the
establishment where banners are flying,
dieval tower beside the field for jousts
nd where I must enter to sign up for
s. I say I'll certainly think about it. I
d sailor's suspicion of aerial move-
en meant to fly, God would have
nd wings.

v two other people, a young
ral others come in for take-
counter. The prime rib is
meat—slightly under-
passable Chablis since
et Key lime pie for
and make a moving
ling. I sit and read
v custom is ap-
Banks at the
ietor and my
er the sum-
t it would
afé front
of the
living
een
ys

Roder. Robin adds, "We're wondering how Liz Winslow is."

(22) Lying in bed, with my ceiling fan revolving at minimum speed, the window half open to let in the night
air, and the blind swaying gently in and out, I listen
to the surf crash against the sand, crash, pause, and
crash again. The effect of this sound—eternal as long
as land and sea last—is to make me consider not only
my own mortality but what a frail, impermanent piece
of land I find myself on. Thank God there are no
earthquakes here!

At breakfast Robin says that if I want to see what much of the Banks looked like centuries ago I should visit the Nags Head Woods, a chunk of coastal maritime forest, marshes, and dunes that have been preserved on the edge of Roanoke Sound, north of Jockey's Ridge. Perhaps she wants me to appreciate that it isn't all environmental and ecological savagery in these parts. And though I have a resistance to conservation combined with education when they try to tell me something that may be good for me, I also have a policy when traveling of remaining open to suggestion. I accept another slice of bacon and tell her I'll follow her advice.

I drive up the Bypass for a mile or so, turn off along a paved road lined with suburban houses, and then take a winding dirt track through wooded, undeveloped land. In the parking lot of the preserve's visitors' center I park alongside the only other vehicle there, a new top-of-the-line pickup truck with lots of chrome trim and Tennessee license plates. A girl sits behind the wheel, two young men on the front seat beside her. She smiles and calls over to me, "Sir—do you have the time?" Sir, slightly abashed by this appellation, does, and tells her; it is a minute or two before nine; **(24)** we are apparently early. She goes on talking with her companions. The open windows of our vehicles allow me to hear that the young man in the middle is about to start work at the preserve. I've already got the impression that the Banks attract young, nomadic people who come and perhaps do several jobs at a time for a season or two. (Later, reading David Stick's history of the Outer Banks, I learn that this has been so for a long time. The inaccessibility of the Banks also made the area a good refuge for those evading the law and for runaways from family or indentured servitude.) In the Tennessee pickup, the preserve recruit in the middle does most of the listening, while his two friends talk on somewhat discordant themes. The young woman is planning a surprise birthday party for a male friend and asking for help in arranging it. The young man next to the nearside window counters this with a reminiscence of time he has recently spent in jail. "They gave us clean sheets, man, they gave us all clean sheets, which I thought was real nice, but this white transvestite, man, he cut up his sheet and turned it into a dress, man, and those guards, they didn't know what to make of that." The girl perhaps doesn't either, for she persists with her party organizing, at last capturing the full attention of the recent inmate, who says to her, with a hint of jealousy, "Girl, you must be in love!"

The surrounding woods have an old, long-planted air, damp, deep in time. But when the administrative assistant of the preserve turns up—a pert and com-

petent young woman in her mid-twenties named René
Walker—and opens the office, she tells me that Run
Hill, a dune to the north of the woods, is constantly
encroaching on the preserve, moving southwest at
some ten feet a year. On the western edge of the woods,
marsh is gradually extending into Roanoke Sound. **(25)**
"There's nothing like this anywhere on earth," she
says proudly. "It's a unique ecosystem. Plants grow
here of both northern and southern species, encouraged by the mixture offshore of warm and cold ocean
currents. Some, like woolly beach heather, are at the
limits of their range. Some of our trees are between
three hundred and five hundred years old. We've got
rare aquatic plants—the water violet, for instance—
and several endangered birds, like the red-shouldered
hawk, and a rare reptile, the yellow-lipped snake. Algonquian Indians made seasonal camps here starting
three thousand years ago. Verrazano was the first European to record his observations of this part of the
coast, when he sailed along here in 1524. White settlers began to move in permanently in the 1700s. Now
the woods form a much needed natural refuge in an
area of rapid development. This is the old normality—
the way the Banks were before lumbering denuded
them."

Members of Dare County garden clubs were prime
movers in saving the Nags Head Woods when, in the
mid-1970s, roads advanced in this direction and building lots were laid out. Now the woods are managed
by the North Carolina chapter of the Nature Conservancy, a national nonprofit organization that owns
much of the land and looks after another part that has
been leased to it by the town of Nags Head—in all,
665 acres. The preserve gets much local support. Many
of the older families in the area have given or sold land

to it; funds are raised by supporters, local firms, and
the Jaycees, with sponsored runs and oyster roasts.
Schools make visits. Scientists come and do research—
for example, in groundwater geology, a study given
urgency by Nags Head's use of water from ponds in
(26) the woods, altering the water table and affecting plant
life.

I walk along one of the trails through the woods,
keeping my eyes open for yellow-lipped snakes and
water violets. I have the preserve's pamphlet in hand.
This means that instead of strolling in bemused self-
satisfaction, ignorant of the wildlife and thinking as I
do when walking of an immense haphazardly associ-
ated variety of things, past, present, and future, I feel
bound—while following the discreet blue arrows
marking the trail—to pause and consult the pamphlet,
to examine the tree in front of me to see if this is the
large sweet gum referred to ("able to live in seasonally
flooded lowlands") or a red maple (which is said to
prefer a slightly higher elevation). The drumming
sound I can hear I assume is being made by a woodpecker. The dark green leaves carpeting the ground
are those of the partridge berry, a plant which needs
the dense shade of the woods. Some trees with shallow
roots have fallen, easy prey to storm winds; some of
their stricken trunks have cavities, rotted out or wood-
pecked, in which dwell raccoons or squirrels, while
insects thrive in the exposed roots. However, the woods
are sheltered from ocean winds and the salt they bear
by an eastern ridge of dunes; there is no sense back
here of beach or Bypass. On a little roadway, once
intended as access to a proposed housing development,
I duck under a twenty-foot-long spiderweb spanning
the road from a tree to a shrub. I look for the tracks
of deer, raccoons, rabbits, and mice, which the pam-

phlet says may be seen in sandy parts of the road, but I don't see them. On a pond, though, fish as suggested are breaking the surface in search of edibles. A frog plops into the water as I approach. And as prompted I notice a double-trunked tree, many of its boughs married together. When I come into an open glade **(27)** and am greeted by a sudden burst of sunlight, I react with a loud, impromptu sneeze.

I drop into the preserve's visitors' center to thank René Walker before leaving. She is talking with a man in his mid-thirties, who introduces himself as Dave McNaught; he has an elderly Airedale with him. He asks where I am going on the Banks. I sketch my plans very roughly, my hopes of seeing the Banks from top to toe, with some walking and perhaps some camping later on. McNaught, who is doing volunteer work at the preserve, expresses interest in hiking and camping and offers to be of help if I need it. René Walker says that if I want to see the conflict between the forces of development and conservation at their most acute, I should get myself up to the very northern end of Currituck Banks the following afternoon, to a public meeting at Carova firehouse. It seems that the Nature Conservancy has recently turned over two large parcels of land up there to the Fish and Wildlife Service, which has plans to limit access for the residents of the area. Many of the residents are hopping mad. René mentions a curfew and gives me the names of some people to see, including a man whose anti-government activities have got him into jail.

The Bypass has a McDonald's, where I lunch. I can't decide whether I am disappointed by finding it here, making no concessions to its Banks surroundings other than a frosted-glass partition decorated with a scene suggestive of dunes and sea, or whether I am reassured by the confident uniformity of the enterprise, which could in other respects be in Dubuque, Detroit, or Doncaster, England.

(28) Replete with a Big Mac, which needs relish and ketchup to give it taste, and a syrupy apple turnover, I visit the Galleon Esplanade, a shopping center with hints of the Alhambra or maybe the Alamo, and in the Harbor Lights Bookstore find two books: *The Outer Banks of North Carolina*, a history by David Stick, and *From Currituck to Calabash: Living with North Carolina's Barrier Islands*, by four geologists, Orrin H. Pilkey, Jr., William J. Neal, Orrin H. Pilkey, Sr., and Stanley R. Riggs. I spend the rest of the afternoon back at the B & B reading these works and begin to feel I know more about the sandbanks which the Algonquian Indians, Verrazano, English colonists, and the McDonald chain have taken an interest in. I then sit for a while on the beach, watching the waves roll in and trying to imagine this coastline some fifteen thousand years ago, when the surface of the sea was about 250 feet lower and the coast was roughly fifty miles farther out than it is now. A forest once stretched out in front of me across what is now the continental shelf and ended at the edge of the sea with a ridge of sand dunes. But as the last ice age ended, as the glaciers melted and the sea rose, the dune ridge was breached and a lagoon or sound formed behind it, flooding the forest. And as this process continued, the dunes—now islands—migrated slowly westward. The process, in fact, still goes on, the sea rising about one foot a century, the Banks getting closer to the mainland by up to ten feet a year. Some of the oyster, clam, and snail shells on the beach beside me once lived in the sound, behind the Banks. The shells are evident here because the Banks passed over them, exposing what was once the bottom of the sounds to the breaking waves of the sea.

There are other dynamic elements in this process. Inlets form and disappear. Particularly in storms, they open in one place, close in another. They should really be called outlets, because less water comes in through them from the sea than goes out in the flow of water from the sounds, filled both by ocean tides and the runoff from mainland rivers. The barrier islands and long peninsulas widen or narrow, affected by how they face the offshore winds and currents, the amount of sand deposited by the overwash of storms, and the way dunes are created. Once the dunes are molded large enough by the wind, they can become attractions in themselves, getting bigger and bigger, joining up with other dunes in dune fields, and sometimes not just moving downwind but oscillating back and forth. Present thinking is that beaches provide their own best protection; no ways have yet been found of ensuring them against the changes caused by winds, currents, waves, and rising sea.

On the Banks, as the Nags Head Woods show, all sorts of plants and vegetation can thrive despite the prevailing sandiness. The sand contains plenty of nutrient minerals, left there after rain has washed away much of the salt and forced down the underlying salt water beneath a basin of fresh water. David Stick writes: "Seeds, carried in the air, or transported by gulls or shore birds, begin to sprout, and the grasses grow and anchor in the sand. Then bushes and trees take root, until finally, as was the case when white men first viewed the Banks, a lush growth of cedar, pine, and live oak, mingled with dense grape vines, covers much of what was once a bare sand beach." The presence of man hasn't made for the stability of the Banks, since settlers have axed the trees for house and ship timber and for firewood. Their cattle have overgrazed the vegetation. In recent times, people have begun to build along the ocean side of the Banks, sometimes **(30)** actually in and on the dunes, as if sand and sea were at some point of stasis, which of course they aren't.

I walk back along the beach from where I've been sitting and turn through the diminutive dunes by the Winslow cottage. In the front yard of the B & B, I use the hose on my feet: the darker sand sticks tenaciously and takes a lot of washing off. I wonder about the route by which it will find its way back to the immediate seaside again.

Within, Roder is sitting with a copy of *Wooden Boat*, a magazine—almost a cult organ—for those interested in vessels constructed of that God-made material. So we discover that we not only have Dayton in common. I own a 22-foot-plus-bowsprit gaff cutter, built in the early 1930s of pitch-pine planking on oak ribs. Roder tells me that he is restoring a big 1950s mahogany-hulled Chris-Craft; she is hauled out in a boatyard on Roanoke Island, where he has just replanked her decks in teak. We discuss the merits of finishing the bright-work in conventional varnish, polyurethane varnish, or Deks-Olje, a Norwegian product derived from fish oils. Robin—who has undoubtedly heard this sort of conversation before—says that television has continued to show scenes of terrible devastation in Mexico City. However, a long-distance operator in Texas has called to check that Mrs. Winslow possesses this telephone number, and they therefore assume that she must be all right, having made a call and charged it here. Liz Winslow was supposed to have arrived in Nags Head several days ago from her home in San Miguel, which Robin says is about three hours' drive north of Mexico City and six hours south of the U.S. border. Roder, still on wood, tells me about the cabinet shop he and two friends are hoping to set up. For several years he worked on fishing boats out of Wanchese, on Roanoke Island, but the living was precarious, financially and otherwise. The Wanchese boats have access to the ocean fishing grounds by way of Oregon Inlet, which Roder tells me is constantly shoaling. Ten feet is the maximum safe draft, and even then, if a boat is coming in laden, it will sometimes bounce between waves on the bottom. In the last few years several boats have been stranded and lost in the inlet. Roder has turned to the other major form of winter employment on the Banks—house building. The year-round population of the Banks is expected to double in the next five years. Yet even though this growth provides employment and a livelihood, it isn't entirely welcomed by those who have been here for some time. "We liked it the way it was," says Robin. "Quieter winters, fewer people." Roder says, "I've been offered a big contract for finishing kitchens." He takes a sip of beer. But then, instead of telling me about the kitchens, he reverts to a technique for cold-molding wood in hull construction, prompted by what he was reading in *Wooden Boat*.

Saturday morning, and I drive northward up the Banks. Getting all the way to Carova, almost on the Virginia line, isn't going to be straightforward; the paved road apparently runs out at Corolla with fourteen miles to go, from which point four-wheel drive is needed. North of the Wright Memorial Bridge the Banks begin to narrow. Sound and sea are often both visible from the road. Development is less dense and of a different character. First comes the entirely residential community of Southern Shores, many of whose well-spaced homes have a year-round look. Next is the village of Duck, and for a mile or so the road twists through little hills, trees are ample and lawns well grassed, and there is an English southern-county sense of dingles and dales. The terrain remains bumpy in the following stage, but the hills are once again sandy, sometimes bare dunes which in many cases have new summer houses on them, standing on pilings. Duck, it seems, has established a trend; the new developments promote themselves with similar ornithological names, such as Snow Geese Dunes, Sea Tern, and Sanderling, and indeed the clusters of still raw shingled houses look like small flocks of gulls perched on the dunes, facing hungrily this way and that. But after a while the tide of construction begins to falter, the **(33)** dunes are increasingly still bare except for scrub. I pass through an Audubon sanctuary called Pine Island, a home for real birds with a name borrowed from an adjacent fragment of marshland in Currituck Sound. Here, roughly where the Banks were once parted by Caffey's Inlet, which opened in the 1790s and closed in the early 1800s, and close to where the line dividing Currituck and Dare Counties crosses the Banks, the road passes through an open gate. Robin has told me that this portal to the northern Banks was guarded until a year ago, October 1984, and only owners of Currituck Banks property and expected visitors were allowed through. Now Currituck County—most of whose 11,000 residents live on the mainland, west of Currituck Sound—has taken over the maintenance of the road, with state help, and the general public has access. This is the point at which, on the North Carolina road map I'd consulted in London, the road was shown as coming to a compete halt, with terra incognita thereafter.

I know that Corolla is close at hand when I see a lighthouse. Cautiously built in 1875 nearer to sound than ocean, it has served to mark the presence of the Banks particularly for southbound ships, which tended to keep close inshore to dodge the north-flowing Gulf Stream. Each lighthouse on the Banks has not only a distinctive light signal but an individual form of decoration, to enable mariners to identify it in daylight. The Corolla lighthouse has been left largely unpainted; its rough brick tower rises 150 feet. Standing nearby is the only other major structure in these parts, a three-story many-gabled mansion that was once the hunting lodge of the Whale Head Gun Club—one of the numerous gun clubs that until recent times owned **(34)** much of Currituck Banks. (The lodge was built in 1922 by Edward Knight, a Philadelphia magnate, who is said to have bought the land and club after unsuccessfully trying to get his wife admitted as a member.) After several inlets like Caffey's closed during the nineteenth century, Currituck Sound waters became fresher, new vegetation grew, and great quantities of duck and geese flew in; many of the local Bankers worked as guides for those who came wildfowling. From the days of first settlement, the area has had a reputation—exceeding that of other parts of the Banks—of attracting those who wanted remoteness from society and proximity to nature. Runaway slaves, criminals, and shipwreckers were among those who dwelt here. The Virginian author William Byrd in 1728 described a Currituck Banks "Marooner" who cohabited with a "wanton female," subsisting on oysters and milk, their bodies covered only by the length of their natural hair.

Corolla's town center is still in embryo: a single two-story building that stands behind some gas pumps and is divided into several units. The post office is at one end, the Kay Cole Realty office at the other, with a small general store and three contractors' offices between. In the post office, the solitary worker is the postmaster, Norris Austin, who tells me he has been postmaster for twenty-eight years—since he was twenty. Mr. Austin says that the total number of year-round residents here isn't much more than 150, but his post office is busier and busier with the arrival of more tourists and seasonal inhabitants—this is despite the difficulties of access. As if cued by this remark, a stranger enters, buys some stamps, and asks if he can drive on north from here into Virginia. "No, you can't," says Mr. Austin. "If you've got four-wheel drive, you can get up the beach to Carova, though. And you'll (35) find a meeting at the firehouse there this afternoon, which is all about why you can't drive any farther." The man expresses his thanks, but says he'll go back down the Banks and across the Wright Bridge again. Mr. Austin suggests that I drop in one afternoon after two o'clock, when business slacks off, for a longer talk.

Phyllis Cole drives me north to the meeting. The Alliance is not equipped for the terrain above Corolla, and Phyllis has a big Jeep station wagon which is. The paved road ends at the dunes, where several new houses are going up in a section called Ocean Hill. Phyllis engages four-wheel drive, steers the Jeep up a wooden ramp through the dunes and onto the beach, and bears hard left. The tide is not far out; the beach is narrow, and Phyllis—an attractively plump young woman in lavender slacks and shirt—is forced to drive in the fine, loose sand at the foot of the dunes. Occasionally we jounce past another four-wheel-drive vehicle parked by the water's edge, its passengers disembarked and casting into the surf; waves of greeting are exchanged as between passing vessels. Now and then the Jeep slithers in deep ruts, the wheels spin, and Phyllis turns the steering wheel this way and that to stay on course. We are going a steady 25 miles per hour. A hot, oily, engine-room smell rises from the transmission. It appears that we are taking the main road to the top end of the Currituck Banks.

Phyllis tells me that she has been working with her mother, Kay Cole, in the real-estate business for the last few years. She was a history major at college and worked briefly in a bookstore. She prefaces most answers to questions from me with "Yes, sir" and "No, sir," and from what she tells me, the situation on this part of the Currituck Banks unfolds roughly in this way:

(36)

For one reason or another, the gun clubs began to sell off their large landholdings in the late 1960s. Some felt that dune restoration work by the Civilian Conservation Corps in the thirties had affected wildfowl, which were coming in smaller numbers. Various developers bought the land, and much had been sold off in small plots by 1974 to people planning to build for the most part vacation homes. A plan with some two thousand lots was proposed for Carova, the northernmost development, and a small number of houses and cottages were built.

There had been talk until this time of a highway south from Norfolk and Virginia Beach to the Banks, joining the large metropolitan area directly to the Carolina coast. This seemed the logical contemporary move. Although the section of Banks in Virginia was already taken up by False Cape State Park and Back Bay National Wildlife Refuge, a road ran down through these and met a track which ran just behind the dunes in Currituck County. However, unless the tide was high—as it is twice every twenty-four hours—and the weather bad, most people preferred to drive along the beach between Corolla and the state line, and for that matter continue up the beach in Virginia to the first settlement of Sandbridge, not far from Virginia Beach. Anyone on the Currituck Banks who wanted to shop in Virginia, or who for reasons of work went there daily, had an interesting twenty-five-mile drive, much of it on beaches.

But just as the development bandwagon was getting under way, a contrary force made itself felt. Some people did not want a continuous highway along the Banks. In 1974 the U.S. Fish and Wildlife Service cut off vehicle access between north and south by prohibiting motor traffic through the Back Bay National Wildlife Refuge and along the adjacent beach. Residents of the Currituck Banks who wanted to go to Virginia had either to drive the long way around, via the Wright Bridge, or else travel by private boat across Currituck Sound to Knotts Island—a route that is sometimes too shallow for passage. Some residents fought back, and some took the fight to court. In 1976 a permit system was introduced, whereby, first for a fee and then without charge, permanent residents of the Currituck Banks and a few long-standing holders of seasonal property were allowed north-south access at certain hours. Presently there are less than fifty such permits. The permits cannot be transferred from one person to another and are declining in number as holders die or move away. At this time the hours of access are from 5 a.m. to midnight, an arrangement that the Currituck Bankers regard as a curfew, constraining their traditional rights of movement.

Access to the north of Carova isn't the only problem. In recent years, two of the big former gun-club tracts between Carova and Corolla—Swan Island and Monkey Island—have been acquired by the Nature Conservancy; both properties, despite their names, are sections of the Currituck Banks that extend across the Banks from sea to sound. Recently these tracts were transferred by the Nature Conservancy to the Fish and Wildlife Service to form a new 6,000-acre Currituck National Wildlife Refuge for such birds as the whistling swan, which winters here. (From what Phyllis tells me, and what I learn later from a staunch conservationist, it seems that during the Carter Administration proposals for acquiring the entire Currituck Banks for Fish and Wildlife, except for a pocket by the Corolla lighthouse, very nearly got through before **(38)** time ran out and Reagan came in. In any event, in 1983 Congress authorized the purchase of the Nature Conservancy lands.) In August of 1985, the Fish and Wildlife Service announced that travel along the Banks through the new refuge would be limited to the beach, except in emergency conditions, such as those created by hurricane or fire, when use of the old, behind-the-dunes sand track (known as the Pole Road because of the skimpy utility poles placed along it) would be allowed. Many Currituck Bankers had been hoping that this track would eventually be turned into a decent road by their county, which had opposed the federal acquisition of the Nature Conservancy land unless an easement was granted for such a road. Now, in nonemergency times, they would have no right to go through the refuge except by the beach, and they perceived this as an attempt by the government to discourage their presence and reduce the value of their properties, leading eventually to federal condemnation and takeover of their land.

Phyllis says that of the two thousand lots planned for Carova, only a hundred or so have been "improved"—that is, built on; another 150 buildings have been erected south of Carova but north of the refuge. Roughly sixty families live year-round on the Currituck Banks; the rest are seasonal residents. Phyllis and her mother, being in real estate, are naturally annoyed that their business opportunities have been, as they see it, limited by government interference. They believe, according to Phyllis, that rapid and unthinking de-

velopment of the Currituck Banks is in any event con-
strained these days by the fact that, for the last five
years or so, no federal flood insurance has been ob-
tainable on properties here, which has meant, generally speaking, no mortgages on them, too. Moreover,
new state regulations for coastal management are intended to prevent building within the dunes and immediately behind them, and rules on sewage disposal
in septic tanks make it impossible to build on many
so-called building lots. Despite this, one new building
at North Swan Beach pokes its raw shingles to the very
front of the dune line. When I ask Phyllis how this
came to be, she says, "Politics. Pull."

The Jeep slows down. Phyllis brings it to a halt close
to a row of dark wooden pilings, each of telephone-
pole thickness, planted deep in the sand and linked
by thick wire cables. It is a fence, roughly eight feet
high, which runs in one direction into the dunes and
in the other out into the water, past the low-tide mark.
It was put up early in 1984, says Phyllis. It reminds
me of barriers seen on the border between East and
West Germany. There is a locked gate—out of sight a
little way inland—to which permit holders are allowed
a key. The permit, a plastic card, must be shown to
the guard at another gate at the north end of Back
Bay Refuge. In front of us on the cable-and-piling
barrier a sign says NO MOTOR VEHICLES BEYOND
THIS POINT EXCEPT BY PERMIT. This is the North
Carolina/Virginia state line.

In the unfinished firehouse of the Carova Beach volunteer fire department, several hundred people are
crammed. The meeting has been called by the Fish
and Wildlife Service to talk about the new restrictions
and—I imagine—to defuse hostility. The hostility, like

a heat haze, is just about visible. The firehouse is really a large new shed, with a concrete floor, double doors wide open—a brush truck, the only apparent fire-fighting equipment, has been left outside. Most people have brought their own folding chairs to sit on, and those **(40)** who have not stand next to the walls, perch on boxes, or lean against bales of insulation that are waiting to be installed. For most, dress of the day is T-shirts and shorts. Many are using Fish and Wildlife leaflets as fans. Several men have radio paging systems clipped to their belts. Parked nearby are the four-wheel-drive trucks and cars or the fat-tired three- and four-wheeled motorcycles known as all-terrain vehicles, in and on which most of the audience has arrived. Despite the up-to-dateness of this mobile gadgetry, the Carova residences on the surrounding bumpy, sandy terrain look more like shanties composed of old containers, trailers, and driftwood, set on stilts, than they do "improved properties." On one inner wall of the firehouse a long map has been pinned, showing the Currituck County development plan for the upper Banks with its two-thousand-some lots. Underneath this graphic display is a trestle table, behind which sit two men, facing the Currituck Bankers and wearing the brown trousers and fawn shirt uniform of the U.S. Fish and Wildlife Service.

One of them, a bearded man in his thirties, introduces himself to everyone as Jack Taylor, manager of the Currituck National Wildlife Refuge. His friendly smile and patient air do not produce any noticeable amicable response from those assembled at the meeting. Taylor says that Fish and Wildlife has been listening to expressions of local concern and is now considering them in the light of refuge objectives, which largely consist of preserving wildlife and wild lands. He believes Fish and Wildlife has made a fair offer in proposing that residents' vehicles be allowed to drive along the sand trail behind the dunes when, in emergency conditions, the beach can't be used. He wants to stress that he and his colleague, Travis McDaniel from Fish and Wildlife's Atlanta office, are here to listen. **(41)**

And listen they do, with stoic restraint, as one Currituck Banker after another stands up to lambaste the entire federal hierarchy—the government, the Department of the Interior, Fish and Wildlife, and all their minions. The first man on his feet says that Interior is clearly set on buying up the Outer Banks, and he doesn't believe Jack Taylor's claim of wanting to be a good neighbor. "We are out here to enjoy our property, but unless there is a permanent easement for a proper road, we may not be able to reach our property or leave it in bad weather at high water." One woman says they are not anti-wildlife—they are here because they love nature—but they love their homes, too. And a public right-of-way is needed, not just access for owners. "What about this lady here in the real-estate business?" says a matron in green Bermuda shorts, pointing to Kay Cole, Phyllis's good-looking mother, who is wearing a peach-colored short-sleeved jumpsuit. "How's she going to get in to look at houses?" Another woman supposes that Fish and Wildlife will be bringing in armed guards, as they have up in Back Bay. McDaniel, older than Taylor, mustached, wearing glasses, remarks quietly that Fish and Wildlife would like to get back to the status quo ante bellum, with neither gates nor guards; but there are covenants in the deeds transferring the land from the Nature Conservancy which make public access out of the question. He doesn't appear to be unhappy that these covenants exist. Various speakers, cheered on by applause and other sounds of approval, declare that the beach often becomes impassable in bad weather. Northeasters are mentioned. Mother Nature is given credit for frequent demonstrations of great power, which might not, however, fit the Fish and Wildlife definition of emergency conditions. The beach, one man says, is more fragile than the land behind the dunes: "The government should get the veehickles off the beach altogether and let them drive back of the dunes." Traditional use of the Pole Road is discussed—the Civilian Conservation Corps improved it; school buses once used it. "You people at Fish and Wildlife have chopped away at us. We've always gone to the stores and worked in Virginia. We want to be able to get to Corolla to the bookmobile, which comes once a month, even if it is high water. We don't trust you. You're out to take our property. Yes you are. We want legislation. Why are you spending all this federal money on new refuges when there's a high deficit?"

Several men in the front row of seats have until now been keeping their heads down, perhaps waiting to see what sort of atmosphere or consensus developed. One, a senatorial staff member from Washington, D.C., says he is speaking on behalf of the two North Carolina senators (neither of whom is here): legislation to obtain a public road is not the best route. Look at the fate of legislation for improving Oregon Inlet, which has been stuck in committee for several years. But he wants everyone "down here" to know that he spent vacations in Nags Head as a child and that the senators want to help "you all" on this issue. "We're not going to drop the ball on this," he says, to a thoroughly skeptical silence.

Phyllis has pointed out for me two local men who

are Currituck County commissioners. (The county is governed by an elected board of five commissioners and a paid manager.) One of the two Outer Banks commissioners, Ernie Bowden, a contractor and livestock farmer, is leaning against the wall behind Taylor and McDaniel, wearing a Stetson hat and alligator boots, and keeping what Phyllis thinks is an untypical silence. Bowden has been in serious trouble with the access restrictions and was in fact elected to the board after serving a jail sentence for driving through Back Bay Refuge after curfew. The other commissioner, whose name is Barry Nelms, speaks: Currituck County has always been in favor of a permanent right-of-way behind the dunes. All these streets on the Carova plan were laid out with that in mind. On the Banks south of the new wildlife refuge, lots are worth $150,000— up here, much much less. The county is losing badly needed tax revenues on the devalued and unimproved property up here.

As the meeting proceeds, several people make inordinately long statements; several shout and storm. But there are remarkably few nuts—of the sort who attend public meetings in my part of London—who want to vent their spleen for other causes in a handy forum. Taylor and McDaniel from time to time interpose the Fish and Wildlife point of view and say that they welcome these expressions of opinion—though clearly they believe that any improvement in public access on the Currituck Banks will lead to more development, and that this won't be compatible with refuge objectives. The people expressing the opinions don't seem to have any trust that such expression will have effect. Taylor and McDaniel may be decent guys but they represent Big Government. The Department of the Interior owns 148 miles—nearly half—

of the North Carolina coastline, and it is after the rest. The federal government already owns more than a third of the entire United States.

Some people, apparently thinking they have heard some of this before, begin to drift away. Taylor and McDaniel are still stolidly sitting there, though not looking quite so patient. I find myself in a departing group that includes Kay Cole, Phyllis's mother. It is a bit like the end of a party, when no one wants to go home. What are we going to do now? A decision is arrived at, and Kay drives me through the sandy hills to Ernie Bowden's house, not far away. It is a modern wooden house on pilings, with an ocean view over the seafront dunes. In the big living-room-cum-kitchen, ladies I have seen at the firehouse serve beer and soft drinks, and people release their aggrieved yet sometimes gleeful feelings: "It was always going to turn out that way." "I told you so—they've got their minds made up." Yet most seem glad of the chance they've had to speak their minds.

Our host remains absent; it seems that he is out with his cattle. So we go to look for him, a small parade again of four-wheel-drive pickups, Jeeps, and noisy all-terrain vehicles, generally referred to as ATVs. South along the sub-Saharan Pole Road for a way and then westward into an extensive area of lean-looking pastureland, with narrow dredged canals and skinny creeks running into Currituck Sound. Kay Cole tells me that Ernie Bowden, who also has a construction and pile-driving business, is the last remaining farmer on the Banks north of Corolla. He appears at this moment, galloping across the savannah in pursuit of a small herd of cattle. In his Stetson and boots, he prompts a thought of John Wayne, though, closer at hand, his features seem more like those of James Cagney. A bunch of what look to me like Charolais are driven into the corner of a field near where we are standing, and cajoled through a gate into the next pasture. Mr. Bowden then makes another circuit to round up and move from field to field five bison—five American buffalo! What on earth are they doing here, so far **(45)** from the Great Plains? When he has in turn cornered the buffalo—shaggy beasts, two of whom flounder in and out of a drainage ditch in perhaps similar bemusement to my own—Mr. Bowden stops for a word with his admiring spectators. Kay Cole has said that he has much to tell about his conflict with Fish and Wildlife, and meaning to ask as well about the bison, I make a date with him for a few days hence.

Kay Cole and I drive back over to the beach and southward for a few miles; her Jeep station wagon is newer and smaller than Phyllis's. The tide has retreated, and the damp sand is wide and flat, smoother than many city streets. As we zoom along, I reflect on the now perceptible good reasons why world land-speed records are won on sand. Kay, slowing down slightly, points out a place where a sand cliff has recently worn away to expose the rusting snout of a car. "That's been in there twenty years at least," she says. "The dunes built up over it, then they got washed away a bit. The beach here isn't being eroded the way it is farther south." The beach sand is, however, prone to traveling southwestward. The first thing Pat Crowder tells me when Kay and I reach the old Coast Guard house Mrs. Crowder and her husband have restored at North Swan Beach is that the dune, looming outside the kitchen window like a giant pet waiting to be fed, has had to be bulldozed back twice since 1971, when they bought the place. On the last occasion, the cost for doing this was three thousand dollars. The Crowders—who were at the firehouse meeting—live between the two tracts that make up the new wildlife refuge, and they feel surrounded. The house is painted white and has resolutely simple lines; it might well suit a picture by Edward Hopper. The post-meeting party **(46)** that began at Ernie Bowden's has rolled down the Banks and gathered here. Among the twenty-some Currituck Bankers is Ernie Bowden's father, William Bowden, known to all as Captain Bill, a cheerful, weathered man of eighty-two who retired from the Coast Guard as a lieutenant commander in 1946. When he was a youngster, he helped build this house, hauling timber over the Banks from a landing on the sound. He recalls—as if remembering the seven ages of man—the various ways he has got around the Banks: barefoot, on horseback, by bicycle, and even, when the wind was right, by a bicycle on which he had rigged a small sail. He has ridden a motorcycle on the beach many times, and used to drive a Model A Ford with some of the air let out of its tires to improve their grip— "slacking the tires," this is called, and is a trick still practiced; alongside a grocery store in Duck, I noticed an air-pressure hose, the charge for its use being twenty-five cents. Captain Bill tells me that he recently found on the beach a number of sixty-pound bales of marijuana. He informed the Coast Guard, which recovered several hundred such bales, apparently washed up from a ship that had dumped them. "I reckon I could have been a very rich man!" He says that I should get his son Ernie to tell me about the rescue of an English yacht which stranded on the beach here several years ago.

Mrs. Crowder and several other ladies active in a local pressure group called the Outer Banks Civic League present me with leaflets promoting their case against the Department of the Interior; no visitor, even from old England, should go away ignorant of their plight. They have published a cookbook, profits from which go to finance their campaign (recipes include Incredible Crab Pie, Carrot Muffins, No-Cook Fudge, Swan Beach French-fried Eggplant, and Gretchen's Salad for seventeen persons). I am given a copy of this and a poster showing a resigned-looking Chief Sitting Bull with the legend "They made us many promises, more than I can remember, but they never kept but one; they promised to take our land, and they took it." A lady named Judy White says to me, "We now understand the lessons the American Indians learned years ago. Fish and Wildlife have told us that if we don't like the restrictions we can move." Another woman says that she commutes daily up the beach and across the state line to Pungo, Virginia, where she owns a beauty salon; as a long-standing resident, she has a permit. The nearest doctor is at Kitty Hawk, twenty miles south of here. When the Corolla Rescue Squad's four-wheel-drive ambulance was taking a stretcher patient through the wildlife refuge recently, a ranger stopped it to examine the patient and decide whether it was a life-or-death emergency. One late-middle-aged man tells me that he believes there is less wildlife in the refuges than ever before; the eelgrass and ribbon grass that geese and duck need isn't growing as it once did. Another says that most people here don't want the Carova lots completely developed; they know that some never will be, because of sanitary problems, and bringing in building materials will be even more expensive now. Most came here, after all, to get away from things. Some bought their land for fifty dollars down and fifty a month. To own one's own land and have a chance at the good life by the sea is surely a slice of the American Dream. Why should the Department of the Interior deprive them of it?

It is almost dark as Kay Cole drives me down the beach to Corolla. The lighthouse fans its warning light across the beach and sea. Some people, standing close to their vehicles, are still fishing. Some have driftwood fires. The tide is a long way out and Kay now and then swerves, avoiding tree stumps sticking up from the sand—the remains, she tells me, of a seven-hundred-year-old forest that once lay behind the Banks. This stretch of beach is called Wash Woods. She drops me outside her real-estate office, where the Alliance waits. (Later, I read in the Pilkey book that more than two-thirds of the twenty-three-mile-long Currituck Banks are designated—by the authors, at least—as dangerous, or to be considered with caution in regard to building.)

When I get back to Nags Head, Roder wants to know about Carova, where he has never been. He says, "Man, that must be desolate up there!" Bad news continues to come from Mexico City. Upstairs, there are lights on under other bedroom doors; several other guests have turned up for Saturday-night lodgings. As I go into my room, the door slams shut behind me; a strong night breeze is blowing off the sea. I think of the English yachtsman who was stranded on Currituck Banks and try to imagine what he felt—horror and shame to begin with, perhaps, and a hope that no one would witness his disaster. But soon enough, as help arrived, gratitude that where he had come ashore wasn't just dunes and seabirds.

At breakfast I share the table with two young couples and a U.S. Army pilot in his late twenties who says that if the weather improves he is going to rent a sailboat for the day on Roanoke Sound. Why not hang gliding? He says, "Well, I don't have the right reactions. Your responses need to be just the opposite of what they are in a plane." It is Sunday, and it is raining—the first rain in a month, says Robin, bringing in more toast. But it has cleared by ten and I take a walk along the Kitty Hawk beach, where some of the ocean-front buildings have been washed away and barely a thin bank of sand exists between the beach and the Beach Road. In one place a hopeful sign, facing the sea, says KEEP OFF THE DUNES—as if the sea might heed it. The cottages on the western, landward side of the road now have an unobstructed—except for traffic—ocean view; but set against this, they are now in the front line. Household garbage cans generally seem to be kept in rustic wooden frames by the roadside, and though the frames prevent them from being blown away, the cans sit at wry angles in them, sometimes inverted, with a disused, end-of-season air.

For lunch I boldly approach the Dare Devil Inn. The early days of flying were no doubt in the minds of those who named this hostelry, and not the venturesomeness of customers like me who enter hoping for good things. I suppose a turkey sandwich ordered on a Sunday is unlikely to be made of fresh bread, but this bread is stale, and collapsing, to boot; the contents taste like cardboard. I ask for a beer, but by North Carolina law this can't be served on a Sunday until 1 p.m. Ten minutes to go. A wall-mounted TV displays the warming-up stage before a football game between the Philadelphia Eagles and the Washington Redskins, who appear, within their ferocious helmets, to be either black or white and not at all red. At one minute past one, when I have nibbled as much of the sandwich as I intend to eat, jugs of beer are brought to the tables of the other spectators and a solitary bottle of Heineken for me.

The idea of flight may well be in the air today. Certainly it seems the right moment to pay my respects to the Wright Brothers memorial a short distance away at Kill Devil Hills. Here, just off the Bypass, the landscape has been formalized: the largest of the dunes, Big Kill Devil, has been bound together with grass, a low museum erected, a neat car park laid out for motorists, and, screened by trees, an airstrip made for those arriving in successors to the Wrights' invention. The memorial, open year round, is run by the National Park Service. A shop in the museum's visitors' center sells books, postcards, and plastic model kits of the Wrights' first "Flyer." In the display areas, there are numerous Wright-related objects—to do with Dayton, their bicycle business there, and life on the Banks in the years from 1900 to 1904. An illustration of the Wright St. Clair bicycle prompts the thought of how little—compared with planes—bikes have changed in eighty years. The first Wright craft is like a Leonardo drawing that has been made to work. In skeletal, almost spectral form, it prefigures the wings, fuselage, and tail planes of current aircraft. Nearby, the flat roof of the museum building has been leaking from last night's rain, and several buckets have been placed to catch the drips.

Among the exhibits is a replica of one of the gliders the Wrights tried out in their first three seasons here. It, and a replica of their first powered aircraft, are housed in a hangar-like hall, with floor-to-ceiling glass doors that give a sense of being open to the sandy ground outside. Here a young woman in Park Service uniform gathers an audience of visitors. She speaks with a Southern accent and with evangelical fervor. "You all have probably heard of men strapping wings to their bodies and jumping out of windows." Picking up a windup-model bird, she demonstrates how wing flapping isn't a very effective way of overcoming considerable weight. The model bird whirs halfway across the hall and crashes. She discusses the technical expertise the Wrights had first to discover, then master, such as the several axes of aerial control. "They had to find out about pitch, roll, and that cute little Southern word 'yaw.' " (This gets an appreciative, if delayed, laugh, as we cotton on to the pun—you all, y'all, yaw.) The young woman wears an identity brooch giving her name as Bev Barta; she has straight blond hair and is quite pretty, despite the Park Service uniform of gray shirt, olive-green trousers, and shiny, flat black shoes with prominent rounded toe caps. She continues her account: ". . . and now Wilbur, he smashed up the plane that flight . . ." Outside, over the trees, a Cessna takes off most ordinarily from the airstrip. Young Ms. Barta arrives at a cold and windy morning in December 1903 and tells us what happened here.

(52)   I am not a passionate flier. I belong to the large body of passengers who have white knuckles from gripping the arms of their seats at landing and takeoff. But as a modern traveler, fly one must, and there's no disputing how marvelous was the conquest of the air. To me, today, it seems especially amazing that this victory happened here at Kill Devil Hills. (Kitty Hawk generally gets the credit—like Waterloo for the battle that took place at Quatre Bras—because the Wrights spent their first season on the Banks four miles north of here at Kitty Hawk, where their first host, W. J. Tate, was postmaster, and from where they often dragged their glider to Kill Devil Hills.) It is also, of course, still a matter of amazement that two bicycle makers from Dayton, Ohio, who finished high school but never bothered to collect their diplomas, were the first to conquer with power the element of air.

Outside, I wander over the sandy ground where sparse blades of bleached, dry grass lie pressed flat; intermingled among them are small green ferns and reddish-brown plants—all forming useful, stabilizing ground cover. A commemorative stone and several distance markers are placed where the Flyer took off from a single wooden rail and landed on its first four short flights on December 17, 1903; the first flight was 120 feet and lasted twelve seconds. Nearby are two sheds, constructed by the Park Service in 1963 to give a close idea of what the Wrights used in 1903 for a hangar and workshop/living quarters. Big Kill Devil is now some fifty yards southwest of where it was at that date;

it stands roughly where it was caught and anchored with grasses in the late 1920s, when the memorial was established. I stick to the path as I climb to the top, one hundred feet up—signs request this, to preserve the grass from bare spots amid which sand leeches in grainy rivulets. At the summit stands a gray granite pylon, sixty feet tall, erected by order of Congress in the early 1930s. It is wedge- or ax-shaped, with a very thirties-looking beacon on top (no longer lit) and, below, an inscription: IN COMMEMORATION OF THE CONQUEST OF THE AIR BY THE BROTHERS WILBUR AND ORVILLE WRIGHT, CONCEIVED BY GENIUS, ACHIEVED BY DAUNTLESS RESOLUTION AND UN-CONQUERABLE FAITH. The all-around view takes in Nags Head Woods, Roanoke and Albemarle Sounds, dunes, housing developments, the Bypass strip development, the conglomerations of cottages, motels, and condos along the oceanfront—and the sea. The humid wind is light, from the south.

When the Wrights first came here, this part of the Banks looked more like a desert. Wilbur wrote home: "South of Kitty Hawk the bar is absolutely bare of vegetation and flat as a floor, from sound to ocean, for a distance of nearly five miles, except for a series of sandhills, the largest of which is one hundred and five feet high." Orville wrote to his sister: "But the sand! The sand is the greatest thing in Kitty Hawk, and soon will be the only thing." A few buildings, including the lifesaving station, stood on the beach. Kitty Hawk was a small fishing village which shipped out its catch and appeared to eat none of it. The arrival of the Wrights unsettled the local arrangements of supply and demand; they had to live off rice, eggs, canned tomatoes and beans, condensed milk and biscuits. They had to trek great distances for water before they got around to drilling their own wells. Among the gear which accompanied them from Dayton—and in the last stages, on a thirty-six-hour boat voyage from Elizabeth City, via Roanoke Island—was a bicycle, of course modified for use on sand. When aircraft parts broke, they fixed them on the spot or shipped them home for repair. Each year they stayed for periods of between five and eight weeks. They never worked or flew on Sundays. Their resourcefulness might have been thwarted by only one local phenomenon—mosquitoes.

Everything that Bill Harrison in Virginia Beach told me about Banks mosquitoes was said—in slightly different form—by the Wrights. Orville: "They chewed us clear through our underwear and 'socks.' Lumps began swelling all over my body like hard eggs." After rain, the minute winged monsters came in thousands; conventional mosquito netting was useless; smoky fires helped, but the smoke itself was hard for the pioneer aviators to put up with. In late September 1903, Orville was reminded of the occasion, two years before, "when the mosquitoes were so thick as to dim the very brightness of the sun, exceeding in numbers all excepting those that devoured the whole of Raleigh's settlers on Roanoke." However, in 1903 it was worse: the rain had made "a lake for miles about our camp; the mosquitoes were so thick that they turned day into night." But the Wrights refused to flee from the bugs.

They were impressive men—impressive, as the inscription puts it, in their resolution. They found that previous students in the field had got things wrong in regard to thrust and lift. They found out for themselves, in a wind tunnel that they constructed during the winter months in Dayton. Unable to obtain an engine of the correct power and weight, they built it themselves. They flew in collars and ties. They were generous with their hard-won knowledge, welcoming other aviation researchers to their Outer Banks camp to share the discoveries, the spartan diet, and the discomforts. And they recognized—without undue trumpet-blowing—their own achievements. Cameras recorded the precarious progress of gliders and fliers, and one of the **(55)** most amazing aspects of those early days is that when the aeronauts at last succeeded, and their first powered plane took to the air, a camera captured the instant. The thrill was almost as great: Would it fly? Would the picture come out all right? The crewman from the local lifesaving station who released the shutter did so at the perfect moment: the camera worked; the film was properly exposed; and the victorious instant was seized forever.

Walking down Big Kill Devil Hill, I think of other curious things about the brothers Wright. Their strange Christian names: Orville. Wilbur. A third brother named Lorin, who wasn't similarly obsessed with the air. Not long after their success, they began to make a living from flight. Bicycles were no longer needed for income. But then—this was twentieth-century America—they were pestered with lawsuits and spent a lot of time having to protect their invention. Although the U.S. Signal Corps gave them a contract in February 1908, and soon after orders came from abroad (from the French first of all), recognition was not total: the Smithsonian for many years viewed them as merely one party among many involved in the conquest of the air. Thus Orville let the Science Museum in London have the first Flyer, and there it stayed from 1928 to 1948, when—the Smithsonian finally bending to bestow rightful laurels on the pioneers—it was shipped to Washington. Neither Wilbur nor Orville married. Wilbur died of typhoid in 1912, aged forty-five. Orville gave up flying in 1918 and went on living in Dayton.

At the foot of the hill it occurs to me that it has taken me a long time to pay my proper respects to the Wrights. Perhaps the Dayton connection is part of what has brought me here. When I spent four wartime childhood years in that Ohio city, evacuated from England, I lived in a big house in the suburb of Oakwood four or five blocks away from Orville Wright's Greek Revival–style mansion, and was only dimly aware of the old gentleman who lived there and was said to potter in his garage with its workbench and lathes, still a mechanic, really—too close, too much a neighbor, even if a reclusive one, to seem important or grand. The Halloween night my friend Fred Young and I got up the courage to knock on the front door under that imposing columned portico and say, "Trick or treat, Mr. Wright?" it didn't occur to me that the wrinkled hand that rewarded our resolution with a silver dollar apiece was the hand that had worked the primitive controls of the first powered aircraft, as it took to the air above this sand.

There is heavy rain during the night, but the wind, though strong, is from the northeast, which means that I, in my room on the southern side of the B & B, don't have to get up to close my window. It is still blowing hard in the morning but there's a clear sky and sun. I am the sole guest again at breakfast—which means more scrambled eggs. Roder enters from the living room, where I can hear a television newscaster talking about Mexico City, and says, "A couple of interesting items on the weather forecast. There's a tropical storm called Henry sixty miles offshore, going north, nothing to worry about. Then there's another, of hurricane force, called Gloria, off Puerto Rico. That may be the one we have to keep an eye on." Roder goes on to say that he is going to be working on his boat today. I ask if he ever gets back to Dayton and he says that he does, sometimes. He was a student at Chaminade High School, where I—aged eleven—used to go for after-school religious instruction with one of the Catholic

Brothers who taught there. Roder's father is county auditor of Montgomery County, in which Dayton stands. In fact, his parents are coming here this week on a short vacation. The push on the boat today may have something to do with a son's natural desire to impress his father and mother with deeds accomplished.

(58)

Robin has let me take up to my room a round garden table, and I sit at this reading and writing letters. I feel very much at home—quite unlike the feeling one usually has in hotels and guest houses. No keys are needed or provided. I walk in and out. No one has bothered to ask for my permanent address. I'm trusted not to leave without paying the bill. I make my own bed without being asked, but Robin, at some point during the day when I am out, vacuums up the sand from the floor and leaves a fresh towel.

I have been trying to make up my mind how I feel about the development of the Banks; it isn't easy. Having seen the ramshackle conglomeration between Kitty Hawk and Nags Head, I am a conservationist. Having talked to some of the people in Carova and North Swan Beach, I sympathize with those who want to live on the Banks. When enough people—like Robin and Roder—want to settle on the Banks, a need for houses and roads and services is created. Since the sixteenth century, this part of the world has been considered with a view to development. Walter Raleigh's Virginia—as this whole area, including the Banks, was named in honor of the Virgin Queen—was merely the first in a long line of real-estate promotions, though the line had gaps when the Banks particularly were valued only by those who had stumbled on them. Now real estate is the second-largest source of employment on the Banks. (House construction is the largest.) Realtors have their notices and offices everywhere you turn. Involved with the brokers are insurance agents, attorneys, property managers, appraisers, architects, surveyors, landscape designers, land developers, and sundry salespersons. Many come here to retire and find themselves selling real estate. Buyers' guides to real **(59)** estate are best-selling items in local bookshops; free bulletins listing houses for sale and rent are placed where you can't miss them in restaurants, banks, and stores, all of which presumably feel they will benefit from more Banks residents, more customers. The assumption is that everyone who comes here is a potential house buyer. The buyers' guides push that notion by telling you what a good *investment* such a buy will be, giving you rental income and tax benefits—everyone who fails to purchase will at least rent. There are subtleties of definition to be mastered: "ocean side" is not "oceanfront"; "sound front" may not appeal so much as oceanfront, but there are "gorgeous sunsets." Some brochures and publicity mention in passing such local problems as floods, storms, erosion, water supply, and sewage. Like government health warnings against smoking, these cautionary words aren't to be dwelt on.

Robin has told me that one of the least offensive Banks developments is Southern Shores, and I take a look at it on the way up to Corolla to see Norris Austin. The merits of the community aren't conspicuous from the main road, where some of the earliest houses, built in the late 1940s near the ocean, are beginning to show their age. But on the winding roads closer to Currituck Sound, with an eighteen-hole golf course and large areas of swamp, marsh, and creeks nearby, are well-spaced houses in well-treed grounds, which look lived-in and cared for. The Southern Shores main sales office is set back from 158, not far from the Wright Bridge, on a gravel drive, with trees and the long arm of a pond in the immediate landscape. SOUTHERN SHORES says a sign. IT'S MORE THAN REAL ESTATE—IT'S A STATE OF MIND.

Frank Stone, the president of Southern Shores Realty, tells me: "What you see out here is happening because many people in America want to live by the sea, preferably in a warm climate—and also because the beaches are saturated farther north." Mr. Stone wears a shirt with the Southern Shores logo discreetly embroidered on it and has the look of a healthy middle-aged golfer. He says that Southern Shores was founded by the artist and illustrator Frank Stick in 1947, and for some time was run by him and his son, David, who has since become a distinguished North Carolina historian. The Sticks went for slow growth; they wanted to establish a year-round community, if possible, with larger than average building lots and a low-key form of local government. These objectives have been more or less achieved—Southern Shores has a population of fewer than two thousand, a three-man police force, local control over land-use regulations, and an efficient garbage service. On the Banks as a whole, the pressures are perhaps less than they were, Stone thinks, because of recent state coastal-management regulations (in whose framing David Stick had a big part), which have prevented greedy developers from squeezing every available lot out of the land. Still, more people continue to come to live and work here, and there is therefore a demand for schools, professional services, and such other concomitants of a complete society as courthouses and jails. Stone says that he is probably in a minority of real-estate agents who don't decry the amount of land the Department of the Interior owns on the Banks and which is preserved in the form of national parks and wildlife refuges, decreasing the room for "growth" and so limiting the tax base. "From a long-term standpoint, I'd say the Department of the Interior has done a lot for the Banks. The land that is left for development has a more stable prospect, and often fetches enhanced prices. And we're preserving nature and space for our children and their children." **(61)**

I stop at the Wee Wink grocery store in Duck for lunch materials. The store is more of a small supermarket and shop for general supplies than it is a delicatessen, but I find a prepackaged chicken-salad-on-whole-wheat sandwich, and a small bottle of apple-cranberry juice. I also purchase the day's *Virginian-Pilot*, which competes successfully with the North Carolinian *News and Observer* for Banks custom. I sit at a trestle table outside on the store's concrete porch and am joined by three other men, who eat hot dogs with chili sauce and drink cola. The oldest of the three tells me he is a building contractor; he is a red-haired, red-faced man with a mustache and sawdust flecking his red T-shirt. He and his two helpers drive daily a hundred miles from the interior of North Carolina to work out here. "Where we live is God's country," he says. It takes them, on average, six weeks to build a house on the Banks. Sometimes there are hitches, brought about by a moratorium on new house building in certain areas because of water-supply problems, or by suggestions that tax reform will disallow interest deductions on second homes. But, basically, house construction is still booming out here.

I find Norris Austin at work in the Corolla post office. "My grandfather served as lighthouse keeper from 1891 until the light was made automatic, in 1929. My father was a market hunter, who killed wildfowl for shipping out, and he made and sold his own ice cream. He was also postmaster here from 1935 to 1959, when I took over the job. I'd tried for the Coast Guard, but I had flat feet, and in any case I had a terrible fear of the water. The outsuck—the undertow—caught me once as a small boy and I've never been an eager swimmer since. The post office business here is really growing. The nearest other offices are in Kitty Hawk, thirty-five miles south, and in Virginia Beach, eighteen miles north, if you can get there that way. Yes, our demand is up, whether you measure it by requests for new postboxes or for forty-four-cent airmail stamps."

Mr. Austin is a mild-looking man with a trim mustache, a gentle manner, and a soft smile. He lives on his own with his dog, Clyde (as in Bonnie and), who is part basset, part German shepherd. Clyde has one crooked leg, and after the day's deliveries he generally spends the afternoon sleeping in the empty sorting bin, beneath open-fronted wooden compartments into which Mr. Austin puts the mail. Sometimes, if Clyde has gone outside, the dog will step onto the bench beneath the post office's front window and look in to make sure that all is well with his master. "He's devoted to me, and I'm devoted to him," Norris Austin says. The building that houses the post office is named the Austin Building after its owner and founder and—with its full complement of grocery store, three contracting firms, the Kay Cole Realty office, and an upstairs apartment for the postmaster-landlord—serves to indicate the burgeoning conditions of Corolla.

Change is something that Norris Austin likes talking about. "One of my grandfathers—my mother's father—had a big tract of land in Kill Devil Hills, where McDonald's and Burger King are now. In those days, Corolla was more of a place than Kill Devil Hills, or so it seemed to me. I used to go coon hunting down there with my uncle, at full moon, the dogs chasing the raccoons through the Nags Head Woods and sometimes treeing them. We'd shoot the coons, skin them, and sell the hides. Of course, up here was all hunting, too, back then. I guess Corolla's population was about two hundred, but it was down to seventy-five after the war, and it's now back to two hundred again. When the Whale Head Gun Club closed, a boys' school, Corolla Academy, took over the mansion house for some years. The next occupant was a company that tested and developed rocket motors. For a while we thought we were part of the space age out here. But that company moved away in the early seventies, and now the property is going to be developed for housing."

I ask Mr. Austin how Corolla came by its name, which is pronounced with two short o's.

"That happened when the first post office was established here in the 1880s, and this part of the Banks was known either as Jones Hill or Whale Head. Three names had to be submitted to the postal authorities and people here were trying to come up with a third. One day the schoolmaster picked one of the wild violets that grow here in abundance in the spring, and he looked into the flower and saw its yellow corolla and thought that was a good name."

And what about the meeting in the Carova Beach firehouse?

"Well, that went about the way you'd expect. A lot of us round here reckon the Department of the Interior is trying to depress property values. They're trying to stop the development of the area by keeping people guessing—is there or isn't there going to be access? I agree it isn't a simple problem—a lot of people, maybe too many people, want to live here. But we believe that

Outer Banks residents have certain inherent rights. And the Fish and Wildlife people just aren't logical. They say they're worried about loggerhead turtles, which lay their eggs on the beach. You'd think they'd want to keep traffic off the beach and have an inside trail. If you call Back Bay Wildlife Refuge and say you've found a wounded bird or animal, they'll tell you to put a plastic bag over its head or hold it by the exhaust pipe of your car."

(64)

Norris Austin is one of the few locals with permits to drive through the gates into Virginia; he has a four-wheel-drive Subaru sedan and regards the restrictions as harassment. "One round trip a day is allowed and you have to be back in Currituck County by midnight. Well, I work till four o'clock, when I lower the flag on the pole in the driveway. Then say I want to go shopping in Virginia Beach, meet some friends, have dinner, go to a movie—it's hard as hell to get back by midnight. We've had this way to and from the north as long as most of us can remember. When I was a little kid, we used to go along the beach in an old Dodge truck. Many Sundays we used to go to church in Virginia Beach. Sometimes we got stuck in the sand and people would stop and help haul us out. They still will, when they see a vehicle in difficulties."

As we talk, a few people drop in for their mail. Two contractors who rent one of the offices in the building come in to discuss a sign they want to add to the board of names hanging by the roadside. Tomi Bowden, brother of Ernie Bowden, arrives barefoot, but wearing a nautical peaked cap, bearing a pair of sea mullet, or "roundheads," gleaming wet from the ocean. He wants Norris's opinion as to whether a certain lady in Corolla would like them. Norris thinks she would. When Tomi Bowden has left on this errand, Norris

Austin says, "This time of year when fish is plentiful, you don't have to go to market for it—someone is sure to bring you some. And in summer, people who have vegetable gardens will share their crops of beans and stuff with you."

He locks up the post office for a few minutes in order **(65)** to show me the Corolla church. It is a run-down clapboard chapel in a sandy lane a hundred yards from the Austin Building. When the church fell into disuse and was threatened with conversion into a vacation cottage, Norris Austin bought it; he hopes to organize its restoration. Proudly he displays the dusty pews and organ. On summer Sundays, a preacher from the Assembly of God comes to conduct an interdenominational service. Outside again, we pause by a small tree with frail, droopy branches absolutely laden with a fruit I don't recognize. "Persimmons," says Norris Austin. He picks up several windfalls and hands one to me. "You're supposed to have a frost before they're ready to eat. It takes the bitterness out of them." The small fruit has a dark peach-like color, but tastes like a mixture of plum and grape, and to me doesn't seem at all bitter. As we shake hands in farewell, Mr. Austin recalls that he has a family recipe for persimmon pudding. It is, he says, extra-special good, and I believe him.

I backtrack to Duck, where Ernie Bowden has agreed to meet me at the Barrier Inn. This is a new sound-side establishment which calls itself a "resort village," slightly distinguished by such Victorian architectural features as gingerbread woodwork on the gables, and with such contemporary leisure-age paraphernalia as tennis courts, swimming pool, sauna, sailboats for rent, and time-share cottages, here—to make a change—said to be available within a "vacation-ownership concept." Ernie Bowden, who is sixty-one and divorced, has been lunching at the Barrier Inn restaurant with an extremely pretty young woman, and when she leaves he pays their bill with an American Express Gold Card. In his Stetson, out on the Currituck range, Ernie Bowden had looked very much like the Marlboro man; now, without his hat, short, curly gray hair is revealed. He is wearing a white shirt, bright orange trousers, white leather cowboy boots, and a large horseshoe-design diamond ring. I drink a beer, and he an iced tea as he tells me that the Bowdens have lived on the Currituck Banks for four generations. When he was a boy, he used to ride a school bus along the beach to and from Virginia Beach, though when the tide was too high the bus didn't run. His father was stationed with the Coast Guard in Brooklyn during World War II, and Ernie Bowden went to preparatory school there and then to Pratt Institute, where he studied mechanical engineering. After a year working in the Portsmouth Naval Shipyard, he felt the call of the Banks; he returned and embarked on his double career of livestock farming and operating a light-construction business, which these days is mostly occupied with installing septic tanks and driving piles for house foundations. When he came back to the Currituck Banks, there were six livestock farmers; now he is the only one. He says the meat market is currently depressed, but there is a seven-year cycle in these matters and he expects it to recover. He has a herd of 150, for the most part crossbred from Charolais and Swiss Simental cattle. Several new additions are a Scots Galloway bull and two Senepol heifers, brought from St. Croix but the descendants of wild African cattle. His five American bison are kept not for the market but because he feels they fit in with the terrain and climate of the Banks. He also feels that the bison—and not the American eagle—is the prime symbol of American wildlife.

Some of Ernie Bowden's construction equipment came in handy when the English yachtsman was stranded on North Swan Beach in his thirty-eight-foot ketch a few years ago. "His name was Martin Pimlott," says Bowden, speaking softly, courteously, in tones similar to Norris Austin's, maybe the voice of Americans who don't live in big cities. "He was making his way single-handed from the Caribbean to Baltimore. He'd been out there in a northeaster for several days, beating against wind and current. He fell asleep and his self-steering gear let him down. When he woke up, it was because his boat was bouncing on the sand, and surf was flying all around it. It was about an hour before high tide. The Coast Guard came and began to haul him off, but the ketch sprang a leak and started to fill, and the Coast Guard didn't want him to sink, so they left him on the beach."

Pimlott's luck, however, hadn't altogether deserted him. He couldn't have run ashore in a more helpful place than that scantily populated section of Currituck Banks. Ernie Bowden arrived with a crane and a huge dolly used for moving houses and at low tide shifted Pimlott's craft to safer ground. Pimlott stayed for a year, living at Ernie Bowden's house in Carova, repairing his ketch and putting his carpentry skills to work on various local jobs. His wife and children joined him from England, and his children went to Kitty Hawk elementary school. Eventually Bowden hauled the ketch over to the Inland Waterway and relaunched it. Pimlott sailed off again. He had got to know a lot of people on the Currituck Banks, and is still thought of fondly.

Ernie Bowden's house is two and a half miles south of the state-line fence that bars the way across the Banks and the beach. His cattle graze to the line on rented pasture. He has a resident's access permit to let him through the gates, and is also allowed to truck his cattle through, so that he can sell them in Virginia, and to move his construction equipment back and forth on business. But he was and remains quietly angry about the constraints. When the Department of the Interior brought in the new rules, in 1976, access north and south through the Back Bay Refuge was for two periods of the day, 6 to 9 a.m. and 5 to 8 p.m., and the permit for a year cost ninety dollars. Bowden refused to pay for the permit or to obey the regulations. He was twice prosecuted for trespassing, but was let off by the courts. In 1981, after receiving an ultimatum from the Department of the Interior that he acquire a permit or be prosecuted, he paid for one. However, in 1982 and 1983 he was twice prosecuted for driving through the refuge after midnight; his permit was suspended. On the first occasion he was fined $475 and sentenced to ten days in prison on each of five counts. He served ten days in jail in Virginia Beach, and forty days were suspended. On the second occasion he was fined $550 and sentenced to sixty days. He served forty-eight days in prison in Williamsburg, Virginia, before being released. Since then he has had to report to a probation officer every ninety days—and will have to do so for a period of three years from his release. The trials cost him "at a horseback guess" $15,000 in attorneys' fees. While he was in prison, his brother, Tomi, and two neighbors fed his cattle. (He has a daughter and two grandsons in Virginia Beach, but they are not allowed to use the refuge-and-beach route.) While he was in jail in Virginia Beach, he was interviewed on local television. In Williamsburg he got less attention; his phone bill—collect calls only were permitted—was over $800. On conviction he had to sign an affidavit relinquishing his rights under federal privacy laws, and thus his financial records and bank accounts are at the mercy of any investigator. Because Bowden was charged with only a misdemeanor, he has not been disqualified from holding public office. In fact, shortly before he started his second jail term, he was elected to the Board of Commissioners of Currituck County.

If Ernie Bowden is a local hero, he seems to have

remained a modest one. His rebellion is as low key as a fairly colorful individual can make it. He says he understands the fragile nature of the Banks, and that any development is limited by lack of water. He doesn't want an arterial highway up to Virginia. But he is in **(70)** a fight to the finish with big government. "You know, this government wants the people of our country in little cells where they can control them. In the last few years we've moved from a democratic process to a bureaucratic process. It's depressing. We elect senators and congressmen and send them to Washington, and though they initiate legislation to help us, they're thwarted at every turn. Bills die in committee. Federal department regulations have the authority of law. Take Interior—the department which has a bison in its logo! They're clearly in the business of empire building, the way most bureaucracies are. When Stewart Udall was Secretary of the Interior back in the sixties, he said these Banks weren't fit for human habitation and should be acquired for the nation. That's what they've been working on ever since, so that now we're surrounded by refuges—there are seventeen in North Carolina—and we're losing our right to use our land. I think my right to travel back and forth to my home after midnight is just as important as Martin Luther King's right to sit in the front seat of a bus. Last week, at 11:30 p.m., coming home through Back Bay Refuge, I was followed by a Department of Interior vehicle driving without lights. In 1978 a young man was run down and killed by an Interior vehicle. The young man's car had broken down on the beach and he was walking back to Sandbridge in Virginia. It took two years for the Department of Interior driver to admit that he'd been driving without lights. He said that he thought he'd hit a deer. He was never prosecuted. For two years a number of us on the Currituck Banks who drive that way were under suspicion. On one occasion, that Interior man actually brought the Virginia police down to interrogate me about the incident."

Ernie Bowden gives a wry smile; he looks like an elderly boxer who is ready to retire. He goes on: "Earlier this summer one of my bison—a buffalo cow— strayed from the grazing area. I'd bought her only three weeks before. A man from False Cape Park Service phoned and left a message on my answering machine to say that he saw her going by, heading north. I must have got home thirty minutes after this. I called Back Bay Refuge right away, talked to the manager, and told him she was docile—harmless. I think she must have been looking for her calf, weaned from her in Harrisonburg, Virginia, a month before. I asked the manager for permission to bring a stock trailer up to Back Bay and collect her, and he said sure. Well, I drove up there and they led me to the animal. She was dead. She'd been shot four times with a .30-.30 rifle— in her right side, her rib cage, and her hindquarters.

"I asked the warden who'd led me there, 'How come she's dead?' He said, 'We killed her.' I said, 'Why?' He said, 'In the interests of public safety.' I thought he was out of his mind and must have looked at him that way. He added, 'I've been instructed not to tell you anything else.'

"I drove back and got my larger truck and frontloader and returned to pick up the body. By then the refuge manager was there. He said that he hadn't known the bison was dead when I called first, but that it had been done in the interest of public safety."

Ernie Bowden delivers this story, which he has clearly told many times, flatly and unsardonically. He finishes his iced tea. I ask, "What happened after that?"

"Oh, well, I requested reimbursement. The Department of Interior refused it. Said I could sue them, if I could get the necessary permission to do so from a federal district judge. You have to show sufficient cause. And I knew there wasn't much chance I'd get permission from Judge Clark, in Norfolk District Court, who'd sent me to jail."

Roder, covered in a light sprinkling of blue paint from his day with the boat, is sitting with a bottle of Heineken, watching TV. He goes out to the kitchen to get me a beer. He calls out toward the bedroom, "Hey, Robin! *People's Court* coming up." *People's Court* is the program from the West Coast in which people involved in disputes present their cases on the screen and agree to accept the verdict of a judge hired by the program. Robin says that it is their favorite TV show. The first case today—in stark synopsis—concerns a quarrel between two neighbors about whether the dog of one impregnated the bitch of the other. The second is a triangular romantic altercation: one jealous woman is said to have put a knife into the water bed of her boyfriend, whom she found messing around with another lady. Both women tell their stories, and so does the boyfriend. I sit as fascinated as Robin and Roder, though it seems to me a fairly crafty California notion—as it were, privatizing justice, while at the same time making it public; that is, turning it into show business. I wonder how Ernie Bowden would have made out with his bison case. I suspect the *People's Court* judge would have found in his favor.

I feel pleased when Robin and Roder ask me to come along with them to dinner. We drive up the Beach Road to Kitty Hawk in their huge six-year-old Cadillac coupe and go into an oceanfront Mexican restaurant called Papagayo. The food is tasty, though the miniature Mexican pizzas we have for starters are, even for Roder's strong palate, powerfully, spicily hot. Roder tells me how houses and cottages are moved on the Banks. He makes it sound easy. It seems that you just have to remember to tell the utility companies, so that they disconnect the power and telephone lines from nearby poles. I-beams are put underneath the building, jacked up, and blocked off half an inch at a time, and then large-tired wheels are attached to the ends of the beams and a tow bar fastened on. A powerful truck or tractor then tows the building to its new site—down the lot, maybe, or across the road, or a greater distance. Some ocean-side cottages in Nags Head have been moved all the way over to the sound. Once the building is on its new pilings, you have to retape the cracks and joints in the wallboard, rehang sticking doors, and check the plumbing for leaks.

I tell the story of Ernie Bowden's buffalo cow. At the end of it, Roder says, "Man, I know how he feels. You'd think we'd all be grateful to the government for preserving all this land on the Banks, keeping it in its natural state for posterity. But, I tell you, gratitude is sometimes the last thing you feel."

Roder, it appears, has had his own encounter with Big Brother—in his case with the U.S. National Park Service, whose large holdings on the Outer Banks include the Cape Hatteras National Seashore. This is made up not only of much of Hatteras Island but most of Ocracoke Island and Bodie Island. (The latter, divided from Hatteras Island by Oregon Inlet, is attached to the upper part of the Banks.) Roder's tale is this: He was driving up from Cape Hatteras one winter night a few years ago in his '59 Ford pickup when he got a flat. He had no spare tire. It was 11 p.m. He drove on for several miles, wrecking the tire, until he found a safe place to pull the truck off the road. Then, fortunately, another late-night motorist stopped and gave him a ride up to Nags Head. Next morning, when he returned to the pickup in a friend's car with a new tire, he found that the parts of a dismantled shotgun he had left under the seat were gone. He went to the Park Service's refuge headquarters to inquire. Yes, they said, rangers had opened his truck, searched it, found the parts of the gun, and confiscated them. Roder would be prosecuted for possessing a gun on national park land.

In court, despite snide comments beforehand from staff of the district attorney's office, Roder defended himself. He told the judge that he pleaded guilty to the charge but wanted to explain how the situation arose. He said that the gun wouldn't work in its dismantled state, that he had no shells for it, and that after getting the flat tire he had driven for several miles in order to leave the truck where no one would collide with it in the dark. Did His Honor think that if he, Roder, stood by the roadside thumbing a ride with a shotgun, even a dismantled one, in his hand, anyone would have stopped for him? The judge said no, he didn't. The judge said, moreover, that the Park Service had wasted everyone's time by bringing the case. He let Roder go without a fine and without having to pay costs. Roder told the DA's men on the way out that he was now going to study law and take the bar exam. Roder says to me, "I tell you, on that one the Park Service were ridiculous. It cost me a day's work but, boy, was it worth it."

On the way back down to Old Nags Head the headlights of the big Caddy pick up sand blowing across the road. Robin, driving, punches a button on the radio, which glows with light. We are in the middle of the news: hospital babies in Mexico City; a plane hijack in the Middle East; and hurricane Gloria, now north of Puerto Rico, on a course for the Eastern Seaboard of the United States. Roder says, with a chuckle, "I don't suppose it will come in here. But if it does, it just might make people think twice about building right on these beaches. Yeah, despite everything that might be really worthwhile."

Tuesday isn't the sort of day to make you think of hurricanes. There's sun and a light breeze off the sea. I take an after-breakfast walk along the beach and on the way back notice five or six kites flying from Jockey's Ridge, flaunting themselves in the air on their invisible tethers. I climb up to the quarters of Kitty Hawk Kites, in the tower above the sports shop, to inquire about hang gliding. A young woman tells me there is space in a lesson at twelve-thirty; the price is $46 for the three-hour beginner course, and this includes a "ground school" class and then five flights. She hands me an application form, which also has information to help me answer the printed questions. "How's your health? You don't need to be an athlete to enjoy hang gliding, but, as with any active sport, you'll get the most out of it if you are in good shape." It seems that by registering in the class I am signifying that I *am* in good health and prepared to run, climb sand dunes, and carry gliders. "In the event of an emergency, are there any special medical conditions we should be aware of? Please describe."

I murmur that I have this thing with my back, which has been known to go into spasm and/or lock rigid. Causes vary, but have included lifting sailing dinghies, putting small children to bed, and reaching for a tube of toothpaste. The young woman blithely asks me to read the other side of the page, which I haven't got to yet and which is headed "Waiver of Legal Rights and Assumption of Risk." Clause 1 thereof is "That I acknowledge that hang gliding is an action sport and recreational activity involving travel in three dimensions and such activity is subject to mishap and even injury to participants. I understand I may suffer a broken limb, paralysis or fatal injury while participating in the sport of hang gliding or ultralight flight." You can't say they didn't tell you. A young man standing nearby sees me wavering and says, "Why don't you come and take a look at a glider?" His name is Chris— he is an instructor—and outside, at ground level, he shows me the nylon-covered alloy framework of the sort in which I would be launching myself three-dimensionally (up, down, and sideways?) off the dune. I explain to Chris that my back is unreliable—good for months but then suddenly letting me down. So much so, that, on trains, I have refused to lift suitcases into overhead racks for elderly women, usually with a loud reference to my injured back and a sweeping gesture for help to neighboring passengers. Chris shows me how to get under the wing, down on one knee in the sand, shoulders braced against the struts overhead. "It only weighs fifty pounds," he says. I grunt like a tennis player serving, and barely budge it. Chris says I will find it a lot easier in a good breeze and maybe I should wait a day or two. I agree.

(77)

In the offices of Kitty Hawk Sports I talk to Kathryn Boeckman, an advertising assistant, who charmingly takes my mind off the disappointing fact that I am not going to follow in Orville and Wilbur's footsteps today. Fifty thousand students have passed through training

here, she says, most of them for the once-in-a-lifetime thrill and so that they can say they have done it, but some have acquired the fever, bought a hang glider for up to $2,500, and gone looking for mountains to soar from. The sand and gentle slopes of Jockey's Ridge make for happier landings than in most other gliding areas; this year there has been only one injury to date, a broken wrist suffered by a woman park ranger who landed badly and was—Kathryn Boeckman says—a great sport about it. The wings of the instructional gliders have a six-to-one glide/sink ratio: in other words, they are not designed for lofty or lengthy flight. However, one Kitty Hawk Sports associate went aloft in a non-instructional glider five years ago, caught an updraft or thermal of warm air to several hundred feet, and glided four miles north to the Wright memorial. Francis Rogallo, the seventy-three-year-old former NASA scientist and wind-tunnel expert who invented the flexible wing from which modern hang gliders have evolved, lives in Southern Shores. He still designs kites and is often seen at Jockey's Ridge, watching the gliders. He has offered a thousand-dollar prize for the first person to fly a hang glider up to the Wright memorial and back to Jockey's Ridge to the point of takeoff. (Roder tells me later that hang-gliding enthusiasts can sometimes be heard scaring themselves in the Updraft bar next door with tales of horrendous thunderstorms in which updrafts seize the helpless aeronaut. Roder says, "One of those will take you up in a vortex to eighteen thousand and then spit bits of hang glider out of the cloud. A frozen body falls to earth." Roder also says that someone experienced in hang gliding was killed at Jockey's Ridge several years ago; he went up on a wonderful updraft but lost control and plummeted. Robin adds that one $70,000 house in the vicinity has recently been advertised by real-estate agents as having a "view of hang gliding.")

I walk across the Bypass to Jockey's Ridge again, dodging through the traffic. Three beginners are near the crest of the tallest ridge and I climb up to watch them trying to fly. Their hang glider—basically a Rogallo wing with the control bar which was an Australian invention—is simpler than the biplane glider the Wrights practiced with at Kill Devil Hills. The apprentices wear crash helmets. Harnessed beneath the wing, one of them runs downhill sending up little spurts of sand, abruptly lifts his feet, stretches forward, and pushes the control bar out in front of him, then gently back toward himself. He is aloft, twenty feet or so above the sand, gliding out, out, then banking slightly, drifting down, until near the ground he seems to force the leading edge of the wing upward. The glider stalls. He drops softly onto his feet.

In half a dozen places along the top third of the Outer Banks, piers stick out into the sea. Except for one, they are municipally or privately owned fishing piers, like that at Nags Head, frail-legged structures which seem to have adapted to the shape of the ocean swells that roll in beneath them. None of them is at all in the class of what I, brought up on the south coast of England, would rightly term a seaside pier, with amusement arcades, bars, a theater for summer variety shows, windbreaks sheltering rows of deck chairs, and wooden staging with numerous levels, for different states of tide, at which passengers could board or disembark from coastal excursion steamers. (I admit that many of these piers, put up in Victorian times, also seem to be on their last legs.) At Duck this afternoon I make a post-lunch saunter on the beach. A sizable swell is running in and young men on surfboards are going through the acrobatic, aquatic motions of the sport—whose exhilaration and brevity of performance seem to match that of hang gliding. In one you can get bruised, excited, and sandy; in the other you can get bruised, excited, and wet. I end my walk by the pier that here projects well out to sea and which has immensely solid legs and a deck as straight as an I-beam. This pier belongs to the U.S. Army Corps of Engineers Coastal Engineering Research Center. It has been built to further the collection of "data" on the behavior of waves, winds, water levels, tides, currents, and the resulting coastal processes. At the head of the pier a low, rugged, hangar-shaped building appears to have been slotted as neatly as possible into the dunes, at little more than dune height. In here, one room is a well-equipped galley whose shelves are crammed with canned and dried provisions. In the adjacent office the walls are covered with gauges and instruments. There is a feeling of being in a well-run ship, and indeed Curt Mason, the chief of the facility, has the look of a naval officer, although he tells me that he and his ten permanent staff members are civilians; he is an oceanographer. He points to the window, which has a view of pier, beach, and sea: "The swells you see out there are left over from tropical storm Henri. We're grateful to storms for the information they provide—we're looking forward to Gloria, if she decides to come this way."

The research center is five years old, and hasn't experienced a hurricane yet. Mason and his crew had to make do with the ten to a dozen strong northeasters that blow every year and that often send waves washing over the twenty-five-foot-high pier, knocking into the sea some of its steel deck gratings and producing interesting data on the office gauges. On these occasions (81) the front window is liberally covered with salt. The center publishes information on coastal processes, the interaction of weather, sea, and land, in monthly bulletins that go to government and civilian institutions involved in flood control, erosion prevention, and dredging projects, and also to local communities on the Banks. The center can now make fairly accurate predictions about the quantities of sediment that will be transported by the sea in certain conditions, and the distance they will travel. Storm water levels can be foretold. The center also does research on its 176 acres of Banks land into various types of dune and marsh grasses, and is studying the effects of salt spray on vegetation. Mason tells me, "We get a lot of people dropping by to ask how much the beach is eroding in such-and-such a place. Should they buy a house there? We try to help if we can. There's no doubt the worst erosion along here in the past twenty years has been in south Nags Head. The Kitty Hawk beach has been fairly stable for the last few years, though historically it's unstable. From here, in Duck, up to the Virginia line, change for the time being seems pretty gradual, though of course a bad storm can alter that in a hurry, for example by making a new inlet."*

* *Pilkey* et al. *put it more boldly: "Currituck Bank has an average shoreline recession rate of 5.6 feet per year. It ranges from 2 feet per year at the N.C./ Va. state line, increasing to a maximum of 8 feet per year just north of Corolla, and decreasing southward to 2 feet per year at the Currituck–Dare County line. The rapid rate of shoreline erosion is blatantly obvious along segments [just north of Corolla] where abundant tree stumps occur on the beach and in the surf zone."*

I walk along the pier, which extends roughly a third of a mile out to sea. On the way I note all sorts of equipment, much of it high-tech, but including a battered, pedal-powered tricycle clearly used for one-person trips on the pier. Life buoys and small one-man plastic surf boats are suspended from the railings. Instead of fishing lines, cables leading to measuring devices have been lowered into the water. At the seaward end, a mobile shed contains recording instruments. Out here the water is thirty-five feet deep. It is a solitary place, or at least it feels so to me, alone with the measuring devices. Big ocean swells glide in, parting in foaming eddies around the huge steel cylinders that support the pier. I can see several miles up and down the coast—northward to Osprey and Sand Hills, southward to Southern Shores. I then look southeastward, out to sea, with the thought of perhaps observing early signs of Gloria, like a Winslow Homer stack of Gulf Stream clouds. But there is nothing special to be seen. It remains a lovely, late-September, coastal afternoon.

Much excitement at the B & B when I return. Mrs. Winslow has arrived. Not only Liz Winslow—as she introduces herself—but her daughter, Ellen, and Ellen's daughter, Erin, who is four, and a Mexican friend, Maruca King, who is the widow of a British naval officer. We all sit in the living room of the B & B and talk while the television shows cartoons and Erin laughs. Ellen and Erin live in Oregon. Mrs. Winslow, who seems a very lively middle-aged lady, has driven up from San Miguel with Mrs. King and met Ellen and Erin somewhere en route to Nags Head. They are all staying in the Winslow family cottage across the road. For a few moments I am a stranger again, a paying guest. But I soon find myself taking part with Robin and Roder in answering questions about how things have been going here. We describe the weekend guests. Robin says, "It's been pretty quiet otherwise." Roder adds, "Of course there has been Tony here," as if that may give Liz Winslow a more cheerful impression of B & B business. Mrs. King has been trying to call Mexico City to find out about some of her family there, but the telephone circuits have been busy or the lines engaged. When the television news comes on and shows the now almost customary shots of men digging in the concrete ruins, and silence being imposed when they listen for sounds of continued existence in the rubble, I see that Mrs. King is crying and I feel suddenly ashamed for having become already blasé about this disaster, which is not much more than television for me but is quite real for her. Soon, the weather. Tonight there are satellite pictures of great white swirls of cloud in the Atlantic. Gloria, still heading north-northwest, with winds now estimated at 100 and 125 miles per hour. Roder says, "*Man*, that's a big one!" Liz Winslow says, "It would be funny if we'd fled from the outer ripples of an earthquake only to find ourselves in the middle of a hurricane."

I dine at a purported Italian restaurant on the Beach Road. An indispensable part of the protocol of dining on the Outer Banks seems to be that waiter, waitress, or management persists in interrogating the customer as to his or her feelings throughout the meal. In my case: "Doing okay, sir?" "Everything all right, then?" Or simply, "How was it?" During the eating of one tuna-fish sandwich recently, the waitress turned up on several occasions to ask, "How y'all doing now?" generally timing this to coincide with a bite just taken. The first time I replied with a cursory nod, trying not to choke. At the last I ignored her, except by following her with a baleful glare as she moved on to a more welcoming victim. In my Outer Banks culinary experience to date, breakfasts are fine, lunches—of which one's expectations are perhaps not great—are all right, and dinners—the meal one hopes will seal with pleasure the day's activities—are downright disappointing. It would no doubt help if I liked such Southern dishes as hush puppies, grits, and "biscuits." It would help more if I enjoyed the common feature known as a Salad Bar, which enables restaurants to avoid offering fresh-cooked vegetables, and which displays various raw and remarkably highly colored items under a thick sheet of glass on which, peering down at what is underneath, one is liable to hit one's head. My needs as a solitary diner are for a table big enough to place an open book alongside my plate (I am reading *Humphry Clinker*, by Tobias Smollett), for enough light to read by, and for a position in the ventilation flow where I am not subject to either the Antarctic blasts of an air conditioner or waves of cigarette smoke. My geniality is affected by these factors. It can also be disturbed by paper napkins that refuse to stay in my lap and by packaging that resists easy opening—and it seems that just about every supplement and condiment at these meals comes in wrappings: half-and-half and tartar sauce in little tubs; sugar in paper envelopes that often haven't stopped it from setting up like concrete in the damp sea air; ketchup and mustard in foil packets, all prone to collapse or tearing too far—if you manage to get them open—and spilling some of the contents onto the table or your clothing. Perhaps tonight my mood has been rendered fragile by one or another of these irritations. Perhaps the house red from California tastes more than ever as if it had been shipped to the East Coast in a tanker which, the previous voyage, carried diesel oil the other way. The perfectly helpful young man who has waited on me brings my bill and inquires, pleasantly and comprehensively, "How did you like it?"

Damn it, for once I am not going to lie by muttering, "Oh, fine." But I give him a chance to escape by asking in return, "Do you want an honest answer?" "Why, yes," he says, already looking a little hurt. I breathe deeply. "Well, in that case—although I'm not a cook—I can say that I've never come across Italian hot sausages—one of my favorite dishes—served in so barbaric a fashion, sliced in half and fried in grease, dumped on a dish with tepid spaghetti, and covered with a meat-and-tomato sauce designed for any eventuality, instead of being incorporated, cooked, and simmered in a sauce of their own . . ." Or do I simply imagine saying this? My criticism is muted; I am a coward when it comes to hurting someone's feelings face to face; and I end by saying that the chilled Key lime pie for dessert was first-rate.

Wednesday comes gray, damp, and windy. The roller blind in my bedroom window is pressed out against the partly opened sashes. Behind them, the wind whistles as it pierces the screen. In the empty front bedroom next door, the windows must also be open, for I can hear the agitated sound in there of metal coat hangers jangling together. From the bathroom window as I shave, I can see the yellow-fading-into-orange-fading-into-red pennant that flies on the hang-gliding tower fluttering fiercely, while a small wind sock stands out straight. East wind. In the kitchen, a hurricane-tracking chart—a newspaper freebie—has been pinned up and a green pushpin marks the eye of Gloria. Robin, pouring coffee from the thermos jug, says that Gloria is now traveling northward at fifteen miles per hour and with winds of 150—"She's a real whopper." I look at the chart and do some simple arithmetic. At fifteen miles per hour Gloria is about a day and a half away from here. On her present course she is aimed directly at the Carolina coast. Robin relates what she has heard on the morning news, that meteorologists are wondering whether the present situation of the jet stream over the North American continent will push Gloria out to sea or draw her into the coast, and at the moment they think the latter is more likely. Robin says there (87) is beginning to be talk of evacuating the Outer Banks. Roder has gone to Wanchese to start looking into what he should do with his boat; it is hauled out at a boatyard on a small creek on the southwest corner of Roanoke Island, sheltered under a shed made of poles and plastic sheeting which Roder erected. I have been treating Gloria as relief from the Mexico City disaster, as fascinating but distant. Now she is getting closer.

Tonight is meant to be my last at the Old Nags Head B & B. I came for two nights and have stayed for eight. In a batch of material I'd received from the Dare County visitors' bureau was a brochure for Roanoke Island that mentioned a guest house in Wanchese named C. W. Pugh's, run by a couple named Wayne and Nancy Gray, who also had a nearby restaurant called Queen Anne's Revenge. This sounded like a good base for surveying the next section of the Banks, and so I have booked into the Grays' establishment for a few days starting tomorrow. Today I have earmarked for talking to David Stick.

Stick's house is several miles back into the woods on one side of the Southern Shores golf course, the grounds fading into the woods, a canoe casually pulled up on the bank of a stream. It is a house—single-story, white-painted brick—that doesn't seem large until you're inside, when you become aware of room after room, and a basement full of rooms, all carefully if dimly lit and the air with similar purpose controlled for temperature and humidity. David Stick lives here with probably the best private collection of early maps and pictures, photographs and books having to do with North Carolina. Every room except the kitchen seems in part a library or study. Even the view, through tinted sliding windows, of the golf course, with golfers trundling by in their electric carts, has the appearance of a picture—perhaps of one aspect of life on the Banks today. Stick is sixty-five. He has the weathered, wiry look of a military man, which he hasn't been for a long time. Both the house and its owner give the impression of well-planned and well-built self-sufficiency and of deliberate solitude: Stick had been separated from his wife for over twenty years; his three sons no longer live on the Banks. Yet as he takes me on a tour of the house the phone rings frequently, and in the course of a long conversation with me he often gets up to answer it, which provides me with an opportunity to look at his marvelous maps—among them a 1590 de Bry engraving of the map John White did of Raleigh's "Virginia," showing the Outer Banks and its inlets with considerable accuracy. Stick, it appears, is involved in numerous commissions and committees, groups and projects. He was among those who helped start the Wright Brothers National Memorial at Kill Devil Hills. He is a member of a blue-ribbon committee established by North Carolina's governor to improve state libraries. He set up an Outer Banks foundation which directs charitable funds toward necessary local services, such as one that sends aid and visitors to elderly people who are housebound. He is also the author of nearly a dozen books and pamphlets, including a fine history of the Outer Banks from 1584 to 1958 and an engrossing account of shipwrecks off the Banks from 1526 to the end of the Second World War.

David Stick—born in Interlaken, New Jersey—first saw the Banks at the age of seven, in 1927, and he remembers his feelings: "Openness—cleanliness—happiness." His father, Frank Stick, whose illustrations accompanied, for example, the fishing tales of Zane Grey, decided to move to the Banks in order to fish and paint, but was soon involved in land development. In 1929, he and his associates owned some twenty miles of the Banks; in the 1930s, he had the idea of establishing the Cape Hatteras National Seashore. David Stick's first employment was as a fledgling journalist in Washington, D.C. During World War II, he served in the Marine Corps as a combat correspondent. Afterward he became an associate editor of the American Legion magazine. But in 1947 he decided that where he wanted to live was the Outer Banks, and he returned, hoping to make a living as a freelance writer. Actually, he found that he spent much of his income going to libraries to do research; he also found that many early books he wanted belonged to booksellers. He began to buy such books himself and, though he kept the first copies for himself, started dealing in them. For fifteen years he was the leading dealer in out-of-print works to do with North Carolina. He has now withdrawn from selling, but he still has a regional collection second only to that of the University of North Carolina, and he hopes to have it housed after his death in a special library in Manteo, on Roanoke Island.

Frank Stick lost a good deal in the Depression and had to sell much of his land to keep his family going. But at the end of the war he recovered, in part by house-contracting work, and he acquired four miles of land north of the Wright Bridge, where he began to develop Southern Shores. His son, David, needed money and was brought in to help, but this involvement—the first of several—lasted only six months. "I'm a perfectionist, and Dad wasn't, outside of painting," David Stick says, explaining their agreement to disagree. But when his father approached retirement, David Stick got mixed up again with the destiny of Southern Shores, turning to the development of the sound front and lagoon area. Although he sold out his one-third interest in the development company in 1976, he wrote into the sale contract clauses which committed the purchasers to continue Southern Shores on the same lines. He is reasonably proud of his work as a self-educated, seat-of-the-pants planner.

He says, "I have tried to leave as much as possible of what nature had provided here, while at the same time making it habitable for man. I also tried to look ahead, to see what it would be like when every lot had been built on, every road driven on, and every watercourse used. I'm glad I did this, though looking back there are things I'd now do differently. Our development was piecemeal—we never had the cash to do enough at once. The area I envisaged for a school and offices next to Route 158 has them now, but so far no shops have gone up on the plot in the middle of Southern Shores, near the fire station, which was reserved for them. But I think they'll come, perhaps with the next energy crisis. We retained riparian rights for one hundred feet back from the mile of ocean that was left for me to develop. In colonial times, new towns set aside from 10 to 25 percent of their land for common use and ensured public access to the water. Here, 10 percent is dedicated as public land. There's also a thirteen-acre swamp, surrounded by forested sandhills, which will remain in its present natural state. Many of our residents don't even know it's there."

From his experience with Southern Shores and his residence on the Outer Banks, Stick saw an urgent need for guiding and controlling what was happening on the Banks. He says, lighting a pipe, "I'm for responsible development and reasonable conservation—the middle ground, which out here can be a lonely position. In the past twenty years, there has been greater man-made change on the Outer Banks than in all recorded history. For a long time man could only get here by boat or on foot. Then, suddenly, there were bridges, roads, and motor vehicles. Soon there were fast-buck operators trying to develop everything and, in consequence, rabid conservationists saying 'Develop nothing.' Most real-estate people failed to steer a moderate course between them. **(91)**

"Well, I know the temptations. I was the first licensed real-estate broker in Dare County. I've seen what realtors get up to, selling lots on which cottages have been destroyed or damaged by storms without telling the new purchasers what had happened, developing low-lying sites that can be flooded by rain or backwash from the sounds and therefore have inherent sewage problems, failing to tell new owners that neither developer nor local government will maintain roads to their houses, bulldozing oceanfront dunes, and campaigning against sensible flood-insurance regulations and building codes. When I started, I filled swamp and killed trees, too—but I learned better.

"I've also served as chairman of the Dare County Board of Commissioners. I felt strongly that Dare would have difficulty surviving as a county—and its residents have difficulty in sustaining life like their fellow Americans—if we couldn't find ways of supplementing commercial fishing as the major source of income out here. Tourism and resort development seemed to be the only options to hand. Yet I can also see that, untrammeled, this could lead to the Outer Banks becoming part of the urban monster, like a lot of the Jersey shore, spilling their refuse, their people, and even their buildings into the ocean on one side and the sounds on the other. I can see saturation point."

David Stick's search for the middle ground led him to work for the passage of the North Carolina Coastal Management Act of 1974, to establish a comprehensive plan for controlling and protecting the fragile coast. Despite the fact that federal law already called for such a program in each of the states bordering water, and despite federal incentives by way of funds and less interference for those states that got on with the job, there was vehement opposition in North Carolina to the coastal-management legislation. It came from developers, lawyers, bankers, contractors, and conservative state assemblymen. Stick says, "At one public meeting in Beaufort, my colleagues and I who were trying to frame the legislation were called Communists. Those opposed to the Act got the support of commercial fishermen, who you would have thought would have favored estuarine-protection measures to conserve their stocks. It was also opposed by farmers, many of whom seemed less interested in protecting prime agricultural land than in the possibility of being able to sell it for housing lots. But in the end we got it through. As a result, parts of the coast were designated areas of environmental concern, and programs were started to preserve valuable resources and ensure compatible development. The twenty coastal counties were encouraged to develop their own land-use plans. I'm all for local powers, where that's possible."

I ask Stick how the coastal management has worked

out in practice. He has been in turn a member, vice chairman, and chairman of the North Carolina Resources Commission, which implements the Act. He says, "You have to remember that before 1969 people could do any damn thing they liked on the coast. The Act required setback regulations, which prevented new building close to the beach—for instance, on many of the Currituck Banks lots already laid out and sold. Some of them, like those up in Carova with no roads and services, people thought they were getting at bargain prices. But there were disappointments, too. Some communities were slow to take action. We wanted the professional planners to find out what people hoped their communities would be like in their grandchildren's time, but we had trouble getting politicians to press for this—and it was hard to prevent the planners imposing on the process a set method they'd been taught in college, and imposing predictable conclusions. Many plans, good or bad, have ended up getting stored or ignored. Officials move on; politicians lose elections—there's little continuity. Then, too, there has been difficulty in tying together all the separate plans in a master plan for the coast. Yet I think our big accomplishment was that local officials were forced for the first time to take an intent look at the effects of decisions they had been making regarding land use and growth. For many, it was a revelation. And even some of the go-for-growth types who'd opposed us began to look at the real cost of providing more water, jails, schools, and roads. They'd always said that putting new property on the tax books would pay for all this, but many started to realize that it wouldn't."

Stick relights his pipe. He looks out across the grass to the golf course, where some golfers are waiting to tee off. He says, "At the moment what worries me most are the problems of water supply and sewage disposal, which aren't being looked at clearly. Most communities out here, except for Manteo, have no sewage mains—it's almost entirely private septic tanks, and after a storm inundates the area, the tanks overflow. Many natural spillways have been built over, so flooding causes damage to roads and houses, and then there are requests for emergency government aid. Dare County is now putting through new taxes—a land-transfer tax and a tourist tax—to help pay for bigger water systems, but that's only going to prompt further growth and more demand for water. We sit out here on a narrow sandbar that is situated between the salty Atlantic and the brackish sounds, and has only a thin layer of surface water, which can only be replenished by rainfall. Yet we not only pump the drinkable water out faster than nature can replace it, we supplant the fresh water with waste from toilets and kitchen sinks— and in such quantities that the fresh water and the waste material are on the verge of becoming one."

(94)

I suggest to Stick that in some ways it might have been better if the Banks had not tried to find ways of matching the living standards of the rest of America— though I could see that it was easy for an outsider to propose this: someone who has a comfortable life asking someone else, whose life seems picturesque and characterful, to keep it that way by doing without.

Stick says, "It used to be that Outer Banks people were invariably competent. If your car broke down, you'd walk along and in the first house you came to someone would be able to fix it. This went with the self-sufficiency we had out here. There just weren't the services. People were accustomed to catching and growing a lot of their own food and doing their own repairs. This self-sufficiency meant pride in an ability to do things and make things, and a feeling that it was sinful to be in debt. Well, maybe it would have been better to carry on like that, and not try to emulate the rest of the country. But I fear it's too late. Development—exploiting the tourist potential of the Banks— seems like a good idea to many who live here, a lot **(95)** easier than having to go commercial fishing. It will be interesting to see what effect this hurricane Gloria has if it hits here. If it doesn't devastate the Outer Banks, people will probably boast that they lived through a hurricane. They'll want to keep building, or rebuilding, in all the wrong places."

In Old Nags Head, self-preservation—if not self-sufficiency—is in evidence when I return in the afternoon. The big plate-glass windows of the café have been taped, crisscross fashion, and a small handwritten sign displayed: *Closed for Gloria. Back on Saturday.* The radio in the Alliance announced as I drove down from Southern Shores that a hurricane watch is now in effect from Edisto Beach in South Carolina to Cape Henry, Virginia, and that visitors are being advised not to go to the Outer Banks. The Cape Hatteras campground is being closed and campers told to leave the island. Robin says that Roder is still in Wanchese at the boat-yard, where he is hoping to get his boat moved into a proper storage shed. At the hang-gliding establishment, sheets of plywood are being nailed over the windows. Across the road, at the Winslow cottage, I find Mrs. King and Ellen battening down the hatches. Maruca King, who is more cheerful since she managed to get through by phone to her relatives in Mexico City and find out that they are all right, is taping the upstairs windows. I help Ellen move the porch furniture around to the rear of the cottage and pile it together, nesting the capsized rocking chairs in each other's arms and putting one upended table inside another. Then I take out the rickety wood-framed screens and attempt to get the shutters to close properly over the front door and windows. But the shutters are old and misshapen, their hinges rusty and the hooks and eyes—which are meant to hold them shut—often missing. In several cases the shutters have disappeared, and Ellen brings pieces of plywood and hardboard to take their place. With hammer and nails I improvise the defenses, once or twice feeling the need to glance over my shoulder at the sea, fifty yards away, and trying to imagine what a wave will look and sound like as it sluices through the gap in the little dunes and across the porch where I am now standing.

Liz Winslow, with Erin, returns from a shopping trip to Kitty Hawk. She reports that the Virginia Dare hardware store is doing a rattling trade in nails, tape, rope, storm lanterns, candles, batteries, and flashlights. I walk around with her as she inspects our work. Inside, the cottage is darker now that the front windows are boarded over. The interior woodwork is in any case dark-stained and the ceilings are simply the unpainted beams and floorboards of the room above. The kitchen, tacked on at the back of the cottage, has the somewhat antique air that kitchens often acquire in vacation houses, full of dated appliances that have survived because they are less used or because they have achieved a special value by association with holiday pleasures, and on that account cannot be thrown away.

The Winslow family home is in Hertford, on the mainland seventy miles from here by road, on a river that runs into Albemarle Sound. Liz Winslow's father was once the state highway commissioner. She tells me that she has spent summers in this cottage since she was a small child; she inherited the ownership of it from an aunt. Built in 1930, it was moved back from the sea some twenty years ago, and now the beach has come right up to it once again. In the great storm that occurred on Ash Wednesday 1962—a northeaster that did more damage to the Outer Banks than most hurricanes—the cottage lost its front porch and kitchen. She remembers that when she was a child the Coast Guard would send men out on horseback to warn residents of approaching storms. Those were the days when they had to bury deeply the garbage they couldn't burn to prevent it from being dug up by wandering pigs. She has been trying to encourage the dune to build up in front of her cottage, planting grass to hold it together, though it is depressed in one place by the path from the beach to her front door. On the southern flank, moreover, the cottage is exposed, because her neighbors on that side have no dune at all but simply an area of flat sand between cottage and sea. They apparently believe that it is better for a storm to drive water under the cottage, which is up on pilings, rather than force the sand of a dune back onto it.

Liz Winslow says that during the Second World War many families continued to come to Nags Head beach. They blacked out the windows so that enemy submarines couldn't see lights on shore. After the war there were still long gaps along the beach up to Kitty Hawk, where nothing had been built. "We thought the land next to the beach would get developed slowly," she tells me, "but we never expected what happened on the inshore side of the Beach Road. I remember when I asked someone where they lived and they told me on such-and-such a street. A street in Nags Head! First the cross streets came, and then a lot more. The beginning of the end was the Holiday Inn."

She bought what is now the café and bed-and-breakfast, but was then the Harris grocery store, when Mr. Harris retired; she wanted to prevent something dreadful happening on the site, maybe a gas station. Nostalgia also had a part in it, she says—her family always shopped at the Harrises'. Early tomorrow the Winslow party will evacuate from the Outer Banks and drive to Hertford to stay with her brother. I am welcome to come and stay with them, if I care to.

I thank her for the invitation, which is unlooked-for and immensely kind. For the moment, however, I have my Roanoke Island plans. Tomorrow morning I will call my would-be hosts there to see what they intend to do, and will then decide on the Winslow offer of shelter.

As I walk back toward the café from the cottage, sirens are to be heard. A police car, followed by an ambulance, comes speeding up the Beach Road and turns into the area by Kitty Hawk Sports. The ambulance attendants rush into the building carrying an oxygen tank. With several other curious onlookers, I wait to see what happens. In a few minutes, a white-faced young man walks slowly outside. He tells me that he was removing an interior neon sign from a window, so that the glass could be taped on the inside. He handed the neon sign down to a young woman, who was helping him—but they had forgotten to disconnect the power supply. She took the sign from him by grasping it at each end, and immediately became part of a live circuit. She collapsed. In a few minutes the ambulance men reappear: No, she hasn't been electrocuted. A severe shock, a couple of bad burns on her fingers, that seems to be the damage. She is apparently the first victim of the preparations for hurricane Gloria.

In the late evening I walk along the Nags Head

beach. It is getting on for high tide. The weather news at 7 p.m. has been that there is now a hurricane warning, no longer just a hurricane watch. Gloria is a definite threat to this part of the Carolina coast. I have the beach entirely to myself as I walk up to the fishing pier and back; not a single other person is to be seen. The wind is from the northeast, blowing about fifteen to twenty, a moderate breeze, though the waves are bigger and stormier than the wind seems to call for. Large, inexorable seas sweep in, slightly athwart the wind, and crash onto the sand. There are more gulls than I've seen before, standing just in front of the dunes and looking more than usually wary. Suddenly all the cottages and motels seem frailer than ever. But even so, before entering the door of the B & B, I do my best to get all the sand off my feet.

It is the night for weather forecasters. Prime time is theirs, and in the living room of the B & B our attention is rapt—save for Erin, that is, who is absorbed with the miniature handbag her grandmother bought for her today; she takes it around the room, showing us all how it opens and closes. Roder switches from one weather report to another, but there is little variety in the news they give: Gloria is just over five hundred miles south-southeast of Cape Hatteras and heading directly this way with a forward speed of twenty miles per hour; the core of the hurricane has a diameter of between fifty and a hundred miles, with maximum winds unchanged—150 miles per hour. There is still a small chance that the hurricane may swing north, stay at sea longer, and perhaps hit land farther up the Eastern Seaboard. On a scale of one to five, five being the strongest, Gloria is classified as a Class 4 hurricane. If it reaches land, it is expected to cause a tidal surge fifteen feet above normal levels. (Roder and I look at each other and say more or less at once: In that case, what if it arrives at high tide?) The island of Ocracoke is now being evacuated because ferries to and from the island are not allowed to run once the wind is over forty miles per hour. The evacuation of Hatteras Island is also being recommended. In its case, a small rise in water level will in many places cover the only road up to the bridge and the upper Banks, making it impassable. One announcer says, "This is one of the more dangerous hurricanes we've had in the last fifty years." Maruca King, who during commercials and repetitive weather statements has been telling me a bit about her life as a convent-school girl, a Paris model, and the wife and now the widow of a British naval officer, says, hitting her forehead with the palm of a hand, "From Mexico to this! Collision course!" At ten o'clock, several hours later than expected, Roder's parents arrive. They have driven from Dayton and in the past hour or so have been coming against a continuous stream of cars leaving the Banks. "What *are* we doing here?" asks Mr. Roderer. He starts to tell a series of jokes, speaking in what from distant memory I recall as a spirit similar to that of someone who has just arrived in an air-raid shelter full of people who are—he imagines rightly—as anxious as himself.

Just before I take myself off to bed, the sailing of the last ferry from Ocracoke to Hatteras is announced for midnight. Furthermore, the gates in the fences at the False Cape and Back Bay Refuges will be left open tonight so that Currituck Banks residents may get most easily into Virginia and away from the coast—a concession from the authorities that speaks of the seriousness of things. In bed, I lie for a long time listening to the surf, wondering if I can detect any change in its note or rote and, if so, what it portends.

Gloria's day. At 7 a.m. it is gray and muggy; the surf sounds as if it is pawing the shore. Traffic is light on the Beach Road, and what there is of it is mostly northbound, with a number of vehicles towing boats and trailers. Downstairs, where I am drawn by the customary smells of coffee and bacon, the television is on and the weather channel is playing to an empty living room. Gloria has not stopped coming. She—as we now are beginning to call it—is less than four hundred miles due south of Cape Hatteras, with winds of 130 miles per hour. If she stays on her present course, she is expected to come ashore in the Carolinas within the next twenty-four hours. A northward turn is still hoped for, but the later it comes, the more chance of Gloria hitting us right here. The present "hurricane warning" status means that people should leave beachfront and low-lying ground, move out of mobile homes, and stay tuned for further safety messages and "advisories." The telephone number of a service called a hurricane hotline is announced, to which one may call for further information; it is *not* toll-free but costs fifty cents for the first minute, and thirty-five cents per minute thereafter, which isn't exactly Good Samaritanship. Some residents of the Outer Banks are interviewed as they leave. One man tells the TV reporter, "I don't mind winds up to a hundred, but 130, that's too much." Coastal boatyards are apparently being inundated with calls from distant owners, asking for their boats to be hauled out.

Robin says that Roder is similarly occupied—having failed to get his boat into inside storage yesterday, he went at dawn this morning to the Wanchese boatyard to ensure that it happened today. Breakfast is remarkably cheerful. The Winslow party come over and say that they plan to leave for Hertford at eleven. According to Robin, she and Roder are going a hundred miles inland to her sister's house in Williamston. Roder's parents are going up to Virginia, away from the coast, to stay with their other son. It seems a good idea for me to call the Grays in Wanchese and ascertain if they are still *in situ*. They are, and will continue to be, says Mrs. Gray. I tell her that in that case I will be over later this morning. Mrs. Gray seems surprised. "You're very brave," she says. Am I? Golly. Liz Winslow repeats her invitation: I am still welcome in Hertford and can come there if Wanchese becomes untenable. When I look at the map, I conclude that this offer is not one I should put off accepting to the last moment, when, in rising wind and water, departing from Roanoke Island may no longer be possible. But for the moment I stick to my plan. Before settling my bill with Robin and putting my gear in the Alliance, I walk across the road to the Winslow cottage. I check my work on the shutters and then remind Liz Winslow, who is packing a suitcase, to turn off the bottled gas, the electricity, and the water. You would think it was my house. And next, not being sure when I will be here again, I take a look at the sea. Large rollers are pounding in from the southeast. It has just started to rain, quite hard. I recall the mariners' rhyme:

> If the wind before the rain,
> Soon it will be fine again.
> But if the rain before the wind,
> Then your sails you'll have to mind.

Finally, goodbyes. It is as if we have known one another for years. I say to Ellen, "I hope for all our sakes this turns out to be simply a lot of excitement for nothing." I can feel the adrenaline starting to flow.

I drive carefully, with the windshield wipers working hard, down the Beach Road and across the two miles of causeway and bridge to Roanoke Island. The causeway restaurants are boarded up. I pass the Tale of a Whale, where Robin waitresses, and where I had some rather undernourished bluefish several nights back, and I wonder what its tale will be tomorrow. If the Banks are low, Roanoke is lower—no dunes or sandhills here; it is as if the marsh which skirts the island has solidified into something slightly more substantial toward the center, but something only a few feet above sea level. The island is sheltered from the direct onslaught of the ocean by Bodie Island, but will that make much difference if the sounds rise eight feet and Roanoke goes underwater? It strikes me that a full fuel tank in the Alliance may be a good idea. I drive to Manteo, the island town which is about halfway up the eastern side of Roanoke, and find a busy gas station. Cars are being filled up in preparation for the trip to the mainland. Then I turn back, down to Wanchese. The intervening land is not overdeveloped. Small dirt lanes run off through swampy woods. An occasional house or trailer sits in an unkempt clearing. I pass the radio transmitting tower of the local station, WOBR, also headquartered in a trailer. Wanchese is an extended and somewhat sleepy village, with fishing docks on Mill Creek, several churches, and a few houses gussied up to display prosperity and a large number that testify to a more general difficulty in making ends meet. Near another creek that winds in on the southwestern shore, I find the signboard I am looking for: QUEEN ANNE'S REVENGE. I park at the rear of the restaurant. But between the car and the kitchen door, despite a nylon jacket over my shoulders, I am well soaked.

I feel like someone who has been in a small boat at sea and is picked up by a larger vessel. I am curious about the ark that has rescued me and about its captain and crew. They have an equal interest in me and my voyage to date. This mutual curiosity is heightened—certainly on my part—by the knowledge that we may in fact be about to undergo an ordeal together. Queen Anne's Revenge is named after the flagship of the early-eighteenth-century pirate Edward Teach, also known as Blackbeard, who for a while based his operations on the Outer Banks. (It wasn't an unusual name for a pirate ship. A number were called *Revenge*, but together with a desire for vengeance against society, masking perhaps a desire for spoils, went professions of loyalty to or at least respect for royal personages. Stede Bonnet, another pirate of that time, had one ship named *Revenge* and later another called *Royal James*.) Queen Anne's Revenge in this case is a long, modern, single-story building of white-painted concrete-block construction, with large tinted double-glazed windows, shaded by canvas awnings; it is set well back from the road in grounds that have been divided into a garden sitting area, a car park, and a horse corral. There are many tall trees. The master and his mate are Wayne and Nancy Gray: Wayne in his early forties, assistant principal of Manteo Elementary School (which in anticipation of Gloria did not open today) and co-owner—with Nancy's father—of Queen Anne's Revenge; Nancy in her twenties, with a little girl, Rheanna, at her apron strings and a smaller boy, Richard, riding on her hip. Other members of the crew who soon appear are Nancy's father, Don Beach, who has driven from his home in Southern Shores, and her younger brother, Jim, who lives in a trailer near Manteo and is accompanied by his golden retriever, named Khaki Jones. Wayne, who seems remarkably relaxed about the approaching hurricane, is the master chef. Don is the bookkeeper and host ("I work the front end," he says), and Jim is chief all-around assistant. Wayne, Nancy, and their children live in a house they've built a hundred yards away and which through the trees looks like a tall barn with a greenhouse on one side. I am meant to be staying in a slightly more distant, Victorian, two-story structure known as C. W. Pugh's—Mr. Pugh having been Wayne's great-grandfather and a lighthouse keeper on the Banks at the turn of the century. Nancy tells me that I am the only guest and that I can decide later on whether I want to spend the night at Pugh's or in company with those who will probably be bedding down at Queen Anne's Revenge.

During a break in the downpour, Nancy takes me over to Pugh's. The upstairs is as yet unfinished and bare, but the downstairs, all mine, is nicely restored:

living room, kitchen, bedroom, and bathroom, with a
screened porch at the side and rear. I look at the newly
varnished floors and nicely picked period furniture and
try to imagine where I will plant myself when the wind
begins to shriek. Queen Anne's Revenge, without antique chairs, is spread lower and has less windage, and
looks altogether more secure. Nancy leaves, telling me
to join them for lunch in a while, and I make a reconnaissance of my surroundings. The road goes on a
few hundred yards, with half a dozen trailer homes on
the other side, but soon comes to a halt at the creek.
Croatan Sound, though not far off, is hidden by marsh
grass. Here the calm before the storm—or possibly a
calm that always prevails in Wanchese—is personified
by a small girl, maybe ten years old, who is leaning
over the stern of a sloppily tied-up skiff, fishing pole
in hand. She gives me a brief glance, a terse "Hi," and
returns to her consideration of the water into which
her line descends. On my return walk, past the trailers
where, to my surprise, no one is making any preparations for the storm, such as tying the trailers down
with extra wires, I try to gauge the rise of ground as I
get farther from the creek. It is not very perceptible.
When I reach the restaurant, I find Wayne in the
kitchen. He tells me that in fact QAR is six feet above
mean high-tide level, and that in his experience water
has never quite come into it. The kitchen radio meanwhile keeps us up-to-date on Gloria's progress: at
noon, three hundred miles from Hatteras and ad-
vancing fast toward us; a storm surge of eight to twelve
feet is expected. Eight to twelve feet! Information is
given about what to do in event of power failure, emergency numbers to call, and a request *not* to call long
distance. The station returns to playing country music.
    Lunch, and it is immediately clear that—if one is

going to see out a hurricane in these parts—I've chosen in this respect a dandy spot. Wayne has broiled some wahoo steaks. This is my first acquaintance with this fish. I consume when in New England much scrod and bluefish. Among my memories of splendid meals, fish figures in many: turbot and loup de mer, cod Portuguese and cod-and-potato pie, salmon in various guises. Wahoo seems to be somewhere between swordfish and sea bass, and as Wayne has cooked it, it is simple and scrumptious. We sit at a table by the window in the large, otherwise empty dining room. Wayne says that one of their waitresses has just phoned to ask if she should come in tonight, but he has told her not to—all her colleagues have gone inland. "That's a real dedicated girl," he says, adding that Queen Anne's Revenge has never closed except on Thursdays since it started eight years ago, and that even though today is a Thursday he will serve dinner tonight to anyone who shows up; but he doubts if anyone will.

The sense of well-being induced by lunch is strong, and is slow to disperse. I seem to be the first—watching the wind stir the trees—to feel time's hurrying footsteps. "Shouldn't we be making a few preparations?" I say, tentatively, and Nancy allows as how it might be a good idea to check on the garden furniture. "What about the windows?" I ask, blessed as I am with a keen imagination for disaster, and able to visualize these large sheets of thermopane glass bowing under pressure and exploding in fragments in all directions. "We'd probably better tape them," says Don Beach.

Outside, Nancy and I round up the Adirondack chairs, tilt them up against the bigger trees, and rope them together. Don Beach starts to tape the windows. I am standing staring at the awnings, which are rigged on permanent hoops of alloy tubing over the windows, when Wayne halts beside me. "I've got those in the back of my mind," he says—then adds "Thanks," as if the awnings might have been brought to the front of his mind by seeing me stand there looking like a sailor who is unsure which sail to strike next. It may be that I am acting like a frightened novice—but, in fact, having been at sea in winds of near-hurricane strength, I believe that we should be preparing for winds of perhaps double that power with the utmost dispatch and respect. I bring my gear indoors from Mr. Avis's car and then park it in what appears to be the best spot, sufficiently close to the restaurant so that it may be sheltered from the wind some of the time but also as far as I can get it from loblolly pine and black gum trees that might fall on it. At what wind speed a Renault Alliance becomes airborne remains to be seen. Then Wayne, Don, Jim, and I remove the awnings, taking turns standing on a stepladder and unscrewing their fastenings while the others bear the weight. Tiny tree frogs jump from the awnings onto the walls and ground. For the moment, all is still, save for rainwater dripping; the wind has completely dropped. The awnings are stored in a shed, and then we help Nancy finish taping the windows. Wayne says that this morning he took the horse, Daniel, from its corral to a field on slightly higher ground. Daniel belongs to his older daughter, Keil (who lives with her mother, Wayne's former wife), and has been hyperactive for the last few days. Possibly hyperanxious, I ask Wayne if he has flood insurance. "Yup," he says, "it's mandatory. I complained about it, since we've never had any water in here. But we may not be complaining tomorrow morning."

As I go through the kitchen to find more tape in a rear office, I hear from the radio that stores are closing in Manteo and that the evacuation of Roanoke Island is now recommended. The clearing of people from the Outer Banks continues. Traffic for the mainland is said to be bumper to bumper on the Wright Bridge. Up on the Chesapeake, the evacuation of the Eastern Shore is commencing. An A.T.&T. commercial. Then music.

Wayne says that he is taking his pickup truck to get some gasoline for the emergency generator and to have a look at the beach. Do I want to come along? We take a swing through Manteo, where pumpkins are piled festively outside Wayne's school and where, at the gas station I had visited earlier, things are now relatively peaceful. The proprietor, a black man whom Wayne introduces to me as Roy Rogers Scarborough, tells us that most Manteo residents have "boarded up and gone ashore." The man who owns the bookshop has moved his stock to the highest shelves. Roy's son—John Wayne Scarborough—fills Wayne's two five-gallon drums. The little plastic pennons that are draped from a rope around the boundaries of the gas station are now fluttering actively; the wind is getting up. It is just three o'clock as we drive over the bridge and causeway, and then turn up the Beach Road toward Nags Head. The road is empty. Wayne stops the pickup in the road and gets out to take a photograph of it in its gray, wet, strangely carless state. All the motels and cottages seem to be deserted, and most are boarded up. On some porches and balconies orange fish-shaped wind socks have been left flying. On plywood covering the front windows of the Nags Head Country Store someone has written: *Realtors Beware. Possible Oceanfront. Not Cheap.* Finally we meet another vehicle, a small yellow fire truck whose crew are warning any remaining residents to leave the Banks. Wayne stops and exchanges greetings with the driver, an old acquaintance. Just beyond the deserted B & B we pass an electricity company gang inspecting power lines. The geese from the ornamental pond in front of the Galleon Esplanade are taking advantage of conditions to waddle along the middle of the road. "During the Ash Wednesday storm in 1962 I came up here with some friends in a flat-bottom boat, powered by an outboard," says Wayne. He points out along the beach some buildings which he reckons won't withstand even a hundred-mile-an-hour wind. Another piece of new graffiti: *Gloria is a bitch*. In the Beach Sentry Hardware Store, Wayne buys some batteries; the last two rolls of tape in the place rest on the counter. Next door, in the Mill Outlet and Ice Shop, I purchase some chocolate bars as emergency rations and a copy of *The Virginian-Pilot*, whose main headline is HURRICANE HEADING FOR CAROLINAS. The plump elderly lady who takes my money for these items says that she is staying put. She has been told that people who depart will not be allowed back into the evacuated areas until public-health officials and building inspectors have given their approval. She says, "I figure I'd kill someone who won't let me return to my store." I figure she means it. Back in the pickup, we turn south again on reaching a point in Kill Devil Hills where a realtor's billboard trumpets the tax advantages of buying vacation property on the Outer Banks.

I am beginning to think it is time we got off the Banks, but Wayne wants to see what it is like down at Oregon Inlet. We bear left at the intersection with the causeway leading to Roanoke and head down the continuation of the upper Banks called Bodie Island— Wayne pronounces it Bah-dee. For the most part this is National Park territory, with little development. Dunes and grass flats on either side of the road. The road deserted save for a solitary police car, headlights on, speeding north. In the marina on Roanoke Sound, just above the inlet, one boat remains where, according to Wayne, more than forty are usually moored. I wonder—this is now a recurring thought—if it will be there tomorrow. We drive out over the long bridge to Hatteras Island and park at the top of the hump of the traffic-free span. Gulls soar above the bridge. The inlet looks rough, and it is hard to see where the navigable channel runs. Wayne takes some more photographs. "I want my children to know what this looked like," he says. The afternoon light—hitherto that of a humid gray late-September day—has begun to change; there is a slightly curdled yellow look to the clouds up high.

Back on Bodie Island just above the bridge, Wayne turns the pickup off the road toward the ocean. He stops to lock the hubs, then puts the truck into four-wheel drive. We turn down a sandy track and out onto the beach, where Wayne halts and switches off the engine. (What if it won't restart?) The wind is steady out of the east, a strong breeze of maybe thirty to thirty-five. Beautiful great gray-green combers are charging in, smashing on the sand, sending up explosions of spray. And along the water's edge, in the almost opaque spray and spume, thousands of small gray shorebirds, waders and sanderlings, are standing attentively, slightly askant the wind, as if waiting for a collective decision to be arrived at. "I've never seen them like that before," says Wayne. "Armies of them. That's weird."

At Queen Anne's Revenge, when we return, the news from WOBR is that the evacuation of all of Dare County, including Roanoke Island and presumably the easily flooded mainland fringe of the sounds, is now strongly urged. The Manteo town water supply will be turned off at 5 p.m., an action being taken, one gathers, to avoid loss of water if pipes rupture during the storm. There will be a curfew after 9 p.m.: liquor stores will shut; the bridges onto Roanoke will be closed to incoming traffic. High tide tomorrow morning at Oregon Inlet is at 7:48. This is significant information. If Gloria strikes, it will be better if she does so as close to low water as possible. In any event, I put my suitcase, backpack, and briefcase on the highest shelf in a pantry behind the dining room, about seven feet off the floor; I reckon this shelf to be about twelve feet above normal high water. I sit in the dining room and read *The Virginian-Pilot*, which says that Gloria is now classified as a borderline Class 5 hurricane, the only one so recorded over the open Atlantic and one of the five most powerful storms ever. (Class 5 hurricanes have winds over 155 mph, and only two have hit the United States since record-keeping began: the 1935 Labor Day hurricane which devastated the Florida Keys and killed 600 people, and Camille, which smashed into the Mississippi coast in 1969, killing 256.) However, *The Virginian-Pilot* adds that Gloria's winds had "dropped" late yesterday from 150 to 135 mph, which I would have thought put it back into Class 4 (winds up to 155 mph; expected storm surge of thirteen to eighteen feet). There is no additional comfort in the photograph the paper prints, taken from a satellite and showing the three-hundred-mile-diameter vortex of cloud, the engine of destruction.

At five-thirty, Don Beach brings over to my table two large goblets of red wine and sits down. He used to be a salesman, he tells me, for the Flexible Steel Lacing Company of Indianapolis. When he retired to go into the QAR partnership with Wayne, Wayne provided the land, Don put up an amount equal to the value of the land, and they borrowed the rest. People said, "A high-class restaurant on a dead-end road in Wanchese! You'll never make it." But there have been few nights since opening when business has been poor—a Super Bowl Sunday was one, a blizzard in '82 another. He agrees with Wayne that Queen Anne's Revenge is open tonight. I say, "I'd like to make a reservation."

Outside, the evening appears strangely calm. From the radio, which has been moved to the bar in the dining room, WOBR tells us the wind is a mere 17 mph, and a few heavy showers are to be expected. Roy Rogers Scarborough, interviewed by the station, says that he is still open for business. Everyone else in Manteo is closed up tight. The forecasters are having trouble deciding whether or not Gloria is making the northward turn, long anticipated, which will spare us and endanger the seaboard farther north. Despite radar, hurricane science isn't completely without guesswork. Don says, "It makes you wonder how the old-timers knew a storm was coming. They must have watched their animals, their horses, like Daniel, who sensed the trouble in the air." He returns to his accounts, taking the opportunity of what he calls a quiet evening to bring his books up-to-date. I go on reading in David Stick's history of the Banks the chapter entitled "Storms and Shipwrecks."

In the nineteenth century the ships that carried most of the passenger and cargo traffic along the coast had no marine weather forecasts, and on numerous occasions many sailed or steamed headlong into destruction. With the wind from the east, the Outer Banks formed a lee shore, made especially hazardous by off-lying shallows, stretching well out to sea, such as Diamond Shoals off Cape Hatteras. Stick estimates that more than 650 vessels have been wrecked, utterly, on the North Carolina coast—a coast which Pilkey and his co-authors point out may get more than its share of hurricane winds, waves, and floods because of the way it protrudes into the Atlantic. One of the earliest storms on the Banks to get into English-language records is the violent gale of June 1586, which hit not long after Sir Francis Drake had arrived with supplies off Roanoke Inlet. (This closed around the end of the eighteenth century but was then roughly where south Nags Head is today.) The main provision ship was blown out to sea and failed to return to the Banks. The colony on Roanoke had been there a year, the second expedition sent out by Sir Walter Raleigh to explore the American coast and establish a settlement; but now, still lacking supplies because of this gale, the hundred colonists under Captain Ralph Lane decided to abandon their Roanoke fort, board the remaining ships, and return to England. They didn't know that another, smaller fleet, under Sir Richard Grenville's command, was to arrive with help a fortnight later and leave fifteen men to hold the fort they found deserted. Drake's storm and Grenville's tardy coming were part of the pattern of unsuccess. When John White arrived a year later, in 1587, with further reinforcements, he found the Roanoke settlement once more deserted, the fifteen gone. And when White, having re-established the colony, was sent back to England for more supplies and colonists, he had evil fortune—it took him nearly three years to return to these parts. The Spanish Armada and other problems intervened. When he did reach the Outer Banks again in 1590, the colony, which had this time included his daughter and granddaughter, was once again truly lost.

Don has switched on the overhead electric candelabra. He and Jim are playing a card game called One Hundred for a penny a point. The radio tells us that the World Trade Center in Manhattan, New York's tallest buildings, will be closed tomorrow just in case, and that traffic is backed up leaving Nags Head. Wayne, who has come in to announce the serving of dinner at seven, looks at me and says "Bullshit." We know that there was hardly anyone left in Nags Head three hours ago. (This is an early instance of "late reporting"—of which there will be other examples over the air during the next few hours.) Wayne says that he has dredged up some weather lore: the right-hand side of a hurricane is the bad one. This is because such storms in the Northern Hemisphere have winds blowing counterclockwise, and thus the wind speeds on the right-hand side of the storm are increased by the storm's forward motion. In other words, if the winds on the right or east side of Gloria are 125 mph, and Gloria's forward speed is 25 mph, as it is now, then those winds are in fact blowing a cumulative 150 mph. On the left or west side, the results are happier: there the storm's forward speed is subtracted from the wind speed, and the effect is winds of a mere 100 mph. Wayne goes on: "If Gloria's eye passes southwest of us across Pamlico Sound, heading toward Engelhard and Columbia, the way one forecaster was suggesting it might, then we're in its east side and in trouble." Jim says, "If it gets too hairy, you'll find me under the bar." Outside, through the tinted glass crisscrossed with tape, the gloomy evening light is fading. It occurs to me that decisions have yet to be made about who is staying where. Wayne says that he, Nancy, and the children have decided to stay in their house. Don and Jim plump for the restaurant, and I accept a renewed proposal to do so, too.

A family dinner. Don, Wayne, Nancy, Jim, Rheanna, Richard (in Nancy's lap), and me. Wayne and Jim bear trays through the swing doors from the kitchen. Crabmeat cocktail. Shish kebab, rice, and zucchini. Blue linen napkins. Led by Nancy we say grace. Don fills our glasses from a big bottle of FJF **(117)** California red. Nancy says to Rheanna, "When you're a big girl, you can tell people you went through a hurricane." Rheanna doesn't look very sure about that being what she wants to do. Only slightly prompted, I hear myself telling snatches of my life story, as fellow passengers are wont to in ships at sea. The lights flicker—go out for a moment—then come on again. As candles are lit, I look at my watch: it is twenty-four minutes past seven. Things are starting early.

After dinner, I go out and stand in the garden. The breeze is still moderate and the rain is not heavy; but a new, almost tropical smell is in the air. It reminds me of the rainy-season smell in West Africa, where I haven't been for thirty-three years. Can Gloria have pushed this dark fragrance ahead of her all the way from her birthplace, perhaps somewhere off the Cape Verde Islands? Wayne's aunt by marriage arrives, a good-looking middle-aged woman named Jayne Gray. She lives in a two-story frame house not far away; her husband refuses to leave it, but she has decided that the restaurant is where she will spend the night. She says that she has heard on the radio that the evening tide in the Delaware is the highest ever recorded in non-storm conditions. The game Trivial Pursuit is brought out and we start playing. Question: "What was the nickname of Haitian President François Duvalier?"

At 8 p.m., Gloria is reported to be less than 150

miles from Cape Hatteras. WOBR tells us that it is blowing 45 mph there now and waves are breaking over the sandbags around Cape Hatteras lighthouse. The island of Ocracoke is already being severely flooded. Gloria's forward speed is thought to be increasing. The leading edge of the hurricane may be making a landfall before midnight. Barometric pressure is now falling fast. Emergency services on the Outer Banks are moving their base from Nags Head to Manteo, and a field hospital is being set up at Manteo Elementary School—Wayne's school. More questions: "What is earth's galaxy called?" "Who was the second actor to die in the film *Psycho*?" Don says, "I always know the answers to the other guy's questions, like 'What stands on X thousand acres of landfill in Jamaica Bay, New York?' " Nancy replants a baby bottle in Richard's mouth and complains, "I keep getting questions about country-and-western singers." The radar at the National Weather Service station at Cape Hatteras has now picked up the eye of the hurricane. Gloria's track is expected to take her over the Pamlico/ Albemarle Sounds area—i.e., where we are. Wayne says, with less than absolute conviction, "Come on, Gloria baby—you don't scare me."

There is a rap on the front door, which nevertheless opens before anyone can go to it. The new arrival is Harry Niser, who is in his late forties, has long sideburns and a trim mustache, and is carrying a can of Budweiser. Something in his appearance makes me think he is a former Coast Guardsman, though it transpires that in fact he was once a printer and is now a mason; he helped build Queen Anne's Revenge, laying many of the concrete blocks for the walls and some of the brickwork for the main fireplace and chimney. "I hope you're planning to stay," I tell him, encouraged by this show of faith in his handiwork. Harry says, "The captain goes down with his ship." (Later, I learn that he once had a bluegrass band and played at square dances where David Stick called the figures. Some thought it exceptional that Harry had arrived to spend the night here without bringing his banjo with him.) Harry lives in a house in the marshes a few miles north of Wanchese. Rheanna says she isn't going to go there again until he gets rid of the mosquitoes. "Well," says Harry, "there ain't no mosquitoes there tonight. They all done gone inland." I suspect Harry is grateful to me for being a new addition to his audience. He tells us that old-timers knew a storm was coming when they saw a pig with a straw in its mouth. He himself has seen a storm or two. Before daybreak there will be some sport, he reckons. Garbage cans going down the road like they had motors in them. Trees flying around like they had wings. He's known a hurricane to set off tornadoes, to blow down even concrete-block buildings. We're going to get wet feet right here for sure.

Challenged by this prospect, I attempt to work out when the eye will be over us and what the state of the tide will be. It seems to me Gloria will be doing her worst about the time of low water—though this may be wishful thinking. However, Harry is perhaps reassured by this notion, for he starts to talk about a book he has been reading on nuclear matters: fission, fusion, core meltdown. WOBR announces that the wind on Roanoke is now gusting to 45, and indeed we can now hear it for the first time through the sealed windows. The sea is overwashing parts of Hatteras Island, where the power is out. No alcoholic beverages are being sold anywhere in Dare County. "Too bad," we say. On our table is Don's jug of red wine, a half bottle of Scotch belonging to me, some beer brought

in by Wayne to supplement Harry's Bud, and an un-
labeled mason jar of nearly colorless liquor, pure corn
whiskey, which is what moonshine is in these parts. It
tastes, to my cosmopolitan tongue, a little like slivovitz.
When I ask Harry where it came from, he says, with
a grin that indicates he doesn't expect to be believed,
"Some Indians upcountry."

At ten, WOBR announces that Gloria is 140 miles
south of Cape Hatteras, but this—given the position
at eight—seems like a tardy report. The barometric
pressure of the storm is given as 27.9 and its course
appears unchanged. We have decided that around
2 a.m. the excitement may begin at QAR. WOBR apol-
ogizes—they are closing down the station and evacuating because they are only seven feet above sea level.
"So are we," says Wayne. We discuss taking over the
station and going on broadcasting. Harry says he'll
play records by the Hollys all night. (The Hollys are a
British group, he tells me, though I've never heard of
them.) Jim says Harry can do this if he runs frequent
commercials for Queen Anne's Revenge. Jim and
Wayne have just beaten Nancy and me at Trivial Pursuit. Nancy decides to put the children to bed and says
good night, good luck. I take a stroll outside where the
wind has got up—it is blowing nearly gale force. It is
also astonishingly hot, with squalls of rain, and the
gusts shake the pine and gum trees. I return to hear
the end of a story Harry has been telling about someone called Bad Jim, a story he has, I gather, told many
times before, but which is met with much laughter.
Another radio station has been found to replace our
fearful friends. This is WWOK, in Columbia, near
Elizabeth City, and as Wayne tunes it in, it is broadcasting an announcement from State Farm Insurance,
telling the firm's clients to contact a State Farm agent

if they suffer damage to their homes or farms. I'm not sure this endears State Farm Insurance to me—or re-assures its apprehensive clients. According to the National Weather Service, a ham-radio operator has reported a tornado in Hyde County, southwest of us in Dare. (So not all of Harry Niser's stories are tall!) The Weather Service goes on to say that in Hyde and Dare Counties it is now unsafe to be out-of-doors.

Wayne announces that it is time for him to go to the house. Don decides to go with him. Wayne says to us, "Make sure you all stay sober so you remember what happens." I go on a long and serious reconnaissance of the restaurant to determine where I may later on kip down. I examine wine cupboards and pantries. I consider the kitchen with its stainless-steel-topped worktables, reminiscent of the indoor Morrison air-raid shelters used in Britain during World War II. I ponder the brick hearth and chimney, which Harry had a hand in building, but he has already said that if the wind gets up to 130 he is going to crawl into the fireplace, and in there it looks like room for one. In my considerations, I take into account ceiling height, the distance between walls, and the proximity of windows. I think about the roof falling in or blowing off, and about the walls imploding (which sounds worse than exploding). Animals should have an instinct for these things, but Khaki Jones, Jim's dog, is asleep, confidently flat out on the mat just inside the glass front door. I conclude that the best refuge is the office, at the rear; it is the smallest of the rooms that have a window and, strangely, despite the danger of flying glass, I continue to want a window for the sense of access it gives to the outside world. I put on the floor a mattress and blanket—brought over earlier by Wayne and Nancy—and slide one end of the bedding under a solid-looking desk. Perhaps that's where I'll lay my head.

Meanwhile, WWOK continues to keep us informed. At 11 p.m. we learn that play at the gaming tables in Atlantic City has been halted. The *Elizabeth II*, a replica of a sixteenth-century English ship that usually berths at Manteo, earlier today took refuge in a creek well inland—"and," says Harry, "is probably roundabout Idaho by now." At 11:20 the eye of Gloria is reported as one hundred miles south of Cape Hatteras, where it is now blowing 75 mph—hurricane strength. Harry starts talking about the *Titanic* (the association of ideas, in his case, is no obscure, deeply buried matter), and when that subject doesn't strike much conversational response from Jayne, Jim, or me, he moves on to the magical properties of cement. In making cement, he says, you should use "sharp" sand, not "round" sand. It requires a little reflection to deduce what has led him to this. I take another sip of moonshine. Ah, of course, he is worrying about the quality of the mortar that holds QAR together. As a diversion, I ask what other major events have occurred in Wanchese recently. Jim, with help from Harry, tells of a major drug bust a year ago. Marijuana was being landed in the creek at the end of the road and trailer trucks were taking it away. A number of people, including a few locals, are now serving time.

Just after midnight the lights flicker again; we light several oil lamps as a more reliable standby than candles. WWOK, quoting another ham operator, tells us that the water has completely drained out of Hatteras harbor. Harry, who has switched from moonshine and Bud to Teacher's Scotch, says, "You can walk in a ninety-mile-an-hour wind but you have to be careful it doesn't slip your feet out from under you. Right here, our biggest enemy is the water." Harry is beginning to scare me. To begin with, he seemed cool and experienced. Now he says, "We're going to get this son of a bitch. I can feel it. We're going to see all sides of it, I tell you." He and Jim nevertheless make a quick foray outside and when they come back report that trees roundabout are "popping off" in the wind. I check to see that they have remembered to lock the front door.

At 12:24 the electric lights go on and off several times and then go out and stay out. In the wavering lamplight it at first seems quieter: the central air conditioning has stopped working with the loss of power. But in the interior quiet, despite the well-sealed windows, I can hear the wind grizzling. The contents of both the whiskey bottle and the moonshine jar have dropped remarkably, and I have a sudden surreal thought that barometric pressure has lowered them. At half past midnight we get a midnight report of conditions at Diamond Shoals lightship, thirteen nautical miles off Cape Hatteras, where there have been sustained winds of nearly a hundred and a peak gust of 110 miles per hour. The eye is now said to be fifty miles south of Cape Hatteras. "That means we're up for it next," says Harry. "In an hour or so."

At 12:40 my conversational abilities collapse. It may be nervous exhaustion, or the effect of the moonshine and Teacher's and California Red, but my eyelids keep closing with a thud. It occurs to me that if the roof does blow off, or the water comes sweeping in, it won't make much difference whether or not I am asleep—I will damn speedily wake up. I take an oil lamp, which is of the sort used for atmospheric dining-table decoration, and find my way to the office, where I stretch out on the mattress. But tired as I am, it isn't easy to fall asleep. The office feels sticky and close. Lying down, at floor level, I can hear the wind as I haven't heard it before, still muted by the effective sealing of the building's joints but increasingly, intimidatingly, audible. The wind hisses as it hits the window glass head on and spreads out. It is as if a beast is snuffling outside, has the scent of us, and is letting off a shrill ferocious whine of pleasure. Will it miss the hole we are in, scent other prey, and stamp away from us?

When I look at my watch it is 1:45. I must have dozed. I take a little walk inside the building. Jayne and Jim have moved into the kitchen, away from the big glass windows at the front, and are playing Trivial Pursuit again. The radio is on. Harry, unmoved, is snoring in his chair in the dining room. Khaki Jones is still where he was, flat out. Through the windows I can see the limbs of the nearest trees dancing tormentedly. There are sharp bangs against the roof overhead—presumably branches blown from the surrounding trees. Curious that the building isn't shaking, though I can feel a strange weight, maybe the low pressure, that makes me feel shaky. As I lie down again in the office, I hear from the kitchen, " 'What country was the scene of the Boxer rebellion?' " Heavy rain begins to beat against the office window with a rhythm like that of waves breaking against a ship. Thunder sounds loud and close, and the room is lit by strokes of lightning. Then there comes a loud crash from the pantry. I dash out and meet Jim on the spot where a huge sack of potatoes has—an act of God—fallen over. Jim and I say more or less in unison, "If this is the worst thing that happens, we'll be all right."

A phone is ringing. It is somewhere over my head. I reach up for the receiver and bring it down from the desk to my ear, noticing that outside it is daylight; a quarter past seven. On the phone, a woman neighbor, wondering if Jayne is here. I get up and find Jayne on a mattress in a storeroom beyond the kitchen. Harry and Jim are asleep on the floor in other parts of the restaurant. Khaki Jones is sitting up, waiting to be let out. I open the front door for him. The wind is blowing a cheerful sort of gale; water covers much of the grounds and laps against the front steps; several trees are down, and broken branches are strewn everywhere. At the rear of Queen Anne's Revenge, the Renault is resting on all four wheels, unscathed, though plastered with wet leaves and twigs. I start singing a hymn which I used to sing with my fellow campers before breakfast in camp in Michigan during the summers of 1943 and 1944: "Holy, holy, holy, Lord God Almighty, early in the morning our song shall rise to Thee."

Wayne arrives in rubber boots and says he slept right

through it. He proposes a short survey expedition. We board the pickup and drive slowly around the neighborhood, much of which is awash, with many roads impassable. At the nearby boatyard, a number of the docks are well underwater, one boat outside a shed has been blown off its cradle, and a temporary structure of wooden poles and plastic sheeting—which I later learn had been covering Roder's Chris-Craft before he got it moved under better cover—is a tangled wreckage. The road to Manteo is under several feet of water, and cars are turning back as their drivers discover this. Here and there on roofs, shingles and tarpaper have come adrift; some windows are broken and storm doors wrenched off; everywhere a lot of yard work will have to be done. But there is no doubt: Wanchese has been spared.

At Queen Anne's Revenge, a celebratory breakfast. Wayne peels and slices potatoes, then fries them on the griddle with onions, ham, bread. The eggs are scrambled. Jayne has gone home, and so has Harry. The ordinary delights of cool orange juice, hot coffee, are this morning extraordinary. From the radio, we learn that Gloria after all took a northward turn just before she would have made a landfall in North Carolina. The worst of the hurricane stayed offshore, the storm brushing the coast with its less fierce, left side. Moreover, Gloria came past with strong forward speed, not lingering. And she did so more or less at low tide. Even so, there has been considerable erosion, overwash, and flooding on Ocracoke and Hatteras Islands. On Roanoke there have been two serious fires—in a house near the causeway to Nags Head and at the largest hardware store in Manteo. A ship just east of the eye reported forty-one-foot waves. Gusts of 120 miles per hour were recorded in parts of the Outer Banks. We were lucky.

I spend the morning helping Wayne and Nancy clear up the grounds. The water gradually subsides. The two large trees that are down are a dogwood, which has fallen in front of C. W. Pugh's, and a weeping willow, which has been uprooted and leans against Wayne and Nancy's house, apparently without damaging it. In midmorning Harry reappears; he can't get into his house in the swamp because the access track is flooded. He parks his car at one side of the restaurant and falls asleep behind the steering wheel. Wayne and I haul the broken boughs of sweet gum, dogwood, willow, and pine to a sequestered spot on the edge of the property. Nancy rakes up the smaller debris and untethers the garden furniture. I'm not usually much of a gardener, but this seems less of a chore than a form of thanksgiving.

By the end of the morning most of the water has drained away from the road up the island. I drive to Manteo for my first extended look at the place. It is a small town which at once gives the impression of being year-round, not a resort, and neo-Elizabethan is the prevailing style. Among other structures a bank, an insurance office, a funeral home, a restaurant, and a movie theater have woodwork stuck to their façades to suggest sixteenth-century half-timbered construction, and here and there leaded glass and mullioned windows intensify the mock-Tudor effect. Today the owners of some of the stores that haven't gone along with so Olde World a trend may be wishing they had done so as, with their large plate-glass windows blown out, they stand in the street sweeping up the fragments. From many buildings, without making architectural distinctions, Gloria has torn off and wrenched away awnings and canopies and carried them off down the street. On the site of the Ace Hardware Store, a huge pile of ashes is smoldering (the fire caused, it seems, by a falling power line, and rendered so destructive by the fact that there was insufficient water pressure to put it out). Schools, offices, and shops are all closed, though people are everywhere clearing up the mess and bringing carpets out to dry.

A few miles northeast of Manteo, close to the top of the island where a highway bridge crosses Croatan Sound to the mainland, a sign points the way to the headquarters in these parts of the National Park Service and several adjacent attractions: Fort Raleigh, the Elizabethan Gardens, and the Lost Colony outdoor theater. The Park Service offices and visitors' center are closed. The Elizabethan Gardens—run by the Garden Clubs of North Carolina—are shut, too, while storm debris is cleared away, so I am unable to sniff around the herb garden or admire the antique statuary given by Ambassador and Mrs. John Hay Whitney. As for the theater, dedicated to performances of Paul Green's "symphonic drama," *The Lost Colony*— which has been seen by roughly two and a half million people since it first opened in 1937, this is open only during the summer. I therefore walk along one of several trails which run through thick woods close to the north shore of the island and converge on the site of what is now called Fort Raleigh. I step over and around fallen branches. The afternoon is humid and warm; the sun is shining; birds are singing; the wind is moderate. Twelve hours ago it was blowing nearly a hundred miles per hour; now it is barely fifteen. My path is paved with reddish-brown pine needles. The trees are cedar, sassafras, loblolly pine, and oak; the woods are fragrant. I arrive at what may have been Captain Ralph Lane's fort, built four hundred years ago in the summer of 1585. It is surprisingly small. The grassed, chest-high ramparts are laid out in an irregular star shape, and now seem less like a defensive earthwork than a green play space designed for children. This is thought to be the spot Lane and his settlers abandoned when Drake stopped by and—the provisions lost—offered the opportunity of a ride home.

The profound disadvantages of the Outer Banks as a place of first settlement are still so conspicuous that it requires an effort to put ourselves into the boots of the Elizabethans and understand why they chose to make the attempt here. At the back of their minds, perhaps, were the words of the charter which Queen Elizabeth had given Sir Humphrey Gilbert—Walter Raleigh's half brother—in 1578, "to inhabit and possess . . . all remote and heathen lands not in actual possession of any Christian prince." Perhaps, too, some knew the words of Gilbert and Raleigh's contemporary Francis Bacon: "Even if the breath of hope which blows on us from that New Continent were fainter than it is and harder to perceive, yet the trial must be made." The explorer Verrazano—a Florentine in French service—had sailed along here in 1524, the first European known to have examined the coast north of Cape Fear, and had conjectured that the water he could see behind the Outer Banks was that of the Pacific Ocean. The English, sixty years later, wanted to avoid places like Mexico and Florida, where the Spanish were already based; but they also wanted a spot from which they could prey on Spanish shipping. And as they met the coast of the New World, what may have mattered most was simply the sweet smell of land after the perils, privation, and suspense of months at sea. Any land would have looked good, and for the moment they set aside the difficulties of landing on the Carolina coast—particularly of negotiating the shoal inlets without grounding or stranding, and of discovering along the shores of the shallow sounds a practical site for a settlement, where water was to be found, food could be grown, and the natives were not unfriendly. They took the first welcoming entrance they came upon and played down the problems. The first party that Sir Walter Raleigh (with a charter similar to Gilbert's) sent out in April 1584 certainly reported the bright side on their return in September. Captains Philip Amadas and Arthur Barlowe wrote as if they had visited Eden. This was "the goodliest land under the cope of heaven," fertile for various fruits and crops, with an abundance of grapes and game, and waters full of fish. There were skins and pearls to be had. "The soile is the most plentifull, sweete, fruitfull, and wholsome of all the world." The timber was fine. And as for the natives on Roanoke Island: "Wee found the people most gentle, loving, and faithfull, void of all guile, and treason, and such as lived after the manner of the golden age." To provide living proof of this, Amadas and Barlowe took back with them two Indians, Manteo and Wanchese.

As a company prospectus, the report of the two captains worked—fresh support and investment for the Raleigh enterprise was forthcoming. The following year, 1585, Sir Richard Grenville led a second expedition to these shores, bringing the two Indians home and leaving his second-in-command, Ralph Lane, on Roanoke with 108 men—a holding party which included the naturalist Thomas Hariot and the artist John White. Surveys and investigations of the surrounding country were made. A fort was built. Lane's men went looking for gold and got as far as Chesapeake Bay—which was recognized as a better place for a colony, with safer access from the sea. But by the time Drake anchored off Roanoke Inlet in June 1586, after destroying the Spanish fort at St. Augustine, Lane and his men had run through their resources—both of food and of tact. They had quarreled with the Indians. And so, when Drake's promised ship and supplies went out to sea with the storm, they cut their losses and sailed home. Grenville arrived shortly thereafter with reinforcements and found Lane and company gone. The small party he left on Roanoke was soon overrun by the Indians. The island was therefore once again deserted—at least by the English—when John White returned in 1587 with the makings of a proper colony: men, women, and children. Even so, it would seem that White wanted to settle his group—116 in number—on the Chesapeake, and it was only his failure to dominate the veteran Portuguese pilot Simon Fernandes that caused them to be left at Roanoke, where they had called in hope of collecting Grenville's men. Fernandes was impatient to get home. One would have thought that the very fact that none of Grenville's party was to be found—save for the bones of one—would have given White strength of argument, especially as the settlers included his pregnant daughter and her husband. White, however, seemed satisfied at finding the dwellings Lane's men had built "standing unhurt," though "the forte was rased down." The birth of his granddaughter Virginia Dare on Roanoke on August 18, 1587, was a good omen. But White was then talked into returning to England for supplies and reinforcements, which he did—and thereafter found himself at the mercy of European politics and human nature. The threat of a Spanish invasion required all the ships Elizabeth could muster. When White did get a vessel and set sail in April 1588, he and the crew were robbed by pirates off the Azores and forced to return to England. After the Armada, he was unable to organize any help in 1589, and it was 1590—three years after he had last been on Roanoke—that he returned to a desolate discovery. He was unable to persuade his sailors—who were keen to go privateering—to make a stay long enough to conduct a thorough search for the missing colonists, and to pursue such clues as indicated that the settlers may have gone farther south along the Banks to friendly Indians at Croatan, now part of Hatteras Island, or had (as White felt likely) afterward gone north to the better locality of Chesapeake Bay. White wrote of that sad return to Roanoke and of how his party "sounded with a trumpet a Call, & afterwardes many familiar English tunes of Songs, and called to them friendly; But we had no answere."

The mystery remains, though there have been ideas enough about what happened to the Lost Colony. Paul Green, in the last scene of his outdoor drama, suggests that Roanoke was abandoned because of a Spanish incursion, and White's people moved away, hoping to live in association with the friendly Indians of Manteo's tribe. Some think that the main body of colonists went up to the Chesapeake, as had always been the hope, and were later exterminated by followers of the great Indian chief Powhatan at the time of the landing of the Jamestown expedition in 1607. Others propose that most of the colonists moved down the Banks to what is now Hatteras Island, and—as suggested by the name CROATOAN White found here carved on a post or tree—intermarried with the Croatan Indians, moving on with them as they traveled about North Carolina. John Lawson, journeying in these parts in 1701, noted that the Hatteras tribe had some sixteen warriors still residing near Cape Hatteras, and that several of these had gray eyes and spoke of a close affinity with the white man. Lawson concluded that members of the Lost Colony had been absorbed by them. Although these Indians are believed to have left the Banks by the end of the eighteenth century, there are others known as the Lumbee Indians, residing in Robeson County, well inland, who have English surnames, blue eyes, and curly hair. But whether this is a result of Indians absorbing whites, or whites absorbing Indians, it is hard to say.

Four hundred years on, the non-flesh-and-blood relics of the lost colonists are several. From 1936 to 1948 excavations were conducted at Lane's fort, and among the artifacts found were a wrought-iron sickle and metal tokens used in accounting. More recently, fragments of barrels have surfaced on the beach near the fort—a beach now, but probably some way inland in the sixteenth century—and it is thought that these may be the remnants of wooden shafts for wells. A Spanish reconnoitering party that called here in 1588 reported finding signs of a slipway for small vessels and a number of wells made with English casks, together with other debris that suggested to the Spanish that a considerable number of people had been here. But in a way the most valuable relics are the writings of Thomas Hariot and the drawings of John White. Hariot studied the ways of the Indians, the local plants, and the native methods of setting and sowing. In his *A Briefe and true report of the new found land of Virginia* (1588), Hariot wrote of the natives: "Doubtless it is a pleasant sight to see the people sometimes wading, and going sometimes sailing in these Rivers, which are shallow and not deep, free from all care of heaping up Riches for their Posterity, content with their State, and living friendly together of those things which God of his bounty hath given unto them." After describing various commodities and grains, Hariot mentioned "an herbe" called by the inhabitants *uppowoc* and known in the West Indies as tobacco. The Indians smoked this "by sucking it through pipes made of claie, into their stomache and heade," and Hariot thought that this activity "purgeth superfluous fleame & other grosse humors [and] openeth all the pores & passages of the body . . . whereby their bodies are notably pre- served in health, and know not many greevous diseases." Little did poor Hariot know. He became a heavy smoker, and died in 1621 of what now would probably be diagnosed as cancer of the throat.

John White's reputation as an artist is more secure than as a leader and governor of the colony. He was a keen observer and an excellent painter—and a skillful mapmaker. His map of the Outer Banks (one of the earliest engravings of which I'd seen at David Stick's) is wonderfully accurate, given that he couldn't have done a personal survey of the entire coast that is depicted. The only main feature unfamiliar to the modern eye is the conspicuous, easternmost promontory elsewhere called Cape Kenrick, which has washed away in the years since and is now marked by the Wimble Shoals; the Banks coastline is generally about a mile to the west of where it lay in White's time. White drew the flora, fauna, and the natives, and from these sketches worked up meticulous watercolors. A number of his drawings made while he was official artist to the Grenville-Lane expedition were apparently lost overboard from a pinnace, when his and Hariot's gear was being ferried out to one of Drake's ships in June 1586. But even when he had the added responsibility of being leader of the next colonial attempt, with the title "governour of the Cittie of Raleigh in Virginia," he managed to find time to record what he saw. From White's work we know the sort of place in which Manteo and Wanchese lived, an Indian village enclosed by palisades, with houses with roofs and walls of matting and bark, and we know what they wore and ate: clothing and ornaments, crops and plants. His watercolors of fish, birds, and fruit are particularly vivid—Portuguese men-of-war, flamingos, pineapples, loggerhead tur-

tles—all novelties to him and his fellow venturers.

I walk down to the little beach, close to where the pieces of barrel were found, and gentle waves from Roanoke Sound are slithering up the sand. To see new things is still part of what travel is about, even if many of the things aren't quite as brand-new and unseen by other North European eyes as they were in White's day. Across the sound I can just make out the glint where sun strikes a flank of the Wright Memorial pylon on Big Kill Devil Hill. Then I saunter through the woods, following a trail named after Hariot, passing a small patch dedicated to growing vegetables as the sixteenth-century colonists might have done (judging by some stringy-looking beans clinging to rickety poles, with not much more success), and instructed by the occasional discreet Park Service placard which tells the visitor that, for example, Hariot called persimmons medlars, because they resembled the English fruit of that name. As I step over the fallen branches and now and then around a downed tree, I think about the people who tried to put down roots here but obviously weren't the best of farmers. There were too many officers and gentlemen, not enough skilled craftsmen and laborers. They depended overmuch on the Indians for food, and the Indians, friendly or awed at first, became less so as they realized that the strangers were going to call on them for provisions at any time, and not just when the Indians had a surplus to give or barter. Moreover, the colonists seemed to expect the same barter rates to apply in times of scarcity as in those of plenty; the naïve citizens of the Cittie of Raleigh may not have realized that at certain seasons the Indians had barely enough for themselves. Then there were Indian feuds and wars, dangerous to get involved in, especially when the wrong side could be taken. And not least, the effects of weather—of a storm like Gloria—when one is living in a primitive hut, hoping for an at best scanty harvest from a plot out of which precious seeds may be washed away. For the modern traveler—his food and shelter more or less guaranteed as long as traveler's checks hold out or credit cards are recognized—the precariousness of their enterprise can be grasped only by a healthy stretch of the imagination.

Tonight I take up my quarters in C. W. Pugh's and walk over to Queen Anne's Revenge for dinner. It is a curious feeling to be greeted by Don Beach inside the front door and shown to a table, where a lissome young woman in a simple black dress hands me a menu and asks me what I would like to drink. I look around at the space in which last night I was regarding tables in terms of their ability to shelter me from falling beams and plaster. The restaurant is full. It is as if people are celebrating their escape. But I am not just a customer—Don sits down for a chat during a quiet spell and we talk about Gloria's further progress: speeded up in pace and diminished in power, she has crossed Long Island and is now damaging boats, trees, and power lines on the Connecticut coast. A dessert of considerable richness is brought to me, compliments of Wayne. I read *Humphry Clinker*. I talk to the waitress, named Georgia, who went inland for last night and who has a ravishing smile. Perhaps I have reached that stage in a journey when all the waitresses look beautiful.

I am up early on Saturday and sit on the porch at Pugh's, watching the squirrels bound on the grass and hesitate at the foot of trees. Morning sun. Nancy, infant Richard on hip and Rheanna at her skirt hem, comes across with a covered basket containing my breakfast: even an egg cup has been found for an Englishman's boiled egg. WOBR, back in operation and heard over the Pugh radio, has an obviously pre-Gloria-recorded commercial for Ace Hardware. Hatteras Island is reported as not yet ready for visitors, with roads blocked by sand, power not yet restored in some sections, and some stores with no supplies to sell. I decide that this is all just as well as far as I'm concerned, since I mean to spend a day or so more in these parts before going down there.

In Manteo, puffs of thin smoke are still rising from the Ace Hardware ruins, and carpets remain out to dry. After a day to recover, people are hard at work in their yards and gardens. I feel that I may be taking a slight advantage of the town, poking around it when it is still shown as vulnerable. But Manteo doesn't strike a visitor as at any time reserved or standoffish. It is a place where—if you call for someone at his place of work and find him absent—you may well be told, "Oh, at this time of day he's at the Duchess of Dare." This, formerly Walker's Diner, has been for many years Manteo's central breakfast, luncheon, and dining place, and the general haunt where you can run into everyone and find out what's going on. Across the street from the Duchess is Ye Olde Pioneer Theater, the cinema where this week *Pee Wee's Big Adventure* is playing. The street is called Budleigh Street and has a number of vacant lots, decently grassed, which suggest that Manteo's prosperity has had thin patches since the town was incorporated in 1899. (In particular, the opening of the bridge and causeway to the Banks allowed a lot of the town's trade to shift to Nags Head and Kitty Hawk.) In Budleigh Street I note that the fragments of glass from a front window of Davis's Clothing Store have been swept into a neat pile and plywood nailed across the gap. Across the way, the awning over the window of the stationer's shop (which forms part of the business of the *Coastland Times* newspaper, published three times a week) is still awry, like a hat that has been stopped from falling off by the tip of an ear. In Davis's, a woman is buying shoes for a child, and old Mr. Vernon Davis, the owner, is standing talking in a lilting accent to two other men. One is his not-quite-so-elderly cousin, Herbert Creef, Jr., who is on the Manteo town council and runs the Duke of Dare Motor Lodge. The second is Bud Cannon, a sandy-haired former history teacher in his late thirties who is the director of the Dare County Tourist Bureau. Cannon, after I've been hospitably incorporated in

their conversation, tells me that the bureau was established in 1952, when cutbacks in traditional Banks
employment, such as fishing and the Coast Guard,
began to make themselves felt. Right now about two
and a half million visitors a year come to the Dare
County portion of the Banks, and both these numbers
and the amount visitors spend are going up by more
than 10 percent each year. "You here for the sportfishing?" Mr. Davis asks me. "That's the big attraction
on this coast, starting 'bout now."

I have to deny any sportfishing ambitions, but to
make amends inquire about the four-hundredth-
anniversary celebrations. These—backed by state,
county, and private money—are to be three years long,
from the July 13, 1984, commemoration of the first
landing on Roanoke Island by Amadas and Barlowe,
to the four hundredth anniversary of the birth of Virginia Dare on August 18, 1987. The local organizing
committee decided not only to spread out the celebrations but to give them an educational thrust, in order
to encourage people to recall the Elizabethan attempt
to make a colony here and understand what this involved. Other non-transient ways of marking the Four
Hundredth took the form of substantial improvements
to landscape and townscape: a new public beach at the
northwest corner of the island; the removal of all billboards along Route 164, which approaches Manteo
from the north, and planting beside it fifteen hundred
live oak and crepe myrtle trees—the latter having scar-
let and violet flowers; the backing of archaeological
research into Algonquian Indian sites and the whereabouts of the Cittie of Raleigh (which may or may not
have been adjacent to Lane's fort); and the setting up
of a permanent fishing exhibition in Wanchese and of
a museum in Manteo focused on life in the sixteenth

century, with the sailing ship *Elizabeth II* as its chief exhibit.

Mr. Creef, who is clearly proud of his town, suggests that we go to look at some of Manteo's waterfront improvements for the Four Hundredth. We stroll down Budleigh Street and around the corner by the county courthouse, where several lawyers or politicians are having purposeful conversations and a wedding party is on the steps, having its photo taken. Across the little street, which is grandly named Queen Elizabeth Avenue, a new development of shops and apartments is "now renting," a three-and-a-half-story structure that makes nice modern use of traditional clapboard but seems a bit high and bulky for its surroundings, perhaps maximizing its waterfront dollar-earning potential. But along with this development has come a public promenade beside Dough's Creek, with berths alongside for yachts, and wooden chairs and benches placed for people to sit and look out across the creek to a wharf where the *Elizabeth II* ties up when she is here. At the southern end of Queen Elizabeth Avenue stands what looks at first like a giant statue of a Rose Bowl football player, ample of shoulder, bulking in front of the Manteo sewage treatment plant. As Mr. Creef and I approach this intimidating form, I see that it is carved out of a single block of wood and is in fact a representation of the chief begetter of English colonizing in these parts, who is now, as it were, setting foot here for the first time—Sir Walter Raleigh. He is shown with one hand on hip, a fierce mustache, beetling brows, and a tremendously determined expression. Not at all sweet Sir Walter. From Mr. Creef I get the impression that there is considerable local debate as to the merits of this totemic figure, whose sculptor, R. K. Harniman, has attached not only his own name but the information that the statue is twenty-four feet high, weighs fifteen thousand pounds, and took ten months to complete. Manteo scuttlebutt has it that it was originally commissioned for a shopping center in Raleigh, the state capital, but not put in place.

"You've heard about our ship, I expect," says Mr. Creef, outside the waterfront shed where the *Elizabeth II* was built. Here Mr. Creef and Vernon Davis's grandfather and great-grandfather, both named George Washington Creef, built many Roanoke Island shad-fishing boats and such other vessels as the *Hattie Creef*, on which the Wrights voyaged to Kitty Hawk. The land here has been given to the town by thirty-six Creef heirs as the G. W. Creef Memorial Park. Since civic pride in Manteo seems to be well alloyed with dispute, I'm not surprised to hear that the *Elizabeth II* has its critics, particularly among knowledgeable boat people like the Creefs, who wouldn't have built her in the same way. She is a three-masted bark, sixty-nine feet long, designed by two American naval architects on the lines of English ships of her time and particularly patterned after the *Elizabeth* that sailed in Grenville's 1585 expedition. She was built in Manteo by a shipwright from Rockland, Maine (which may have aroused local jealousy), her planking fastened in the proper sixteenth-century manner with seven thousand wooden trenails, but with hatches enlarged to allow for easier access for visitors and a better view for the helmsman, who in the original models was stuck unsighted below decks, dependent on advice from above. The *Elizabeth II* draws eight feet and, when launched, couldn't reach navigable water in Shallowbag Bay until a channel was specially dredged for her— which some locals say was poor planning and others claim was clever, since deeper access to the waterfront

was needed, anyway, and the Corps of Engineers dug
it. To date, the *Elizabeth II* hasn't shown much sailing
ability, though that may be because the handling of a
sixteenth-century vessel is a lost art. The regional press
seemed to have enjoyed her misadventures on her recent voyage to other ports in the state, when she took
nearly five days to get from Manteo to Beaufort, even
with the towing assistance of the state tug *Albemarle*.
On this trip the decks leaked, the crew's sleeping bags
were soaked, and a woman crew member fell overboard while cleaning a portable toilet (both were recovered). Even so, the *Elizabeth II* looks like being a
considerable draw for tourists curious to know what it
was like aboard a sixteenth-century ship. The sleeping
bags may be an anachronism, but I imagine the leaking
decks are not.

Out on the jetty Mr. Creef introduces me to Harry
Schiffman, the young owner of the Salty Dawg marina,
on the other side of the bay. Schiffman, Manteo's
mayor pro tem, is looking for any damage Gloria may
have caused. There is discussion as to the correctness
of the County Water Department's decision to turn off
Roanoke water before Gloria hit, which meant that
there was insufficient pressure to fight the Ace Hardware blaze. Schiffman says the town's 250,000-gallon
elevated storage tank was pumped full before the department shut down on Thursday afternoon, and must
have been nearly drained by residents filling bathtubs
and jerricans as reserves before the hurricane arrived.
"We're all wise with hindsight," says Schiffman. "I
think we're lucky somebody didn't get hurt."

My tour with Mr. Creef seems to have established
for him that I may be a suitable person to see what he
wants to show me finally, and especially: a Roanoke
Island shad boat he has bought in order to restore. It

is in a shed behind the movie theater. As he opens the shed doors, Mr. Creef rattles off a chronology of the Creefs and their relatives the Davises, five generations involved with boatbuilding, the most recent being Ralph "Buddy" Davis, Jr., whose Wanchese boatworks turns out costly sportfishing cruisers. The boat in the shed bears only a distant relationship to these. Its name is *Paul Jones*; it is twenty-four feet long and open save for modest side decks; and it is painted a faded white, without brightwork. But a brief look at its lines gives me the feeling of shivery pleasure that one can get on encountering any artifact that is recognizable to sight and touch as the apogee of a type or form. "She was built by George Washington Creef, Jr., in 1882," says Mr. Creef, patting the gunwale and nicely adhering to the convention that a boat—whether with a male name or not—is "she." "In those days they arrived at work in the mornings while it was still dark. They sharpened their tools by lantern light till daybreak, when they got going on the boat. Her last state registration sticker is for 1979. I bought her in 1980. Her owner was elderly—the boat needed recaulking and a lot of repair—and the days were past when a man could make a living taking one of these boats out daily and catching eight boxes of fish."

I recall a photograph which was printed, I believe, in a work by the marine historian Howard Chapelle. It showed a bearded North Carolina boatbuilder outside his weathered shed with two shad boats. Could this have been one of the George Washington Creefs? In sepia and white the photograph prompted a sense of a real man who had lived, a real way of life that had passed.

The *Paul Jones* is a snug fit in the shed, but there is just room to edge around her, to sweep one's hand along her rail and feel the considerable sheer, to sight along the waterlines and admire the way the garboards tuck back in at the stern. "You see how clean the decks are," says Mr. Creef. "No fittings on them at all. That's so you could haul in the nets without them snagging." In the decks, holes are placed to take pegs on which sheets and tackle were made fast but which could also be easily removed when the nets were hauled in. There is a feeling of a nautical golden mean having been achieved. Mr. Creef attempts to explain this to me: "It's all thirds in her lines. She has a third of her length in her entry, a third in her run, and a third in the tuck. These proportions made her sail well, made her handy to turn, and made her a good load carrier. The mast is a third back from the stem. She had an easy motion and didn't bob overmuch." Mr. Creef isn't sure if or when he is going to relaunch the *Paul Jones*, but he is enjoying the pleasures of possession, of looking for old juniper stumps with the right curves from which to fashion new knees and frames, and, impelled by contact with the shad boat, of recalling his first rowboat and the adventures he had in it as a boy sixty years ago.

After a late lunch, I drive over the bridge and causeway to Old Nags Head to see how the Winslow establishments have fared during Gloria. In the vicinity, the lofty metal-columned signboard of Kitty Hawk Sports has been blown down, and the police are towing away an abandoned car from the Updraft parking lot. No one is in at the B & B, where nothing seems to be amiss, but across the road I find Ellen shoveling sand out of the cottage. Liz Winslow is upstairs sweeping up glass and sand. They arrived this morning from Hertford and have been busy since. Our defensive works worked where they were put in place, but the strongest winds hit the cottage not at the front but at the back, where there were no shutters and new windows had been installed not long ago, apparently without being properly fastened in place. They had simply been jammed in, trim tacked on around, and no nails or screws actually put in to fix them to the structure of the house. Thus several windows complete with their frames blew into the interior. The wind then knocked pictures and mirrors off the walls. Great quantities of sand blew in thereafter. "Still, it could have been worse," says Liz. Because wind and water came from the northwest rather than from the sea, some houses on the sound side of the Banks have suffered considerable damage. Yet in south Nags Head, below Whalebone Junction and the causeway to Roanoke, erosion has been such that several cottages may have to be condemned. "Now tell us how *you* made out in Wanchese," Ellen says.

I dine down by the Mill Creek docks in Wanchese, at a restaurant named Fisherman's Wharf. I do so because I feel guilty for gustatory inertia—eating happily in the same place several nights running. But my venturesomeness is not rewarded. For one thing, Fisherman's Wharf is dry. For another, the broiled trout I order turns out to be a small gray or speckled sea trout—also known as weakfish (had I but known it!) —served in a pool of cooking oil, of which it largely tastes. I leave a lot on my plate. However, the menu contains a printed *cri de coeur* from the fishermen of Wanchese about the dangers of Oregon Inlet, their access to the sea. This plea and complaint is entitled "A Story of Betrayal," and despite my dissatisfaction with the local catch as tried tonight, I put the inlet on my list of things to inquire into on the morrow.

Sunday morning. I sit in a sunny chair on the Pugh porch with coffee and warm blueberry coffee cake (brought over by Nancy), and then, feeling a need to give thanks for deliverance from catastrophe, I walk half a mile up the road for the eleven o'clock service at Bethany United Methodist Church. An obvious stranger, I am welcomed warmly by others entering. The church is wooden, wainscoted within, with stained glass that is not too gaudy and fans overhead turning slowly so that one can just feel the movement of air. The church is broad rather than long; the pews make embracing sweeps from one side to the other, and the altar—rather than being lost at the distant end of a nave—is at immediate center front. The pews are crowded. Perhaps they always are for this service, although I overhear many expressions of good fortune and I imagine that this may have brought forth a few infrequent churchgoers like me. The congregation is made up of people of all ages in their Sunday best, with a number of elderly couples but also a lot of young ones, many with babies that are remarkably well behaved. I can see Nancy with Rheanna and Richard across the church, and Nancy gives me a quiet smile. The service is led by the pastor, W. T. Clarke, who

speaks with cheerful confidence. He is backed up by a choir whose members wear bright red cassocks and, in turn, are helped along by a small organ. The first hymn, "Tell Me the Stories of Jesus," is a bit sugary for my taste, but is sung with plenty of feeling by choir and congregation—who indeed also put themselves strongly into the Apostles' Creed. Nothing shy and withholding about the members of Bethany United. I try to take heart from this as I see that in the Order of Service, the item following the Gloria Patri is called Recognition of Visitors. Pastor Clarke calls all visitors to their feet. I have to stand up and be recognized and am glad to see that other people are doing the same; but I sit down quickly. A young woman who hails from another part of North Carolina and a family visiting from out of state take the heat for a few minutes, while the good pastor prods them gently to say something about themselves. But it is not to be so easy. An elderly gentleman, whom I had encountered in the vestibule on the way in, fingers me. He calls out from the back, "We have a visitor from London, England."

So I stand again. This is worse than a hurricane. The Reverend Clarke genially asks me what I am doing in these parts, and I say that I am touring the Outer Banks and just happened to be in Wanchese for Gloria. Yet, suddenly, the spotlight of attention seems less dreadful than I had feared. People roundabout are looking at me kindly, and Nancy among others is smiling reassuringly. The pastor wants to know if I am a member of a Methodist congregation in London. I reply that I am more or less Church of England these days (for this doesn't seem the moment to trace my entire religious or irreligious history, which starts with baptism as a Roman Catholic and meanders through various shades of doubt and quirks of belief). I say frankly that I came here because Bethany Church was close to where I was staying and seemed friendly.

After another hymn, " 'Tis So Sweet to Trust in Jesus," there comes a solo, "Special Delivery," sung by a plump and pretty blond teenager named Randi Harrell, who steps forward from the choir. It is a country-and-western sort of song, albeit with religious overtones, and Miss Harrell—with a recorded accompaniment—projects it sweetly and yet powerfully. It is a stirring moment. Anyone nervous about standing up in front of a large audience might feel a little abashed by the example of this young woman, so unprofessionally poised. It is a pity that being in church inhibits one's urge to clap and shout "Encore!"

The pastor's sermon, on the theme of spiritual fitness, ranges wide. It encompasses the need for racial harmony (though I see no blacks in Bethany), the slow modifications being made to apartheid in South Africa, and what the pastor considers to be the overemphasis in our time on the "externals" of life at the expense of the "internals." References are made to the white teeth of the Osmonds' singing group, to *Madame Bovary* (a quick synopsis of the plot, highlighting Emma's misdeeds and fate), and to Ralph Waldo Emerson, who provides a relevant quotation that fails to stick in my mind. The concluding hymn has some guts to it: "Come, Thou Almighty King." I sing staunchly—I can hear myself singing. On the way out I am greeted by many people who shake hands and introduce themselves. There are lots of Midgetts, Daniels, and Tilletts.

Several say, "Come again—you're very welcome here."

On this part of the Atlantic seaboard, inlets come and go; coastal scientists call the area "inlet prone." The report to Raleigh made by Captain Arthur Barlowe in 1584 said that the expedition sailed through the first entrance that appeared to them, "though not without some difficulty." When John White mapped the area in 1585, he drew two inlets, one which he called Hatorask, or Port Fernando (after the pilot), the other Port Lane. These inlets disappeared by the mid-seventeenth century, but others opened and closed thereafter through Bodie and Hatteras Islands. Now, since the last of several Currituck inlets also closed more than a century ago, the first inlet one comes to proceeding southward on the Banks is Oregon Inlet. This formed between Bodie and Hatteras Islands in 1846, when a September hurricane washed great quantities of ocean water into the sound, which was then forced back out by a southwest gale. A paddle-wheel steamer named *Oregon* is believed to have christened the inlet by being the first vessel to pass through it. In time Oregon Inlet has moved south roughly two miles, as from littoral drift Bodie Island extends itself and the top end of Hatteras Island (here called Pea Island) wears away. The building of a road bridge across the inlet in 1962 is thought by many to have hastened this process, the numerous support pilings seeming to trap sand on the north side of the inlet and on the south side causing eddies which wash it away. Some also think that Oregon Inlet has reached a point in its natural career where, at the age of 140, it is on the point of closing back up again—though this is not what the fishermen of Wanchese like to hear.

Mill Creek—the fishing hub of Wanchese—is an

indirect nine miles' voyage up Roanoke Sound from the inlet. But it is hard to imagine any activity other than fishing going on here. Residents weren't surprised when, a few years ago, students on an archaeological dig excavated what the locals call "the thicket lump"— in archaeological terms, a remnant hummock—outside the Moon Tillett Fish Company waterfront building, and radiocarbon dating of the remains showed that there had been a summer fishing village here from roughly A.D. 460 to 800. Moon Tillett's is one of four perennial fish companies at the landing, the others being Randall Tillett's, Willie Etheridge's, and the Wanchese Fish Company, which also owns Fisherman's Wharf restaurant. The landing—as I walk around it on this Sunday afternoon—makes a thoroughly pungent and picturesque declaration of *laissez-faire*: collapsing sheds, rotting pilings, and derelict vessels squat, stand, or are moored amid up-to-date structures, new concrete wharves, and modern steel trawlers. The cycle of birth, maturation, and decay is evident in forms that are nudgingly real (though as allegorical as you like of some twentieth-century dreams of progress). The eye wanders over rusting refrigerator trucks, ancient hulks, broken boilers, cracked-up car chassis, with weeds and shrubs growing up through the foundations of former packing sheds. Some canny waterfront property owners appear to have a long-term policy of abandoning old craft and dumping old machinery at the water's edge and allowing the land (and their property) to build up around them. Few people are to be seen at this hour on a Sunday, though several cats are prowling through the debris, many seagulls are sitting atop pilings, and overall from the modern sheds comes the whir and hum of refrigerating machinery.

Around the top end of the creek, the scenery

changes: abruptly all is resolute improvement. There are well-built fences and gates, new prefabricated buildings, concrete roadways with curbs. This is the Wanchese Seafood Industrial Park, backed by the state of North Carolina and federal funds, and opened in 1981. And yet, despite signs of work in the state ship-repair yard (full of ferries and tugs) and several buildings occupied by crab packers and a marine-equipment service firm, there is an air of wait-and-see; many lots are undeveloped; potential tenants are unsure what is going to happen in the battle to keep Oregon Inlet open.

Wayne Gray has given me the impression that this struggle has been going on for so long that it is a fixed item on the local scene, like the summer play *The Lost Colony*, and that, also like Paul Green's drama, it is one that looks as if it will go on forever without offering the audience a definitive ending. Evan Wilson, general secretary of the fishermen's association which is campaigning for the construction of jetties to preserve a navigable inlet, has a loquacious role in the drama. His upstairs office at Moon Tillett's is reached by more of a ladder than a staircase, but the height, once gained, provides a comprehensive view of Mill Creek landing. The kempt and ill-kempt surroundings are reflected in Wilson's office, where charts, posters, and photographs are pinned haphazardly on the plywood walls; a sofa with torn cushions provides a Hobson's choice of seating for visitors, and—when I sit down on it—a venerable spaniel named Bo sniffs my shoes and familiarly falls asleep at my feet. Wilson is barefoot, in jeans and T-shirt, with a mustache and short beard, a Camel-smoking sportscar enthusiast in his mid-forties. He was born in Florida, he tells me, grew up in Washington, went to Johns Hopkins, served in Army

Intelligence in Europe, wrote a book about Alfa Romeos, and arrived in Wanchese four years ago on a twenty-five-foot-long wooden sailing boat, in which he was heading for Mexico. Wanchese is where he ran out of money. It is where he went to work, first of all, packing fish for one grueling winter. It is where— rather like Roder—he has ever since found it hard to consider moving on. He says, "I've been off Roanoke Island and the beach maybe ten times in these four years."

The jetties were authorized by Congress in 1970, and the fact that they haven't yet been built arises from opposing circumstances. Wilson spells it out, as he sees it: "A later law gave greater power to Fish and Wildlife not to surrender government land. And the jetties need to be anchored on land—north and south of the inlet— which belongs to the Department of the Interior. That's part of the problem. In addition, our opponents claim the jetties will cost too much. Plus they say the jetties won't work anyway. We're up against academics, so-called environmentalists, and officials of the all-powerful, mean-spirited Department of the Interior, none of whom has roots in the area. Right now they're saying go on with the present method of keeping the inlet navigable, which is by dredging—though it doesn't work satisfactorily and is very expensive. If they can keep us stuck with a year-by-year solution, one year they may just cut off the funds for dredging. And that will be it."

At the height of the winter season of 1963 there were seventy seagoing fishing vessels working out of Wanchese. Now, at the best of fishing times, there are eleven. Fishing vessels have generally got larger and deeper and can no longer navigate the inlet safely. In the past sixteen years, a number have grounded or capsized as they tried to make the passage; some boats broke up; and nine fishermen have died because of conditions in the inlet. One moment a boat is in the channel, the next it has been lifted by a swell and dropped onto a newly formed shoal. Wanchese could (154) be considered well placed as a base for fishing, with the meeting place of the Gulf Stream and the south-bound cold current only twelve miles offshore, forming a funnel in which fish congregate. Yet because of the state of the inlet many Wanchese boats are now fishing out of Norfolk, Virginia, which is farther from the fishing grounds and where costs are higher, leaving at risk many of the backup services here. Roanoke Island Steel and Boatworks, which built many Wanchese trawlers, has moved to Beaufort. The local economy is suffering and the Seafood Industrial Park looks more and more like a white elephant. Wilson says, "Right now there are a lot of expensive streetlights over there shining down on very little."

Wilson insists that fishermen are interested in the environment, too. "Sure, they make mistakes—they don't always do the right thing—but they make a living out of their understanding of wind and tide. Fishermen were here before the National Park Service, before the condo developers. Fishing is just about the only thing—apart from house building—that keeps this area going in the non-tourist season. You hear people say it would be cheaper to give Wanchese fishermen a million bucks apiece rather than build the jetties— let the old ones die rich, and let the young ones sell insurance or goggle at computers! Some people think food grows in supermarkets. They look down on men who work with their hands. Well, I say an American has the right to try to earn a living doing what his father did, in the place where his father lived."

Precisely what the jetties and their maintenance would cost is a matter of argument. The bill for dredging in 1985 was more than seven million dollars. The two three-quarters-of-a-mile-long jetties are estimated by their proponents to need nearly $100 million to build, while the jetties and the channel between them (155) would need some $500 million for maintenance over fifty years. Sand would have to be dredged from where it would build up in front of the north jetty and pumped through a pipeline to the area by the south jetty, where sand would tend to wash away. The Corps of Engineers has tried to work out the financial benefits of having a fully navigable inlet, for the inlet is used not only by big trawlers but by roughly four hundred smaller commercial boats and sportfishermen from the Albemarle/Pamlico area. To be taken into account are not just increased fish landings but the profits of many support businesses, and such other factors as lower insurance premiums for boats using an improved inlet. Geologists and coastal scientists like the Pilkeys say that the system to pass sand from the upstream to the downstream side of the jetties will not work, particularly in the face of storm action, that erosion will be severe, and that continued dredging will cost less and do less damage to the Banks. The great Ash Wednesday storm of 1962 caused the inlet to "blow out," widening it for a time from half a mile to a mile. The Pilkey team ask, "What will happen to the proposed jetties in another 1962 storm?" The Wanchese fishermen claim that erosion is worse with the present dredging system than it would be with the jetties, and that in any event the present efforts to keep the inlet open, often by three big dredgers at once, clearly don't work. The inlet has recently had to be declared closed for weeks at a time. Evan Wilson thinks that a country which can put men on the moon—and puts up condos on the beach at Kitty Hawk—can build two jetties to keep Oregon Inlet navigable.

The political background to all this is a confusing, many-sided tussle between federal departments, con-

gressional committees, and politicians. Some of the latter have attempted to get the land needed for anchoring the jetties to the Banks transferred from the uncooperative Secretary of the Interior to the Secretary of the Army, who would set the Corps of Engineers to work. Jetty opponents say that the Corps of Engineers is able to consider only structural solutions to such problems. In Wanchese as in Carova, citizens denounce the Department of the Interior for land-grabbing and empire-building. In Congress, pro-jetty legislation that gets through the House, generally as amendments to other bills, fails to survive passage through the Senate—where, according to local Dare County Democrats, the two North Carolina senators, both Republicans at this writing, have been inactive on the issue. Inactive Evan Wilson is not: he writes op-ed pieces for any papers that will publish them, broadcasts on local radio, and puts out a frequent newsletter called the *Oregon Inlet Alert*. And meanwhile the Wanchese fishermen who continue to use the inlet have to wait for daylight, high tide, and calm conditions to get in and out, holding their breath as they do so.

"Fishing is the oldest occupation in North America," says Wilson. "Fishermen should be able to return safely to their harbors with their catch." I feel almost persuaded. As a consumer resident in the European Community, paying above world prices for this and that item of food, I help to protect the livelihoods of the small farmers of France and Germany and Wales, knowing that there is more to life than efficiency—and that perhaps the land is in better hands with them (who live and work in a specific place which they know and care for) than with giant landholding corporations, owned by pension funds and investment trusts, who go in for factory farming. On the other hand, if God wants to close Oregon Inlet, neither the ramshackle charms of Wanchese, admiration for its fishermen, the skills of the Corps of Engineers, nor the persuasiveness of Evan Wilson is going to keep it open.

On my way back to C. W. Pugh's, I call in at the boatyard at the head of the creek on the other side of Wanchese, where Roder has his boat. I find Roder and a couple of his friends dismantling the wreckage of his painting shed and picking up tatters of plastic sheeting. Roder seems pleased to see me and, offering me my choice of a beer or a soft drink from a portable cooler, leads me into the big boatyard building to which his Chris-Craft was moved on Thursday afternoon. In the way that one notes resemblances and correspondences between people and their dogs, so I can see Roder in his boat, all curving surfaces, stocky rather than sleek, and strongly built. The craft was first launched in 1952 and now reflects Roder's enthusiasm and effort in glowing paint and varnish. Roder shows me where he has caulked the seams. He tells me about the two new diesels he has installed and the shade of blue he is planning to paint the cabin top. The boat's name was *Dixie Reb* when he acquired her, and having removed that from the broad mahogany transom, Roder is seeking a new one. "What's French for 'done at last'?" he asks. "*Enfin fini*, I think," I reply. "Sounds good," says Roder. He hopes to launch her the coming spring. (However, Nancy tells me later that Robin, whom she knows quite well, is beginning to talk houses, not boats. Wayne also knows Roder, whom he has apparently tried to engage as a craftsman but found elusive, and says, "If you really need help, Roder will turn up and set to work. But if you try to give him a contract in advance, he isn't interested—though he may sound as if he is. He goes his own way, works on his boat, fits in odd jobs. He's a character, Roder is.")

Wayne has spent the day refencing the corral for Daniel, his older daughter's horse. Business tonight at Queen Anne's Revenge is not overwhelming. I dine on wahoo, which I will now always think of as not simply a fish but as an exclamation of delight: "Wahoo!" It is just as good on this occasion when I am paying for it as it was when I was a guest at the pre-Gloria lunch. After I have eaten, Wayne comes from the kitchen and sits down. Don has sent Georgia over with a complimentary after-dinner drink for me. Wayne wants to know how I manage to operate as a writer, and I duck out of answering by asking about *his* career. Being a teacher and school administrator and a chef-cum-restaurant co-owner seems to me arduous, if well balanced. But Wayne—one reason for his initial question—has a third occupation as a writer of verse. He has put out six self-published collections, slim paperbound books whose titles all speak of what really matters to the author: *Love Songs from the Outer Banks*, *Wanchese Wharf*, and *Outer Banks Boy* are three I note in the small stack he now hands to me as a gift, and which in following days I dip into. In one introduction Wayne says that his poetry is "written about those things I am most familiar with but comprehend the least—love and the sea." It seems that the man I have seen as an excellent, unboastful cook and unruffled restaurant owner is in his poems an overt romantic. He likes walking beaches, staring at the surf, and remembering summers as an adolescent spent drinking and joshing around with friends. He recalls quarrels with the women in his life. He rues lost love. The poems are a bit raw and self-indulgent, but some- times they have the simple, indisputable directness of popular song:

> *I learned when I was twelve*
> *you have to make life yourself.*
> *You have to make it work for you.*
> *You have to make it beautiful.*

I'm impatient to get going south of Oregon Inlet, but no one is encouraging me to do so. A motelkeeper in Buxton, near Cape Hatteras, to whom I speak by phone, tells me it will be another day before they have things straightened out. Four-wheel drive may still be needed on the road down. But since it is Monday, a working day, I decide to return to the Cape Hatteras National Seashore headquarters near Lane's fort, north of Manteo, to get a report from the Park Service of conditions on Hatteras Island. It also seems to me time that I encountered at first hand those regarded by Roder, Evan Wilson, and Ernie Bowden as minions of ever-expanding federal government, with whom they are locked in a battle for survival. The National Seashore is eighty miles long, and takes in not only most of Hatteras but the better part of Bodie, Pea, and Ocracoke Islands. A number of local people are employed by the Park Service in looking after the National Seashore. Even among those who are not, there are many

who feel in no way antagonistic to the body which is—
on behalf of the American nation—the largest local
landowner. (One young architect in Manteo told me:
"The Department of the Interior has saved us from
the worst ravages of overdevelopment. The land they
own is now protected in perpetuity. In a hundred years'
time, we'll be something special on the Eastern Seaboard because of this.")

The two Park Service men who talk to me certainly
don't give the impression of bureaucratic arrogance,
but rather of being thoughtful individuals who are
trying to cope with complex problems created by nature: by the interaction of land, sea, wildlife, and human beings. Robert Woody is a very tall Park Service
officer in his late thirties with the title Chief of Inter-
pretation, which I gather has to do with interpreting
policy to the public. Kent Turner, fair-haired and
younger than Woody, is a biologist who now concen-
trates on environmental planning. Both wear Park Service uniforms. Woody says, "Right now we're busy
recouping our losses from Gloria. Fortunately, much
of it is minor stuff—sand overwash, roads eroded,
beach-access ramps buried or damaged. There's several weeks' work for front-loaders. All our campgrounds are closed, either because sand has to be
moved or they are without power, water, or sewage. If
you're heading down there, it might be a good idea to
take some water and food."

From what Woody and Turner tell me, it seems that
there has been considerable erosion of the Park Service's traditional management policy for its large area
of the Banks. The Cape Hatteras National Seashore
was first proposed in 1933, with the idea of retaining
much of the area in its natural state and confining
development to villages left outside the park. A great

deal of the land for it was acquired—and donated—
as a result of a campaign led by D. Victor Meekins,
the publisher of the *Coastland Times*, who believed
tourism was needed to save the Banks from poverty.
The National Seashore—first of its kind—opened in
1958. However, in the mid-1930s, nature on the Hatteras Banks was already being tampered with, or at
least given a helping hand, by the Civilian Conservation Corps. The previously unemployed youths and
transient workers of this New Deal agency lived in
camps on the Banks and built a continuous low dike
of sand all the way from the Virginia border to the
middle of Ocracoke; they put up sand fences and
planted dune grasses in an attempt to protect the narrow barrier islands from erosion and flood. Until the
1970s the Park Service made a determined effort to
preserve this dune line, although it was frequently
breached by storms—each such occasion generally
being followed by demands for emergency appropri-
ations to make good the damage. In the 1970s the Park
Service began to shift its objectives. Research into the
formation and movement of the Banks was making it
evident that sea levels were rising and the barrier islands were migrating naturally. The opening and closing of inlets was part of this process, and so was littoral
drift and the phenomenon called overwash, which
rolled sand over the islands from the sea toward the
sounds. (Apart from the dunes, much of the National
Seashore is less than five feet above mean sea level.)
The Park Service has therefore decided not to try to
alter or impede what it calls "natural shoreline processes"; the policy now is to go with nature rather than
fight it.

Some people on the Banks had regarded the CCC
dune building as evidence of government commitment

to holding back the sea forever, and the Park Service's change of mind was taken hard: there were cries aplenty of being abandoned to nature. Woody and Turner say that in fact the Park Service is aware that the service corridor of roads and power lines down the Banks requires its assistance. It works with the state **(163)** to ensure that spoil dredged from ferry channels or overwash sand removed from roads is deposited on dunes or beaches where it may buy a little time. Yet in recent years several sections of the one continuous road down Hatteras Island have had to be abandoned and new stretches built. Small storm-created inlets have been given Park Service help to fill in again. Nevertheless, the Park Service realizes new inlets may form which would be beyond its powers of restoration, and several spots on Hatteras Island are viewed as strong possibilities for such natural engineering as time and the elements reshape the Banks. The only spot where the Park Service is currently reluctant to take a passive approach is at Cape Hatteras lighthouse. The defense of the tower against the encroaching sea may be a never-ending job, but is one which, right now, the service must undertake because of the lighthouse's historic and cultural associations. The service also recognizes the contemporary influence on the National Seashore of the actions of people, whether in developing land adjacent to it or by coming to visit it. With more than a million and a half tourists passing through the National Seashore each year, a lot of planning and steering has to be done so that human beings don't—in Park Service terminology—"impact" wildlife and vegetation.

"The Cittie of Raleigh" is still on my mind. Even though the fate of the Lost Colony looks as if it will

remain obscure, surely one should be able to determine exactly where John White's little band of settlers
lived. I walk again through the woods on Hariot's trail,
from which Gloria's debris has now been cleared, and
stand brooding on the grassy banks of the recon-
structed fort. "We passed toward the place where they
were left in sundry houses," wrote White on his return
in August 1590, "but we found the houses taken
downe, and the place very strongly enclosed with a
high palisado of great trees, with cortynes and flankers
very Fort-like." Then, having soaked up as much as I
can of local knowledge by breathing the air and having
my feet on the ground, I walk back to the Park Service
visitors' center to get what help I can from Philip Evans, a young park ranger who keeps up with research
in these matters.

Evans tells me that archaeological efforts have been
sporadic. Some people believe the settlement to have
been on Dough's Creek (where Manteo now is), but
majority opinion favors the neighborhood of Lane's
fort, which was first surveyed and dug by an amateur
archaeologist in the late nineteenth century. It wasn't
until after the Second World War that a professional
archaeologist investigated the area. This was J. C. Harrington, who worked for the Park Service, and as a
result of whose investigations the fort was recon-
structed. Harrington hoped also to find the site of
White's settlement, particularly the palisade White
had mentioned, but uncovered only some soil stains,
thought to have been left by decaying posts, which
didn't create the anticipated pattern. In 1965, however,
another dig revealed what archaeologists call a "feature," nine feet square, which had had a large vertical
post at each corner and walls or a fence apparently
attached at each flank—this was close to the fort on

its landward side. A later dig at Wostenholme Towne, Virginia—a settlement founded roughly thirty-five years after the Roanoke attempt—uncovered a similar feature, which was identified as in all probability a palisaded gun platform with flanking post-and-rail fences. In 1982, a team of Park Service archaeologists brought up-to-date scientific equipment to the Roanoke scene. A proton magnetometer was used to seek subsurface items, such as metal and pottery remains. A resistivity meter—which measures the flow of electricity through soil—recorded the differences found underground: decaying matter in a buried rubbish pit, for example, would record less resistance than the drier soil around it. These results were fed into a computer and a map of the research area printed out on which the archaeologists looked for patterns or anomalies. One such anomaly was then partly excavated: signs of posts, or post molds, were found. But no artifacts related to the Raleigh expeditions and colonies were discovered. Evans says, "What's here seems to date to the right period, but we need to keep searching. It's possible that the settlement is now underwater, off the beach—though those who suggest this have to discount the location of the fort, which you would think would have been between the settlement and the threat of the Spanish, arriving by sea. Of course, it's hard for us to know what mattered most to sixteenth-century people. There isn't much money available but we hope to carry on following up the clues. I'd give a lot to know one way or another, so that I don't have to answer the question I get all the time, 'Where did the colonists live?' with, 'Oh, somewhere around here.'"

I spend the night in Manteo at my first motel of this trip, the Scarborough Inn. My room is furnished with what strikes me as unusually solid period furniture, though there is also a television set. Weather forecasts aren't of urgent interest to me now, *People's Court* isn't on, and I'm left with the rather droopy cinematic version of John Fowles's novel *The French Lieutenant's Woman*, a book I remember liking when it came out, but the film of which, with extra-added directorial contrivance, seems to be pulling the strings of its characters visibly and hard. Perhaps I am at too great a remove from the cliffs of the Dorset coast, the quaint charms of Lyme Regis, and the curved stone jetty of the Cobb on which Meryl Streep peers forth, looking winsomely windswept, to care about making the sympathetic, imaginative leap back. An early night, therefore, and I wake early for a stroll down Budleigh Street to scrambled eggs for breakfast at the Duchess of Dare.

And then I drive out to the Banks to Whalebone Junction and turn south.

The name of the motelkeeper I had talked to in Buxton is Jack Gray—no immediate relation to Wayne—and last night when I called him again he was sounding more cheerful. Things were getting back to normal— **(167)** in fact, by this coming weekend he was expecting his motel to be full of visiting surf fishermen. As Vernon Davis had suggested, the Banks fishing season begins in earnest with October; for the next two months bluefish, flounder, mackerel, channel bass, sea mullet, and grouper will be sought from pier, beach, and boat. And as I drive the Alliance over the long arch of the bridge spanning Oregon Inlet—the water calm, the breeze light, the morning sunny—many fishermen and fisherwomen are to be seen, rods and buckets at hand, on the south side of the inlet. A number of pickup trucks and four-wheel-drive vehicles are also heading down Hatteras Island, with fishing rods like lances carried over the front fenders in holders made of plastic pipe. Two young men with long surfboards are thumbing a ride toward Cape Hatteras, but I leave them to the charity of an accommodating pickup truck.

The first fifteen miles of Hatteras Island form the Pea Island National Wildlife Refuge; they give one a feeling of what the upper Banks around Nags Head and Kitty Hawk must have been like before development. There are no houses, shops, or billboards, only low dunes on the sea side, the green of marshes between the road and the sound. Apart from the road, man's handiwork takes the form of twin crossbar utility poles carrying power and phone lines south, Crosses of Lorraine that here and there have been knocked awry by Gloria. The road itself provides one lane in each direction; it is mostly free of sand, though in places the sand which has recently buried it is banked up on the ocean side, and big yellow-painted graders sit with blades dug in behind their last push into the pile, as if recovering from their labors. The few small prefabricated-looking structures of the refuge head-quarters are closed, presumably because the staff are out working on what Robert Woody had called the recovery situation. But I leave the car in the nearby parking lot, among cars with license plates from all over the United States and Canada. Then I cross the road and walk through a small gap in the dunes, where a few placards on posts explain that this was the site of the Pea Island lifesaving station from 1878 to 1947 and give a little of its history. On the beach, men and women stand or sit in folding chairs with their rods angled out over the low surf. Sun hats are the order of the day.

Time was when hundreds of ships carried people and produce along this shore. In pre-loran, pre-sonar, pre-radar days it was a coast which shoals and storm and current made perilous; plenty of vessels came to grief in what Alexander Hamilton (who as a young man made a harrowing voyage through these waters) is thought to have been first to call the Graveyard of the Atlantic. During the Second World War, when U-boats found it good hunting ground, it also became known as Torpedo Junction. In the nineteenth century lifesaving stations were planted roughly seven miles apart, so that there were ten of them and one smaller lifeboat station on Hatteras. For several generations of Banks men the U.S. Lifesaving Service provided a ca-reer. Each of the twenty-five stations on the Banks had a stationkeeper and six surfmen. A station rivaled the local church and general store as the focal point of its community. The surfmen took turns patrolling the beach and manning watchtowers, while to reach ships in trouble they launched surfboats from pony-drawn wagons. In the library of the Park Service headquarters on Roanoke, I had browsed in some of the late-nineteenth-century annual reports of the Lifesaving Service, covering its activities all around the coasts of the country, and read some of the terse accounts of operations on the Banks. Lives were indeed saved, sometimes by the lighting of flares to warn ships of the proximity of shore, sometimes by more arduous action; danger was routine. On December 5, 1898, for example, the Wash Woods station on Currituck Banks reported that the American sloop *Harp* had "dragged her anchor and stranded 2 miles WSW of station during a westerly gale. On the 6th instant, surfmen from Wash Woods and False Cape stations went to the stranded sloop and succeeded in floating her without damage. Her crew of two men were succored at False Cape station during the storm." On December 29 of the same year, men of Ocracoke station went to the aid of the American schooner *Vennor*, which had "stranded on a reef 4 miles NW of station and hoisted a signal for assistance. Life-saving crew went out to her, discharged part of her cargo of wood, laid out her anchor, and hove her afloat undamaged." On March 7, 1899, there was a more dramatic rescue—though the courage remains between the lines—when the American schooner *Alfred Brabrook* hit near Gull Shoal station. "About 3:40 a.m. patrol discovered this vessel ashore 2 miles NNE of the station. He at once reported to the keeper, who called up Little Kinnakeet and Chicamacomico stations, asking their assistance. Arrived with beach apparatus opposite the vessel in about ½ hour. The gale was very heavy and the surf too high to make an attempt to board the vessel; the keeper accordingly fired a line over her. The line was found and the crew bent on a heavier line which was hauled ashore. Then sent off the whip, but, owing to strong current, it fouled so much that great delay was occasioned in clearing it, and the same trouble occurred in sending off the hawser. It was nearly 11 a.m. before the gear was in readiness for work. Then made 8 trips of the breeches buoy, landing the 8 persons who comprised the crew of the schooner. Took them to the station and supplied them dry clothes from the supplies of the Women's National Relief Association. Next day boarded the vessel and brought off all of the personal effects. The vessel was a total loss. The master remained at the station for 13 days; the remainder of the shipwrecked men remained but two days."

This should be read while trying to imagine the detonation of the surf, the scream of the wind, and the pulverizing effect of the sea as it hit one like bucketfuls of buckshot, and drenched one, too. Arbitrary and democratic in its violence: What care these roarers for the name of king! Although in these parts such names as Etheridge and Midgett resounded as powerfully as human acclaim could manage.

Richard Etheridge—part black, part Indian—was for a long period the keeper of the Pea Island lifesaving station, where his crew of surfmen were all black. This was exceptional on the Banks, for in most stations black personnel were generally given menial tasks, like looking after the ponies. In the period from the end of November 1879 to January 1915, ten vessels were wrecked off Pea Island; six hundred lives were saved from them and only ten lost. The crew of the Pea Island station had the reputation of being one of the tautest on the Carolina coast. At the next station to the south, Chicamacomico, the keeper in August 1915 was John Allen Midgett, Jr., who led his surfmen to the rescue of forty-two survivors from the British tanker *Mirlo*, torpedoed by a German U-boat within sight of the shore. For their bravery in the turbulent seas and blazing oil, Midgett and his men received Grand Crosses of the American Cross of Honor—six of the eleven such medals ever awarded. In his village of Rodanthe Captain Midgett also acted as unofficial physician, pulling teeth, setting bones, even stitching up people now and then.

At the south end of Pea Island Refuge I stop for a look at Chicamacomico station, which still stands. It is a noble shingle-clad house, once painted white, whose hollow-columned porches and weathered dormers put one in mind of the big old summer houses that grace the shores of New England resorts like Magnolia, Marion, and Quisset. The ground around it is still saturated four and a half days after Gloria. A huge bell sits on its base in the yard and, when I tap it, gives off a forlorn *ding*. Large wooden cisterns, ringed with iron bands, stand near an outhouse which was once either kitchen or stables. The last rescue effected from Chicamacomico was in May 1954, when the cargo ship *Omar Babun* came ashore three miles to the north and fourteen men were taken off by breeches buoy—the last sizable ship, so David Stick believes, to have stranded on the Banks. The station was abandoned in that same year by the Coast Guard (which was formed out of the Lifesaving Service and Revenue Cutter Service in 1915). It is now being looked after by a local historical association, which opens it to the public three days a week during the summer and in the off-season for a few hours at weekends.

Rodanthe is the first village the southbound traveler comes to on Hatteras Island. One is alerted to the fact that the Park Service doesn't own the entire island from shore to shore by the appearance of roadside billboards—and not only billboards but cottages, motels, an abandoned filling station, and a seemingly derelict amusement park, whose parking lot is delimited by old tires buried on edge so that only the top half shows. Several rusting trailer homes provide an introduction to some newly erected real-estate advertisements, one of which proclaims the advantages of "Interval Ownership." (Who gets the mosquito season, or is there a worthwhile discount?) In the ensuing eight miles—before the Park Service reclaims the whole width of the island—I drive through two other settlements, Waves and Salvo, which have tackle and gift shops and new resort cottages among older homes and a few gnarled trees. "Insiders predict a real estate boom here soon," says a local guidebook I'd seen at Queen Anne's Revenge. Pilkey & Co. give an on-the-other-hand warning that much of the Banks from Rodanthe to Waves—despite the loss of Cape Kenrick, still protruding farther eastward and seaward than the rest of the Banks—is liable to considerable erosion and has "high inlet [formation] potential."

In one respect, Waves and Salvo don't call for criticism: they have evocative names, and are certainly less of a mouthful than Chicamacomico, which is what Rodanthe was called before it acquired a post office in 1874. Although the local citizenry in collaboration with the postal authorities ducked out of that tongue-twisting challenge, many Indian names in these parts have been simplified rather than replaced in the course of being written down in English. Kitty Hawk, for example, is thought to stem from an Indian place name, "attested"—writes David Stick—"by the appearance on maps as early as 1738 of the name 'Chickehauk.'" (This reasonable notion hasn't quite stifled suggestions that the name derives from the alleged presence in the area of large numbers of mosquito hawks—"skeeter hawk" becoming Kitty Hawk.) Several legends have developed to account for the name of Kill Devil Hills, one being that a shipload of unwholesome or kill-devil rum came ashore here in a shipwreck. Nags Head, according to the story that is just about unavoidable on the Banks, got its name from the practice of Banks wreckers driving a pony by night along the beach with a lantern tied to its neck. A writer in *Harper's* magazine of May 1860 found this plausible, because "the up-and-down motion resembling that of a vessel, the unsuspecting tar [at the helm of the endangered ship] would steer for it." Why a helmsman would steer for another ship at sea, unless under the influence of kill-devil rum, is unclear, though another version of this explanation says: "As soon as a ship's captain saw this light, it appeared [to him] to be from a ship riding at anchor in a sheltered harbor." Yet again, *The North Carolina Guide* tells us that "mistaking the light for a beacon, ships were lured to the treacherous reefs, there to be boarded and looted by the wily shoremen." The guide comments: "Those who hold to this story should try tying a lighted lantern around the neck of a banker pony." (Or perhaps ask themselves why a beacon light would be expected to bob up and down.) For the moment, I'm prepared to go along with those who have noted that one of the highest pieces of land on the Scilly Isles, off the Cornish coast, is Horse Point, locally called Nag's Head, and for many sailors was the last they saw of old England as they steered west. However it got its name, Nags Head nearly lost it altogether in the time of post-office rechristenings, becoming the village of Griffin for a few months in 1915, before confusion and complaints made it Nags Head again.

No one seems to have bothered to dream up a story of "Why Griffin?" though generally, one may conclude, more energy appears to have gone into explaining these names than went into choosing them.

(174)   Apart from the occasional utility pole skittled sideways, sand piled here and there at the road's edge, and a Park Service display hut capsized in Salvo, no great stir has been caused by Gloria's passage—or so I think until, after another fifteen miles of National Seashore, I get to Avon, which was formerly Kinnakeet. Avon is a mess. The village—noteworthy for possessing Hatteras Island's one movie theater—sits in a broader patch of the island, though it would have been better disposed had it been higher than broader. Avon was undoubtedly not beautiful before Gloria; it has the air of a squatter camp slowly and penuriously improved, the sort of place that was into do-it-yourself before handyman home restoration became modish. And now much of the improvement has washed away. Most of Avon's three hundred homes have been flooded above floor level. It is going to claim the largest share of financial damage in Dare County, more than a million of some two and a half million dollars reported in the county as a whole (a figure which includes the damage done in the two fires on Roanoke Island)—and which goes to show what things cost to replace when they have been ruined by water. Many things—like refrigerators and television sets—are still to be seen standing out in yards as if to dry, while carpets and couches air on front porches. Avon's houses are mostly single-story. Some homes are former trailers, and many of them have been lifted off their concrete-block foundations and are now lying at various angles of heel; one is on the verge of sliding into Pamlico Sound. A

man at the fish dock, on the little harbor that gave original impetus to Avon, tells me that if Gloria had come at high tide most of its houses might have blown out to sea. As it was, most had four or five feet of water in them; the owners of two hundred homes have lost their major appliances; salt water has damaged a great deal of wiring and plasterboard beyond repair; and many carpets and pieces of furniture will never be the same. An emergency kitchen run by the Salvation Army and the Red Cross has been busy over the weekend, since with no electricity and their fridges and stoves out of action, the people of Avon found it hard to put a square meal together.

What Avon looks like is daunting enough: the very embodiment of wet-through and raggle-taggle misery. What Avon smells like is even more persuasive. Avon stinks. When several hundred septic tanks are flooded and the floodwater becomes general, the entire area becomes a cesspool, somewhat diluted and dispersed maybe, but overwhelmingly and foully pungent, like a giant latrine. At the fish dock, where hauls from Pamlico Sound crab pots and pound nets are landed and trucked to Elizabeth City, Norfolk, and New York, any long-accumulated odors that might have wrinkled the nostrils of sensitive visitors have been, by comparison, washed clean away. The ambient tang is rather that of the marshes flanking the sound. Close to where I have parked the Alliance, a hose runs water unsupervised by human hand into a dockside tank; two men in work clothes stand leaning against the front end of a big old Mercury coupe, cans of beer in hand, chatting; and several battered boats lie upturned amid nets, floats, and crab pots in a disorder that is possibly no greater now than it was last Thursday, before the storm. But in the small harbor not all the wrecks are old. One modern fiberglass motorboat, clearly a Gloria victim, sits with its bow up on a jetty and its stern underwater. Near the jetty, a young bare-chested man is examining the rough cross-planked bottom of a beached skiff, hammer and nails in hand. I ask him **(176)** what he means to do with the skiff. "I'm sort of thinking of fixing it," he says. "Maybe fiberglassing it. But I don't know if it's worth it."

I think, as I drive on, that whether fixing is worth it is a question which may be pretty general in Avon today.

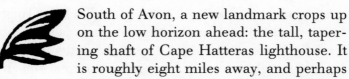South of Avon, a new landmark crops up on the low horizon ahead: the tall, tapering shaft of Cape Hatteras lighthouse. It is roughly eight miles away, and perhaps because the day has become overcast, its light is visible. There are seven and a half seconds between each flash. Since I am on the only road going south, I don't need the light to tell me I'm on course for the cape, but it is nevertheless encouraging to see it there, marking the elbow of the Banks and forming a milestone on my journey. And after I have booked into Jack Gray's Tower Circle Motel on the edge of the extended village of Buxton, I set out for the lighthouse. The motel is only half a mile away from it, but Coast Guard housing within a fenced compound lies between the Tower Circle and the pharos, and I have to take a roundabout route through more of Buxton. On the way, the need for lunch strikes me. The only place that seems to be open is the bakery-and-sandwich shop, where the motherly lady in charge apologizes: All the sandwich

makings in the deep freeze have been thrown away, "to be on the safe side," and deliveries are still awaited. However, there are some sweet items freshly baked, and so I buy a blueberry muffin, a doughnut, and a small carton of milk. The lady says that she and her husband went all the way to Nashville, Tennessee, to get away from Gloria, and also "to see our folks." The hurricane brought about a good many, sometimes long-delayed, family reunions. Outside, I sit on the shaded porch of the bakery and consume my purchases. A great number of butterflies dance through the warm midday air. What had *they* done during Gloria?

The topography of this part of Hatteras Island merits explication. Buxton village lies mostly on the sound side, apart from one finger of land (on which the Tower Circle and Coast Guard housing stand) poking into Park Service territory along the beach. Hatteras village is, confusingly, twelve miles to the west, near the end of the lower arm of the island. Cape Hatteras, the outer bump of the elbow, is generally referred to as Cape Point—and Cape Hatteras lighthouse is about two miles north of the point, accessible by way of a road through National Seashore property. An immediate contrast with Buxton, therefore—grass, trees, and no commercial clutter on each side of the approach to the lighthouse. Then a nicely laid-out parking lot, with not many cars today; a Park Service information booth, closed because of post-Gloria staff problems; the handsome double house which served two lighthouse keepers and their families, also closed for restoration and termite removal; and—looming over everything—Cape Hatteras lighthouse itself. Its tall tapering shaft is painted in spiral bands of black and white, as it has been since 1873, when the Light House Board decided to make the four main Outer Banks lighthouses readily distinguishable in daytime (thus, Cape Lookout is painted in a checkered pattern, Bodie Island is done with horizontal bands, and Currituck Beach has been left undecorated brick). To seaward, the surf is breaking loudly near a small dune, which on the north side is banked against the stone plinth of the lighthouse. I walk to the door, full of anticipation. At eye level a printed statement has been pinned up: CLOSED TO THE PUBLIC UNTIL FURTHER NOTICE.

It is a common case—to put off an action until it becomes a necessity; the prospect sometimes becomes more pleasurable. So I have made no attempt to explore the lighthouses at Corolla and on Bodie Island. I have been saving my lighthouse visit for here and now. Cape Hatteras light is the tallest in the United States, set near this crucial cape, a National Historic Landmark—a structure and symbol that is for the Banks what the Eiffel Tower, St. Paul's Cathedral, and the Empire State Building are for their cities. For the light to be automated and therefore unmanned—that I expected. But to be shut out, deprived of a climb to the top, of the view, of the ensuing sensations . . . Damn it! There is, fortunately, a public telephone nearby which is not shut or being restored, and I get through to the local headquarters of the Coast Guard, about a mile away between the lighthouse and Cape Point. This is the right thing to do, for although, as I soon learn, the Park Service is now the owner of the lighthouse structure, the actual light is the responsibility of the Coast Guard. Lieutenant John DeLong, the Coast Guard group commander, will be happy to make his weekly inspection of the light this afternoon and let me accompany him.

While I'm waiting for the lieutenant, I sit on the concrete lip of a groin running out into the sea and one of several anti-erosion devices placed at this spot.

I watch half a dozen young surfers. This is clearly a favored place, what surfers term a "break," where the shoaling water compels waves to crest in a useful manner. The surfer of course has to paddle hard to move at almost the same speed as the incoming wave, then time precisely his crouching, getting up, and standing on the board, one foot in front of the other, so that he swoops in on the curling front of the wave, often shouting with glee. It seems that this is one of the best places for surfing on the Eastern Seaboard. Here the continental shelf is closer to shore, and ocean swells arrive at greater speed. Here, too, are frequent storms to help create swells. And here, close in, the groins at the lighthouse divide the swells into three separate surfable waves. As I watch, one lad who has been waiting perhaps five minutes for his thirty seconds of thrilling ride chooses his wave. Up, he weaves in along the face of it, and suddenly—just before it pounds him against the beach—whips around over the diminished crest, drops down on his board, and is paddling out to sea again before the wave has completely collapsed on the beach. Novices look on in admiration.

What is good for the surfers is evidently less so for the lighthouse. The sea and the beach are altogether too dynamic for it. Robert Woody and Kent Turner at the National Seashore headquarters gave me the facts for appreciating its present perilous position. It was the second built in this area, replacing an 1803 lighthouse 600 feet to the south—which developed cracks. The new lighthouse, rising 191 feet above the sand, went into operation in 1870, at which time it stood 1,500 feet from the sea. Its builder, Dexter Stetson, originally intended to drive piles to support its granite foundation but found that the sand underlying the water level was too hard and compact. He therefore had his men lay several courses of massive yellow pine timbers as a base (which, because it was always submerged, would not rot). On this solid wooden raft the stone foundation was built, seventeen feet to the surface, and then a stone-and-brick octagonal plinth, on which stood the circular brick tower. By 1935, despite groins that had been put in place, the sea was a mere hundred feet away. In 1936 the Coast Guard decided to abandon the lighthouse—it was handed over to the Park Service, and a steel skeleton tower was built in the woods, a mile from the shore. A light from this prosaic structure proclaimed the presence of Cape Hatteras to mariners until 1950, when it seemed as if nature had relented and the eroding beach had "stabilized." The Coast Guard then reactivated the 1870 lighthouse. But after another fifteen years it was realized that the remission was temporary. Since then, various measures have been taken to try to keep the ocean at bay: more groins, rubble ramparts, and nearly two million cubic yards of sand pumped over from Pamlico Sound or from the ocean beach to the south. At the moment the sea is within fifty feet of the lighthouse.

It is a place where the struggle between man and the elements is only partly visible. Not far off the shore an experimental device called Seascape has recently been installed. This is a series of long, gravel-filled tubes, with fronds attached which wave about underwater and cause passing sand to stop and drop to the seabed. The hopeful idea is that a sandbar will form and protect the beach behind it. Also underwater are large scour-protection mats, put down to defend one of the groins that is presently threatened with an out-flanking movement by the sea. Conspicuous around the lighthouse is a dike made of big black-and-white polypropylene sandbags. Elsewhere the Corps of Engineers is currently testing with models in a wave tank a revetment that might be built to encircle the lighthouse. And meanwhile the sea continues to tease, sometimes giving the impression that the beach is building up again, sometimes that none of man's inventions are going to stave off the fatal blow much longer. There are seasonal variations in buildup and erosion. None of the authorities involved is sure whether any of the devices are having a positive effect or whether a natural cyclical pattern is at work. One thing is certain: the sea level continues to rise. As I sit on top of the groin, with my toes cooling in intermittent splashes from the sea, a working party from the Park Service arrives. The men unroll a paling fence and drive in stakes to support it on the narrow beach, hard against the plastic sandbags. One tells me that they are replacing a similar fence damaged by Gloria. It seems a brave gesture—or a symbol of human impotence.

Lieutenant DeLong is wearing blue overall fatigues, very shiny bulky black shoes, and a blue peaked cap with the legend *Graveyard of the Atlantic Group Cape Hatteras.* He has a small mustache and, most importantly, carries the key to the lighthouse door. As we go up and around, up and around, I count the steps, but listening to what DeLong is saying I lose count. DeLong tells me that all the Outer Banks lighthouses are now closed to the public, in Hatteras's case because of cracks in the tower and failing ironwork; last year, a forty-pound chunk of iron fell from a window frame. A private engineering firm is advising on remedial action. Stone landings between sections of wrought-iron stair alternate between the front and the back of the tower. The brick walls are whitewashed within, and although a few cracks are perceptible one would call them hairline. On the way up, DeLong checks the window on each landing. Several have broken panes, and though mesh screens are in place to keep birds out when the windows are open, some screens are holed and there are signs of pigeons on the inner sills. After several hundred steps we reach the top, the deck on which the lantern apparatus sits, and where it is hot with a greenhouse-like heat. I am puffing. The lantern is in fact two beacon lights separated by a board so that the brilliance of one doesn't interfere with that of the other; it revolves once every fifteen seconds, thus giving out two flashes of light in each revolution. The 1,000-watt bulb on each side has a backup bulb which comes on in the event of a burnout. The apparatus is switched on by a photoelectric cell when daylight diminishes below a certain level, and an electric motor turns the beacon lights. "It has been electric for over fifty years," says DeLong. "In the old days, the two keepers each had to carry up five gallons of oil when they came on watch. They had to check the lamps, trim them, light them, and turn them out. I think those men would have been older than me, but in tremendous shape. The turning machinery worked like a grandfather clock, with weights that had to be wound up. Although the light is automatic now, it's the job of our officer of the watch to keep an eye on it. But if it did fail for some reason, I'm sure it wouldn't be out for more than a minute before our phone would ring. Someone in Buxton would be saying, 'Do you know our lighthouse is out?' People are very possessive about the lighthouse around here." (Later I hear that a Buxton man, Frankie Laguna, rode down here on his bicycle during the passing of Gloria's eye, to see how things were with the lighthouse. Asked why he rode his bike, Laguna said that he didn't want to get his car scratched.)

Outside, on the iron balcony that surrounds the lantern, I don't rely on the railings—they look okay, but it is about 180 feet to the sandbags. From up here the surfers look like brightly colored waterbugs. The sea is white-flecked, though the small waves seem more than the onshore breeze would call for. Perhaps it is the result of the warm Gulf Stream on its way north bumping into the colder Virginia coastal current as it goes south, the waters joining, dancing, and stepping on one another's toes. Looking out to sea I survey great fields of water, some brilliantly lit, others darkened by cloud shadow. On the horizon, in a patch of sunlit sea, I can just make out the spindly shape of a Texas Tower, Diamond Shoals Light, nine and a half miles away. This replaced a lightship on the seaward edge of the shoals in 1967 and, with its insistent flash every two and half seconds, has a greater importance for deepsea shipping than Cape Hatteras lighthouse. Up the island coast toward Avon the view is wide and clear, as it is from the other side of the balcony down the last two miles of beach to Cape Point, where the island makes an abrupt turn westward and the shore dips back into Hatteras Bight. Behind the lighthouse I can see the deep green of Buxton woods, a baseball field near the Coast Guard houses, and the Tower Circle Motel. On the ocean side once again, DeLong looks down and says, "We sure lost some beach during Gloria. I guess we were lucky not to lose the lighthouse. *National Geographic* had a photographer down here who set up a camera to take photographs every three minutes during the storm. They must have been hoping to catch it on its way into the waves. I can understand how the people around here feel about it. It's a national treasure, though goodness knows what's going to happen to it in the years to come."

The Gulf Stream air has given me a holiday feeling. I loaf around at the Tower Circle, talking to Mike Finnegan, who stands in occasionally for Jack Gray when not teaching at Cape Hatteras School, and chatting with the surf fishermen who are staying at the Tower Circle as they clean their fish on outdoor wooden tables. I walk along the beach looking for remains of shipwrecks, like a few exposed ribs and timbers of the *Altoona*, wrecked in 1878, uncovered by the surf in 1963, the last relics of which have been washed to a spot on the inner edge of a pond behind Cape Point. On the beach I admire the wavy patterns the retreating surf leaves on the sand, a bit like the tracings on a recording barograph, sometimes in interlaced lines and generally decorated with fragments of reed, seaweed, and eelgrass. I also hang out in such Buxton bistros as Lee's Steam Eatery, a one-man roadside restaurant known until recently as Daddy White's—a name which is still attached to a faded Pepsi-Cola sign outside. Lee heats up some crab cakes, which I have ordered from his hurricane-restricted menu (the other "Gloria's Special" being twelve chicken wings or "peglegs"), and tells me that he previously owned an exterminating business in Richmond, Virginia. He was making good money but he wasn't happy. He decided to "retire" to Hatteras Island and—hoping to live off a percentage of the future profits—handed over the exterminating firm to his son, who promptly ran it into the ground. Lee says, "In six months the IRS had stepped in and I was pretty near bankrupt. We were out here with no money, living on welfare and food stamps. I dug ditches and worked at the wharf in Hatteras, lumping fish." But Lee, as he puts it, slowly got straightened up. Now he runs the eatery and is editor, publisher, and printer of a free news and advertising sheet, the Hatteras Island *Happening*. I like the thought that a man can paste up his wife's typed account of local events one moment and wield a slice and skillet the next. However, as the crab cakes are put before me, it occurs to me to ask how they survived the recent power cut. "No problem," says Lee. "They remained frozen." I yield to Lee's persuasion. The crab cakes taste all right and, indeed, there is no problem.

I also take walks in the interior—in Buxton woods, for instance, along a winding trail which has been laid out for the purpose of observing nature, keeping a wary eye open for Eastern cottonmouth moccasins and canebrake rattlesnakes, and carrying a stout branch with a forked tip, which I have broken from a tree, for use as a snake dissuader. (Cottonmouths are a poisonous viper whose name arises from the fact that their mouths look as if they are lined with cotton; they are said to be friendly, at least until alarmed or put on the defensive.) Signs, which alert walkers to the possibility of snakes, tell as well of the Eastern mole, the South-east five-lined skink, whitetail deer, the hooded war-bler, and the downy woodpecker, but fail to mention mosquitoes and no-see-ums, which are prevalent. The path is paved with cones and needles from loblolly pines, which grow among dogwood, cedar, and the evergreen yaupon, a shrub with bright red berries and small glossy leaves that used to be dried for making tea. I also spot the ever-perilous poison ivy, whose berries are enjoyed by birds. Through the trees there are glimpses of malarial-looking swamp, of marsh and sedge. Vines grow tangled, and in places the woods seem interwoven at the top, scalp hair brushed short and dense by sea winds, the height of the trees stunted by salt—either in the wind or in the brackish water that creeps in where there is insufficient fresh water in the ground. I hadn't thought of trees as suffering from stress, but one sign tells me that they do, and are kept from full growth by stressful conditions. The lob-lolly pines are perhaps an exception to this, for at least where they stand on hummocks they grow tall, even if this exposes them above the other trees to the winds. (187)

I make a more organized excursion one morning to look at birds. Near the Park Service camping ground at Cape Point I rendezvous with a Park Service ranger, Marcia Lyons, who is petite, has fair hair and tanned skin, and wears a broad-brimmed, round-domed Teddy Roosevelt felt hat. Marcia, who is in her twen-ties, says that sometimes forty people turn up for these bird walks; it is a big social event in the locality. But today, in the wake of Gloria, she doesn't expect many. In the event, only two others arrive—Jack Mitchell and his wife, Ruby, who have retired here from Connect-icut, where Mitchell worked as an advertising writer for the Remington Gun Company and served as pres-

ident of the Connecticut Audubon Society. ("The bird-
ers thought I was a gun lover," Mitchell says. "The
gun nuts thought I was soft about birds.") Mitchell
carries a small telescope mounted on a gun stock, with
an Audubon Society sticker on the butt, which he says
helps prevent it from being confiscated during plane
flights. Marcia and Mrs. Mitchell have conventional
binoculars. Since our numbers are small, we pile into
Marcia's four-wheel-drive wagon to reach the far side
of the great pond behind Cape Point, where we get
out to look at birds.

The Outer Banks are home—at some point during
the year—for more than 250 species of waterfowl.
Some, like black ducks and gadwalls, nest on the seashore; some, including the American and Arctic per-
egrine falcons and bald eagles, are in danger of dying
out; and some are migrants, simply passing through.
Greater snow geese, Canada geese, whistling swans,
and twenty-five species of duck winter on Hatteras
Island. Every time I have walked on the beach, I have
had for company hundreds of small wading birds—
dunlin, plovers, sandpipers, stilts, oystercatchers,
sanderlings, knots, and dowitchers—pecking and
probing in the sand for food, running ahead of the
final inrush from each wave, occasionally reaching a
sudden collective decision to take to the air, where, in
blurred squadrons, they wheel out over the sea before
coming in to land on the beach again, not far beyond
me. I would like to be able to give proper names to
some of these waders before I leave the Banks. Jack
Mitchell refers to them all as "peeps"—not a bad idea
if you can't always identify one from another.

Out over the Gulf Stream tower pillars of billowing
cumulus. On the margin of the beach the vehicles of
the surf fishermen are spread out in a thin line as their

owners patiently attack the sea, generally standing one foot forward, and sometimes with stomachs well forward, too; a few in swimsuits and one in high rubber wading boots as a vanguard out in the water. I have the impression that Americans want to drive their cars to the very edge of the continent. If Diamond Shoals got shallower, they'd drive out there. Some four-wheel-drive vehicles are air-conditioned. Most, however, are now open to the air, tailgates down to allow access to coolers, folding chairs, bait pails, and tackle boxes. One has a Confederate flag flying from one of six fishing poles stuck in the holders on its front bumper—not just lances but a pennon! The greatest number of rods I've seen so flaunted is twenty. Some vehicles have bikes hung in brackets on the back and cowcatcher-like extensions on the front for boxes and buckets. Marcia, who is from Boston, says, "When I first came here I couldn't stand the sight of four-wheel-drives on the beach. It's no fun to walk a beach all grooved with tire tracks. But now . . ." She says that the Park Service, while trying to balance the demands of all forms of beach use, has closed a number of vehicle access points in an attempt to prevent the four-wheel-drive vehicles from injuring the toe of the dunes. Jack Mitchell says a number of fishermen wouldn't come here if the Park Service prohibited them from driving on the beach—as it has done in the Cape Cod National Seashore.

In any event, Hatteras at this time of year is fishing mad. Mitchell says, "You tell someone on the beach they're missing the World Series, they'll reply, 'Oh yeah, the king mackerel are running.' " And it isn't just the addicted amateurs. On the southwest side of Cape Point, several men in a pair of big dories are setting seine nets, while their pickup trucks and trailers for the dories wait on the sand. This is known locally as "swipe fishing," and sometimes involves a dozen hauls a day. Lines from the nets will be fastened to the trucks when the men come ashore, beaching the dories and waiting for the nets to gather in their catch.

"There are fish stories on top of fish stories down here," says Mitchell. "Last winter I was told the seiners got one hundred thousand pounds of sea trout here in a single day's haul. Once their nets were so full, the trucks were pulled down into the water."

We walk beside the pond. Marcia, with a bird guide held in the small of her back between her leather belt and her khaki shirt, says we should see some of the migrating birds that are still coming through, some of the nesting birds that live here, and some birds that are just arriving to winter here: a good mixture. I spot a bird standing almost invisible in the grass and Marcia congratulates me on my perception—it is a female gadwall, she adds, realizing that I have no idea what sort of duck it is. The Mitchells point out on the pond a blue-wing teal and a pie-billed grebe. An egret seen on the far edge of the pond is identified by Marcia as a snowy egret; that it is one of this year's young is shown by black on the front of its legs, and yellow behind. Marcia says that, because it is dancing as it feeds, she knew it wasn't a great egret, a bird whose actions are of a more stalking kind—as Jack Mitchell puts it, "more CIA-like." At the turn of the century, the plumage of egrets was in demand for women's hats and the birds were nearly wiped out. Defense of the bird against annihilation by fashion was one factor that helped bring about the formation of the Audubon Society.

Hundreds of terns are standing in the shallows of the pond, all facing into the wind. Marcia adjusts a telescope she has set up on a tripod; she has thin tanned arms with a faint down of blond hair. When she has got the telescope successfully focused, she tells me to look through it: "There are four different terns in view right now." It seems they are the common tern, royal tern, Caspian tern, and sandwich tern. I note—though will I remember?—that the Caspian has a blood-red bill, while the black bill of the sandwich tern has a yellow tip. "I call it the mayonnaise tern," says Mitchell, generously providing a mnemonic. Some birds, like the knot, are already in their winter plumage, and doing their best to confuse newcomers to the identification process. Even so, I begin to feel a benign glow when I attach the right name to a bird. Two pelicans fly over, the first I've seen on this trip, Concorde noses attached to jumbo bodies, the tips of their wide wings upturned as they stroke slowly through the air. High above them, a falcon flaps fast across the pond—too fast for either Marcia or the Mitchells to be sure what sort it is. "I think it's a merlin," says Marcia. (The merlin, a bird of prey, is also known as a pigeon hawk, though merlin sounds fancier.) Around the pond we find a number of birds who are victims perhaps of Gloria or of summer exertion. Close to the beach are several dead pelicans and a blue heron lying with its head tucked in to the body, feathers bedraggled by wind and water, spackled with sand. At the end of our circuit, a fish crow stands officiously on a sign that directs traffic toward the Park Service camping area, where several newly arrived tents and trailers indicate that other visitors have decided that Gloria is well past.

Jack Mitchell and I have lunch in a Buxton diner. His particular post-Gloria worry is how to dry out several hundred books in boxes that got soaked when a storage space under his house was flooded. He says, "We build houses on pilings down here so they're above the water level, but then the space seems useful and gets walled in." Mitchell tells me that he finds life in Buxton a great contrast to what it was in exurban Connecticut. "In Fairfield, where we lived, maybe 365 cars a year are stolen. Here it's a crime wave when a surfboard disappears. Up there the air is visible, almost tangible, from pollution. Here every day it's crystal clear. Of course Hatteras Island gets pretty cleared out in winter, the beaches are empty, restaurants are closed. I tell Ruby I'm going downtown to see if there's anyone to talk to—but then people here have time to talk. I may have a gam with Zander Brody, who is an artist and local sign painter, if all else fails about the weather or the price of fish. Quite a few people down here are living on marginal incomes. Local youth tend to move away, looking for a better standard of life, and other youth—refugees from the metropolis—move in, thinking this life looks good. They surf, they pack fish, they paint—and most of them remain. I thought at first I'd be worried about how unkempt it all is—there isn't much planning, and there ought to be, but fortunately we're insulated from complete self-destruction by the National Seashore. The natives kick about the Park Service, but people come here because of what's been achieved and preserved by it. I like the isolation. Hatteras is about as far as you can go without getting close to somewhere else."

Marcia Lyons told me that her husband, Jim, is a teacher of third grade at Cape Hatteras School, which takes 470 island children all the way from kindergarten to graduation at the end of twelfth grade. Jim Lyons is also to be found after school sitting in his bright blue pickup truck at Hatteras Harbor Marina, on call for any jobs cleaning fish when the sportfishermen land in the late afternoons—looking to bolster his income from teaching and apparently not damaging pedagogical status in these parts as I—with a perhaps prissy English view of the matter—would have thought at first such hands-dirtying moonlighting would have done; in fact, in the eyes of his students, probably the contrary. Most young teachers here seem to have second jobs, like Mike Finnegan, who teaches fifth grade at Cape Hatteras and whom I occasionally talk to when he is manning the reception desk at the Tower Circle. "Of course, the guy you really should have met is Dick Lebowitz," says Finnegan. Lebowitz taught English at Cape Hatteras and was a local stringer for *National Fisherman*, a monthly devoted mostly to commercial fishing interests, but he has, according to Finnegan, quit teaching and gone to Vermont to be an editor of a bi-monthly called *Small Boat Journal*. While he was at Cape Hatteras, Lebowitz was mentor of a student-produced, once-, twice-, or thrice-a-year magazine called *Sea Chest*, in which a great deal of Outer Banks lore was printed. "People around here were really proud of *Sea Chest*," Finnegan tells me. "Many of them have kept every issue."

(194)

National Fisherman, as it happens, is a magazine I receive, and a few years ago I came across a mention of *Sea Chest* in it—presumably planted by Lebowitz. In the course of my Outer Banks ponderings at home in London, I wrote to *Sea Chest* c/o Cape Hatteras School, saying that I was hoping to get to the Banks and asking how I could subscribe. I got a courteous letter back from one Greg Neilson, saying that *Sea Chest* had ceased publication but welcoming me to the school if I ever got to these parts. I had assumed Neilson to be a teacher, but Finnegan now tells me he was a student, a *Sea Chest* editor, and had graduated last year and gone off to college. "But you'll have to come to the school," Finnegan says to me. "You can look through the *Sea Chest* files. And you can stand up in front of my class and say something in English."

Thursday afternoon is when I do this. The school is on the road down the island, beyond the cape, between Buxton and the next small community of Frisco. As with most American schools, the parking lot—here still heavily puddled—is prominent, as is the playing field, and there is nothing unusual about the one-story buildings, joined by walkways, that form the school. I present myself first to Grady Austin, the assistant principal: gray-haired, glasses, open-neck shirt, pipe-smoking. He tells me he was a member of the school's first graduating high-school class in 1956, worked for thirteen summers as a park ranger, is addicted—"like everybody else down here"—to fishing, and has spent his entire teaching career at Cape Hatteras School except for one year at a school near Elizabeth City. Until the early fifties there were separate schools in Rodanthe and Hatteras village; now children are bused here from both ends of the island (the Rodanthe bus leaves at 6:45 a.m.). Cape Hatteras School and Ocracoke School, which is a good deal smaller, are the only all-the-way-through schools in North Carolina.

"We closed last Thursday and Friday for Gloria," says Austin, "but we started up again on Monday with a borrowed generator. There wasn't much damage, though I wish architects had never gone in for flat roofs. We're more than a school—we house Boy Scouts, Girl Scouts, and all sorts of local recreation and community facilities. Most of our students go on to college or trades schools. Not many want to take up teaching. We don't have much of a discipline problem. There are few drug cases and not many dropouts. We take in the children of quite a few itinerant families, especially the kids of fathers who are down here fishing. We run several extracurricular projects. *Sea Chest* was great for the students who worked on it, though eventually they used up the memories of just about all the older people on the island. We now have a marketing program in which students go into part-time jobs while still at school. We also build a house every year, out on the edge of the playing field—both boys and girls work on it. We then sell it—last year's went for $36,000—and the purchaser takes it away to his lot, where a foundation and utilities are ready. It generally costs a couple of thousand to move it. One man took his house all the way to Manteo with his own moving rig, but he spent a long time on the highway with blown-out tires."

Finnegan's class is a mixture of fourth- and fifth-graders: dimples, freckles, bumps, and bruises; many smiles and wide-eyed wondering stares. A fashionable hair arrangement with some boys is to have it tied at the nape of the neck in a "rat's tail." I am introduced as someone from across the ocean, but this status may not be as exotic as I might have imagined, for one ten-year-old girl has Sicilian parents and, she says, has been to Europe, too. Sample questions for the English visitor are:

"Do you have celebrities in England?"

"Do you have VCRs in England?"

"Do you have shopping malls in England?"

"Have you met Princess Di?"

From this you might conclude that the younger generation on this part of the Banks desires nothing greater than to join the rest of the developed world in TV-thralled consumerdom. But a few gentle queries posed by me in return elicit deep strata of outdoors interests. Beach and boat fishing is popular with this age group, too, both male and female. One small boy tells me that if I come across a cottonmouth in my travels, I should stomp on it. He, he says, has killed several this way.

The *Sea Chest* archives are in a room which is in use for a high-school English class, but the woman teaching it kindly takes a moment to show me the relevant drawers in a filing cabinet, offers me a table and chair, and then goes back to composition. *Sea Chest* started in 1973 and continued for eleven years. It was one of some fifty school magazines in the United

States that followed in the pioneering footsteps of *Fox-fire*, of Auburn, Georgia, getting students interested in the lives and histories of their own localities. The teacher who founded *Sea Chest* was Mrs. Mildred Jeranko, who retired not long after doing so and handed on the job of advisor-encourager to Richard Lebowitz. The students looked at local habits and customs, past and present; they interviewed, researched, wrote, took photographs, selected material, and laid it out. They bought a typewriter, camera, and three tape recorders. They solicited subscriptions. They mailed out the magazine. *Sea Chest* won prizes. The first issue, that of Spring/Summer 1973, began with a forthright anti-tourist piece. "There are 3200 of us and there were 750,000 tourists here last year." Tourists, said the *Sea Chest* journalists, do dreadful things: act as if they own the place. Clean fish in motel bathrooms. Build picnic fires in private driveways. Dig up shrubs and flowers in private gardens. Tourist surfcasters interfere with the activities of commercial fishermen. They steal nets, mess up boats, and block a haul. Some park their trucks on haulers' nets. They leave trash all over the beach. They ask where's the lighthouse when it's looming right over them. They ignore signs saying DEEP SAND and get their cars stuck. They drive too fast. They ask, "Is it a long walk out to Diamond Shoals?" or "Where's the shopping center?" Family tourists are the worst. They have screaming kids. In restaurants, they want to be the first ones waited on, even if their order is in last. They want it *right that minute*. Some don't have the money to pay for the food they order.

Sea Chest recorded Hatteras Island superstitions, many of which are similar to those of the Old Country—for example, "If you tell your dream before breakfast, it's going to come true." Bankers used to know a storm was coming "when the crabs leave the sound side and seek higher spots" or "when the ocean is 'frying.' " Many of the idiosyncrasies of Hatteras speech seem to be the slightly fossilized and somewhat contrary usages one finds in other isolated maritime communities, reminding me of those current into recent times in Newfoundland. Here "biddable" is docile or obedient (as in "she's not a biddable girl"). A "flaw" is a gust of wind and "wind" is air ("You'd better get some wind in that tire"). "Everwhat" is a Hatteras stand-in for whatever ("I don't know everwhat it was he wanted"). To "haul off" is to act or move ("He hauled off and went to Buxton"). "Up north" is any place off the island, while the worst thing a mother can say to a Hatteras child is "You little Hessian!" "Like the feller said" is to quote an authority, as in "Like the feller said, they'll raise the taxes anyhow." Some pronunciations seem designed to fool the terrible tourists: "Go up to the rough and fix the chimney." The word "vine" often came out as "woine." A vowel in the middle of the word was frequently turned into a *y*, as in "Ocrycoke" and "hurrycane." Some words, say the student scholars, are of unknown origin, like "catisnined," an adjective meaning "in bad shape" or "beyond repair," though I'd hazard it has a lot to do with the effect of a cat-o'-nine-tails. I like "disremember" ("I disremember who she is"), and I can see the uses of the verb "sull," meaning to pout or sulk ("He sulled all day"). Another handy term is "prowser," nicely combining prowler and browser, for one who walks around at night. Such mother-country words as "daffy" and "frock" were long in use here. And that not all of these usages have disappeared is borne out by the father-in-law of the artist Zander Brody, who,

Brody says, continues to call a frying pan a "spider," which is the old name in these parts for a small three-legged frying pan that was placed over a fire. Some Hatteras folk refer to instant coffee as "snuff coffee."

Many *Sea Chest* stories have to do with "Back when . . ." Back when there were gun clubs, and geese were plentiful, and the roads were sand, and the mail came by boat, and a man could make a living as a hunting guide or as a fisherman, crabbing with fifty pots a day. Times are marked by the proximity of a hard winter or a hurricane. Time was when home remedies had to suffice for many an ailment—"For an animal bite, take a piece of chewing tobacco and chew it up and soak it in whiskey and place it on the bite." In Rodanthe they celebrated Old Christmas, the Epiphany, by having an oyster roast and carrying about the figure of a bull, made of a blanket over a wooden frame. One elderly resident, Con Farrow, who from the roar of the ocean could "tell pretty well what direction the wind would be the next day," says that he misses the sound of back then: "the chopping of wood, the honking of geese, the cranking of the brant, and people in the morning grinding their coffee beans." That was before snuff coffee and cans with no wind in them.

Other aspects of Banks life investigated by the *Sea Chest* staff were the Lifesaving Service, the lighthouse, fishing, food and its preparation, and hunting. Traditional instructions were recorded for how to tie nets, how to make quilts, and how to turn an apple-butter jar into an oil lamp ("oil" pronounced "ill"). The young journalists learned to take criticism—"We were in hot water on the Tourist story with everyone but the tourists, who for the most part thought it perhaps too mild." And they learned that disappointment could be turned into copy—"Our scheduled interview with Mr. Jack Gray had to be canceled because he was pumping sea water from a recent storm out of the driveway of his motel." In time, however, pickings grew slimmer. Local residents were perhaps all talked out. Subscriptions were down and publication costs up. Working for *Sea Chest* ceased to be a standard part of the English course; there were new school programs in sports and computers. Richard Lebowitz wrote to me, in reply to a letter in which I asked him about the circumstances of *Sea Chest*'s suspension: "My students were discovering other interests—wrestling, plays, music, art—whatever new programs our school offered. Also, the complexion of the community changed over the years I was there. A lot of new construction was going up, including the first condos, and a lot of new faces were appearing in the community. My impression was that there was more interest in making a buck than in preserving the beauty and traditions. And I can't say I blame the people—if they didn't make any money off their land, then outsiders would."

Before leaving Cape Hatteras School, I walk across the playing field to look at the house which this year's carpentry classes have under construction. It is still skeletal: plywood floors in place, raw pine studs rising from them, and a few joists overhead; the framework of a large box in which people will live. The students are going with the times, constructing the present rather than continuing to reconstruct the past. But, like Lebowitz, I don't have it in me to condemn them. In any case, they built in *Sea Chest* a well-carpentered repository that will continue to hold Hatteras memories and habits for a long while to come.

Hatteras Island has had a weather observation post since 1874, though in its early days the station had constant trouble with the telegraph line that conveyed its reports. The weather station's journal for September 17, 1876, records:

The storm of yesterday continues today, with rain. It became very moderate during preceding night, but increased in fury this a.m. Winds reached a maximum velocity of 72 miles per hour from 9:30 to 9:45 a.m. No cautionary signals ordered. Telgh line not working. The sea is very much agitated and breaks in heavy pools over the beach from S.E. Anenometer Cups blown away from Spindle 10:35 a.m. from the extreme violence of the wind & the wind increases in force to 12:30 p.m., at which time it blows 100 miles per hour [presumably a guesstimate], picking the water up from the surrounding pools and changing it to spray dashes it against the houses like rain. At 3:30 p.m. put up another set of cups, wind having moderated to 73 miles per hour. They done well until one of the cups blew off the arm. Wind veers to westward moderating all time. At 9 p.m. wind only 7 miles per hour. The day ends clear. No aurora.

The present U.S. National Weather Service station is in a two-story concrete building on a back road in Buxton, identifiable by the radar scanner and sundry other devices outside that measure wind direction, wind speed, temperature, humidity, and atmospheric pressure. It was from here that the reports emanated which, somewhat tardily, reached the apprehensive radio listeners in Queen Anne's Revenge on the night of Gloria. And here, in a second-floor control room, among visual display units, radar screens, electronic recording instruments, and overflowing ashtrays (indicating a preponderance of chain-smokers on the staff), a cheerful, red-haired, thirty-three-year-old meteorological technician named Bonnie Terrizzi is happy to relive for me her Gloria experiences. "We were very very lucky," she says. "If the storm had gone twenty miles west of us, instead of twenty miles east, we might not be here now. This building is meant to withstand 150-mph winds. But we were holding our breath, hoping we wouldn't have to find out if it would."

(202) For the big night, eight station staff were on duty, including Wallie Demaurice, the chief; Bonnie's husband, Frank, on radar; and technician Jim Cox, whose wife's name is Gloria. (Jim says, indiscreetly, "Once I heard the name given the storm, I knew it was going to be a tough one.") Bonnie's job was putting out reports and updates—sending details to the National Weather forecast office in Raleigh, which then fed them to the "weather wire circuit" for press, radio, and TV use. Bonnie says, "We were boarded up in here like in a bomb shelter and watching it come on radar. Our screen covers about 250 miles, and Gloria filled half of it—it was awesome. When the eye got to sixty miles offshore I was putting out reports every twenty minutes. The eye was shaped like the iris of a human eye, from twenty-five miles to eight miles across. The tighter the iris, the more severe the storm, and that was pretty tight. We were so busy in here we didn't have time to think about what might be going to happen to our homes. Out in the Atlantic, Gloria had been blowing a hundred and fifty. But it was also moving fast, not hanging around, and then, just before it got here, the cold front which was coming through gave it a nudge and Gloria followed the line of least resistance and went up the coast. The eye just raked us. The main storm surge and the worst winds went offshore."

Even so, the weather station lost several of its recording facilities when the power lines failed. The tide gauge ceased to function. But most of their instruments were kept going by an emergency generator. At just after 11 p.m. on Thursday, the station recorded a sustained wind speed of 64 knots, which is 74 miles per hour, with a peak gust of 87 miles per hour. Out at Diamond Shoals light tower at midnight, the wind was 98 miles per hour, gusting to 120. In the eye as it brushed Cape Hatteras at 12:30 a.m., the wind dropped to 8 miles per hour and the pressure fell to 27.98 inches. "Then the pressure went up again so rapidly our ears popped," says Bonnie. As a souvenir, she gives me a barograph tracing—a printout of the change in atmospheric pressure; it looks like a drawing of an undersea abyss. During the passing of the eye, Wallie Demaurice released a fifteen-foot-diameter, hydrogen-filled balloon. This carried up to a height of twenty miles an instrument which radioed to the station readings of pressure, temperature, and humidity. Demaurice felt fortunate, Bonnie says, to have the eye come that close to the station. She adds, "Close enough, when you see what it's like in Avon. I live just down the street here, and we lost a few shingles and bits of screen from the porch. A neighbor found a bluefish in his pond."

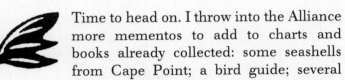 Time to head on. I throw into the Alliance more mementos to add to charts and books already collected: some seashells from Cape Point; a bird guide; several copies of *Sea Chest* which Grady Austin gave me. From the road, there is a scrappy picturesqueness about the landscape of the lower arm of the island between Buxton and Hatteras village. Although there are a few upmarket housing developments, marked by rustic nameboards and gateways, such as Brigands Bay, where Jack and Ruby Mitchell live, the more general scene is made up of trailer homes and shacks set among palmettos and live oaks with Spanish moss growing on them. The air of impoverishment is similar to that in parts of rural Maine, though here the climate makes possible in all seasons a more outdoor life. On one rickety porch a man with long, bedraggled hair is playing a banjo; the dogs fretting in his front yard are undoubtedly hounds. Little marsh-bordered creeks appear on the sound side, with the occasional weath-

ered dock and weathered skiff alongside, in many respects recalling the scenery in the comic strip *Pogo*. The pickup trucks standing in driveways are, to put it kindly, older models; it occurs to me that I haven't seen a Mercedes south of Nags Head. The single hamlet that intervenes between Buxton and Hatteras is Frisco, but there is nothing else to make one think of the great California city named after the good saint. In recent history this section of Hatteras Island has been notable mostly for the fact that General Billy Mitchell chose the sandy airstrip near Frisco as the place from which to fly his bombers in 1923, when demonstrating the advantages of air power over sea power, adding a number of derelict naval sitting ducks to the several thousand vessels that have sunk in these waters.

In the village of Hatteras I book into the Hatteras Harbor Hotel, owned by the Caldwells. Mark Caldwell is a soft-spoken, bearded man in his early forties who came here from West Virginia thirteen years ago, spent some time as the wrestling coach at Cape Hatteras School, and now with his wife runs the motel and an insurance agency. He says, "Right now we've got four loss adjusters looking into claims because of Gloria. They're amazed at how cooperative people are around here. Some even don't want to take the money they're being offered. Of course a few get mad when they are reminded that their homeowner's policy doesn't cover water damage from flooding. They knew this, but didn't do anything about it, since flood insurance costs an extra forty-five cents per hundred dollars. Once they've got over being mad, they may buy more insurance. Historically, it has been shown that a lot of insurance gets written after a bad storm."

The Hatteras Harbor Motel is similar to the Tower

Circle, with skinny single-story buildings forming three sides of a U, outside walls of brick veneer, and flat roofs. As seems to be the case with most motels on the Banks, a Stars and Stripes flies from a flagpole; the rooms are decorated with garish seascapes. However, my room is comfortable, the bed is firm, a light is provided over the desk, and hot water is plentiful. In the middle of the courtyard there is a small swimming pool in which I take a mid-afternoon dip. As the motel's name implies, the harbor is near, though out of sight behind some buildings by the fish dock.

I have a few days of almost complete failure of momentum in Hatteras, which is not suited for anyone unprepared for a period of inertia. For those who aren't drawn to fishing or beach activities, there is little to do in Hatteras. In a motel, unlike a hotel, if you are on your own, you are on your own. My room has a television, but there is little on it except game shows. For several days rain sets in. I read. I take occasional damp strolls through the village, whose prominent structures are motels, restaurants, gas stations, and boat wharves. From a civic point of view, Hatteras is favored by a post office and a library, but no sidewalks, a lack which enlarges the feeling of roadside dereliction. Sand, puddles, and mounds of ineffectually grassed earth greet the feet of the pedestrian. A tiny weed-ridden graveyard, crammed with the ancestors of Hatteras's present population, has been nearly subsumed into the adjacent Midgett Brothers Garage. A large billboard overshadows the dead. Each business seems capable of maintaining only its own property, if that, with no outgoing largesse to spare for the surroundings, which, therefore, are invariably scruffy. Within, things may be otherwise. I enjoy visiting Oden's General Store, whose claim to be non-particular is indisputable. Its dimly lit, narrow aisles allow passage between shelves stacked from floor to ceiling with bronze bolts, light switches, stopcocks, pliers, beer, wine, T-shirts, papers, magazines, paperbacks, bread, canned goods, postcards, toothpaste, sunglasses, Timex watches, garden shears, boat shoes, fishing hats, life jackets, cigarettes, and candy.

I also spend a good deal of time in Sonny's, the nearest restaurant, waiting for a table, waiting to be served, and—eventually—eating. Sonny's is generally full, and at breakfast time overfull. A queue to get in has often formed by 8 a.m. Most customers seem to be men here for the fishing. I have provided for the wait by first getting a *Virginian-Pilot* from the dispenser on Oden's porch. While pondering the breakfast menu (it will be some time before the young woman returns for my order), I waver between hot cakes (i.e., pancakes) and scrambled eggs with English muffins. I choose the former, and my coffee cup is topped up three times before the hot cakes actually arrive—by then I am affecting an interest in the *Virginian-Pilot*'s small ads and recalling the impatient tourists derided by *Sea Chest*. In the evening—dinner is served from five until nine—the pressure is off. Sonny greets me at the door: "Alone again tonight, sir?" He leads me to a table. I have remembered to bring my own wine, bought from Oden's. Hatteras Island is dry to the extent that it has no package stores specifically selling alcoholic beverages, no hard liquor is on sale anywhere, and you have to buy your own beer or wine before dining—brown-bagging, this is called. I'm not sure how the managements of Hatteras restaurants would feel if one brought in one's own bottle of spring water, but given the taste of the tap water, that—for water drinkers—might be a good idea.

As I enter with my brown bag, I feel slightly furtive. I slink to my table, obscuring the bag with book or newspaper, and smile with a touch of embarrassment as I ask for a corkscrew—or reject the kind offer of an ice bucket. My bottle tonight is Gallo's Special Reserve Hearty Burgundy.

Solitary travel has its advantages. On the long way down the Iron Curtain from Lübeck to Trieste, I read *War and Peace*. On the Banks I've been finding *Humphry Clinker* excellent company, and now, that work sadly finished, I've turned to *The Adventures of Tom Sawyer*. A journey of this kind gives one a chance to reread books one hasn't read since childhood (*Robinson Crusoe* is next on my agenda). Unaccompanied by either a Johnson or a Boswell, I have to do without much mealtime conversation, but on the other hand am not insulated from my surroundings as, when traveling, one sometimes is by the company of family or friend. On his own, the traveler flings himself more boldy into encounters with strangers, and strangers respond with greater readiness than they would if the traveler had backup companionship.

It may be that I also look around me and at my fellowmen with what is sometimes more asperity, sometimes more sympathy, than might be so were my viewpoint not one of solitude. Tonight at Sonny's I am impressed by the extremes of physique displayed by the other diners. People here seem to be either very thin or very fat; some jog daily, some shuffle through life. One normal-sized elderly couple, with nothing otherwise to draw attention to them, are each wearing ordinary spectacles to which green sunglasses are attached at the top, presently rigged so that the sunglasses stick out toward those of the person opposite and filter a green light onto their plates of food. Many of the tables are taken up entirely by fishermen, whose conversation is—from what I can overhear—about fish: bluefish, Spanish mackerel, marlin, bluefish, bluefish . . . They wear long-peaked fishing caps (possibly they even go to bed in them) which have a mesh fabric top and an elastic back. Over the peak, some caps have promotional badges for companies making drinks, fuel, or machinery, while others have slogans like *Keep the South Beautiful—Give a Yankee a Bus Ticket*. One man at a nearby table sits happily tucking into a steak under a cap with the boastful or hopeful legend *Bass Buster*.

I walk down to the harbor wharves the following day to look for Captain Ernal Foster, who Mark Caldwell tells me is credited with getting Hatteras started in the big-time business of charter fishing. Soon after the Second World War, Captain Foster used to talk to guests in the lobby of the Atlantic View Hotel here and, finding out that they didn't know what a blue marlin was, set about convincing them that going out and trying to catch one of these great game fish was an exciting thing to do. Pretty soon Captain Foster had three boats, which he called the Albatross Fleet, taking out private fishing parties. Now more than twenty such charter boats work out of Hatteras; it is an hour-and-a-half run to the Gulf Stream and its fish. As it happens, today Captain Foster is out fishing, though probably not for marlin at this season, and for his views I am restricted to a clipping from the *Los Angeles Times*, whose reporter was more successful in tracking down the captain: "Our Outer Banks way of life is disappearing—being replaced by yuppies, condos, and miniature golf courses. People are buying property on these islands like crazy. They come from Virginia, Maryland, Pennsylvania, New

York, and Ohio. They're paving up the islands. A person can hardly breathe. We had something precious here, but it will be gone in a generation, swallowed up by outsiders."

Captain Foster shouldn't have spread the word about the blue marlin.

I have lunch on the upper deck of the new marina, looking out over sportfishing boats' wheelhouses, spotting towers, and lofty permanently attached rods with struts and stays that prevent them from collapsing under the strain of a giant catch. I have a smoked-marlin sandwich; it tastes similar to smoked mackerel. The lady who runs the marina coffee shop says that she and her husband (out fishing) spend the midwinter months on their boat in the Bahamas. Then I walk on, past the slip where the ferries sail to and land from Ocracoke, the next island. The inlet between Hatteras Island and Ocracoke is three miles west-southwest of here, but the last buildings on Hatteras before one reaches the inlet belong to the U.S. Coast Guard lifesaving station—one of three such stations on the Banks, the others being at Oregon Inlet and on Ocracoke. Here, an attempt is being made to throw grass around the utilitarian brick-and-concrete buildings. Alongside a dock, two trim white craft are moored and are identified for me by the station commander, Chief Warrant Officer Rob Sanderson, as a forty-four-foot motor lifeboat and a thirty-foot surf rescue boat, both designed to go out in heavy weather and survive a rollover. "They'll just pop right back up and keep going," says Sanderson, as we stand at the controls of the motor lifeboat and I hang on unnecessarily to a polished brass safety rail. Sanderson is thirty-two, with a sandy mustache, and comes from Oregon; he trained on the Pacific coast at the national motor-lifeboat school near Cape Disappointment, Washington, where the surf, he tells me, generally runs twenty or so feet high and in a strong winter storm reaches forty feet. "That's real good training water," he says.

At Hatteras Inlet rough winter weather occasionally provides what Sanderson calls "cases," but the summer, generally calmer, keeps the Coast Guard busier. Sanderson says, "We monitor Channel 16, the distress frequency. We also get a lot of calls from people saying a friend's or relative's boat is overdue—though most situations of that kind correct themselves before we respond. Before we go out, we do some extensive checking at boat harbors and marinas. In summer, much of our work is what we call Go-and-Tow—go out and tow in boats that are disabled, have run out of gas, or are simply disoriented and need help. Just before Gloria, we started working what we thought was an overdue. A nervous relative called us. Fortunately, we didn't launch any resources to look for him—it turned out the guy was in harbor all the time. Today we've heard from Cape Hatteras there's a pleasure boat out there, a guy who is in some sort of panic— he thinks his clutch is slipping. Our helicopter from Elizabeth City has looked for him but hasn't found him at the location the guy reported—so for a start he isn't where he thinks he is. The forty-one-footer from Oregon Inlet has now gone to see if they can find him. In winter, we get more calls for help from fishing boats, a lot of which aren't in such good shape as they would be if fishermen were doing better financially. Then we're also in the law-enforcement business—for instance, out looking for the elusive weed. Florida's got too hot for some of those people and they're heading north—not that they generally mean to get close to Hatteras on the way."

Like lifeboatmen everywhere, Sanderson and his men are proud of their vessels. The pride is visible in the bright white paint, the coiled warps on deck, and below, the gleaming cooling water pipes of the big diesel. I am impressed by a bulky tubular framework, covered with steel mesh, behind the position where the helmsman stands, which is intended to protect him if a towline snaps. A set of crash helmets is hanging on a nearby bulkhead. Safety harnesses are also often buckled on.

"It can be a rough ride through the inlet," Sanderson says. "During the marlin tournament this June, a blow came up. All the competing boats stayed in harbor except for a thirty-two-foot Cigarette—one of those racing machines. He went out with five people aboard and capsized in the inlet. We took out both boats, picked up all the people, and saved the boat, too. One night recently, we got a call that a boat was sinking offshore. We went out to it and on the way found another boat capsized in the inlet with three people in the water. So while we took care of them, we called back for our other boat, which rushed out to the sinking one, and rescued them."

I ask Sanderson for the secret of staying upright while running an inlet.

"Wave avoidance," he says. "And managing to stay out of the curl. If you're heading out to sea, you want to let the surf break ahead of you or behind you. One way of avoiding the breaks is by going to where the shoulders of the seas are—where the seas are running with solid, round tops, not curling yet. If you're coming in, it depends a bit on the speed your boat will do. Often the seas here come in at twenty to twenty-five knots. The surf rescue boat will do thirty-three knots, so it can outrun the breaking surf. This motor lifeboat has a top speed of fourteen knots, and so in this we try to get on the backside of a wave and stay on it as long as we can. If you can see the sea is going to break, slow down."

"Can be scary, I suppose."

"Now and then you get bounced around real good. But a number of our guys here go surfing in their spare time."

I have a 1974 chart of this part of the Banks, which I intend to compare with the inlet when I reach it. It is a blustery afternoon, hinting of rain. From the top of a dune I survey the broad end of the island—in shape something like a dragon's head—which was once largely the property of the Gooseville Gun Club. In 1954 it was sold to the Park Service for $47,000, which seems little enough for fifteen hundred acres. Much of the gunning took place on the shallows in the sound just north of here, a place called the Reef, where blinds, batteries, and sinkboxes were established. Sinkboxes were made of concrete and had canvas upperworks, which helped disguise the hunters from the geese, brant, and duck. Batteries—or "lay-down boxes"—were built of wood and looked like lidless coffins; the hunter lay inside, almost awash, paying for his prey with cold and discomfort. A hundred or so wooden decoys would be set out around these gunposts. And Gooseville was well named. Yet another of the Austin clan, Luther Austin, who was once a manager of the club, told *Sea Chest* ten years ago: "The geese, they used to be so plentiful, they were in clouds. They just jumped in clouds and when you scared them they'd be like clouds. They were clean to the shore then. Take a calm night and you could hardly sleep for them hollering along the shore. But nowadays there ain't no fowl." Luther Austin thought their favored eelgrass had disappeared, and this had driven the fowl inland to feed on farms. During the hunting season of November, December, and January, many Hatteras men "back then" made a living as guides and as market hunters. "They would kill boatloads of them," said Mr. Austin. "You could go out there and kill a hundred or so a day, but you could sell them all in them days, and ship them out of here. Of course you didn't get much for them, probably seventy-five cents or a dollar for a pair of brant, fifty or seventy-five cents for a goose."

No geese are about this October afternoon, though there are plenty of "peeps" and terns along the shore. As the island narrows to its end, I can see the water on both sides. A single pelican glides over the low ocean surf, while in a small pond by the sound an egret stands, just getting his feet wet. I am the only person walking. However, there are plenty of surfcasters with their vehicles and equipment. One woman is sitting in a folding chair so far back from the water that I don't realize she has a line out, and as I walk past, exchanging friendly greetings, I bump my head into her almost transparent nylon line. For a moment she looks a little less friendly. Nearing the inlet, I consult the chart and then regard my surroundings. Hatteras Island seems to be longer, the inlet narrower, than the chart showed it to be eleven years ago. Moreover, a solitary sandhill which is an islet part of the time is in process, so it seems, of becoming a permanent addition to Hatteras Island. I walk to it across a sand flat, over which the tide will rise, joining sea and sound and renewing the islet's surrounded-by-water-on-all-sides status for the time being. I do this after a moment's cogitation, as I work out the present state of the tide—just about low water, I believe—and whether I'll be able to get back without swimming. Half a dozen four-wheel-drive vehicles are on the part-time islet, but they may scamper before me, and without me, when the tide rushes in. At the tip of the land I stand at the water's edge. The inlet looks as tricky and tormented as an inlet can: buoys leaning over, almost underwater for a moment before bobbing back up—crisscross seas—whitecapped breakers foaming in. At my feet, brown flecks of spume whisk across the sand. And on the other side of the inlet, I can see another surf-fringed beach, low dunes, and dark specks which I take to be fishermen—almost a mirror reflection of this side, though it is a different island. Ocracoke.

Proceeding to the next island is this time an immediate adventure: there is no bridge. The island I am going to is therefore truly such. The ferries follow the Currituck Sound practice of being named after worthy public servants of North Carolina; one that is coming in as I drive up to the slip is called *Alpheus W. Drinkwater*. The Alliance and I board the *Conrad Wirth* with twenty other cars and their passengers, nearly a full load. The half-hour voyage is free. Away from the ferry slip, we pass a tiny island whose beach is packed with pelicans, and more pelicans are aloft, patrolling the channel with their leisurely wing beats. Looking back, I see a sign on the dock we have come from: *Dare County Welcomes You to America's Birthplace.*

The first seventeen miles or so of Ocracoke—which is part of Hyde County—are National Seashore. It has the same open, sandy beauty as the upper Pea Island end of Hatteras Island, with low dunes between road and ocean on my left as I drive southwest, and on my right, marshes bordering Pamlico Sound. For several miles sand which had recently blocked the highway has been pushed back to the ocean side by machinery which sits there as if waiting for the next blow. In fact, in places sand is already edging forward across the road again in arcs and crescents; it gives the impression of doing so when it thinks it may not be noticed. Ocra- coke village is at the far end of the island, next to the harbor called Silver Lake, and this is where nearly everybody on Ocracoke lives. Just beyond the halfway point along the island I stop for a stretch, and also for a look at the last surviving representatives of Ocracoke's herd of Banker ponies. They are kept in a corral of several acres on the sound side of the road. Four are in view, part of a herd of twenty or so maintained by the Park Service—a memento of what was. These four are small shaggy brown horses, though perhaps not so small as the Banks ponies used to be when they depended entirely on salt marsh grass for their provender. Early this century some 250 wild ponies grazed on Ocracoke and are said to have found fresh water by gathering in a circle, pawing shallow holes in the ground, and lying prone to drink. Between the wars the island had a mounted Boy Scout troop. At one time more than five thousand horses are believed to have roamed the Banks from Oregon Inlet to Beaufort, North Carolina; in the nineteenth century pennings took place twice a year on the Core Banks, at which colts were branded and horses sold—though not all of them took to life and the less salty forage on mainland farms. In the second half of the nineteenth century, a Virginia agricultural scientist named Edmund Ruffin visited the Core Banks and watched a horse-breaking:

After the captured horse has been thrown, and sufficiently choked by the halter, he is suffered to rise, mounted by some bold and experienced rider and breaker, and forced into a neighboring creek, with a bottom of mud, stiff and deep enough to fatigue the horse, and to render him incapable of making more use of his feet than to struggle to avoid sinking too deep into the mire.

(218) On Portsmouth Island, at the upper end of the Core Banks, there were 175 horses earlier this century. They were periodically driven toward the village, penned, and sold to mainlanders for fifteen dollars a head. David Stick recalls taking part as a boy in one of the last all-day pennings on Bodie Island, and says he hasn't been able to sit on a horse comfortably ever since. The pennings came to an end when state laws in the 1930s required the fencing of lifestock to control overgrazing and consequent erosion, and the horses began to go.

The origin of the Banks ponies is a matter of dispute. Some think they are descended from Spanish mustangs, brought to Florida by Ponce de León and his men in the early sixteenth century. Ninety horses were part of the expedition Lucas Vásquez de Ayllón made in 1526 from Florida northward to establish a temporary colony, believed to have been in the vicinity of Cape Fear. Measurements of equine skulls and skeletons by a scientist named William Stabler in 1973 and 1976 showed similarities between the Banks ponies and sixteenth-century Spanish mustangs, both having five lumbar vertebrae rather than six, as other horses do. But the Banks breed may also have had ancestors in the horses Sir Richard Grenville picked up in the Caribbean in 1585, and which were brought ashore on the Banks when his ship, *Tiger*, grounded off Ocracoke Inlet. Other strandings, and landings from captured ships carrying horses, may have added to the Banks stock. Certainly there are known to have been horses on Ocracoke in 1733, for the will of Richard Sanderson, the absentee owner of the island at that time, mentioned them. However, eighteenth-century settlers on the Banks brought their own horses—and these are thought by some to be the dominant strain in what became the Banks breed. In recent years, the road down the island and increasing traffic made life harder for horses. A fenced pasture and smaller numbers brought about inbreeding. The Ocracoke herd was down to five horses in the mid-1960s, when new blood of the Spanish mustang line was brought in. Now the policy of the Park Service is to maintain a small breeding stock of a few stallions and a dozen or so mares. Wildness is gone.

The human tendency to improve one's surroundings—to fix things up by, for example, painting fence palings and planting flowers in the front garden—and the not uncommon urge to encourage dereliction and decay—say, by throwing one's rubbish as far as one can into the back or side yard—have been at conspicuous odds for some time in the village of Ocracoke, and it is still too early to say which tendency is going to emerge victorious from the struggle. I book into the Island Inn, one of the older hostelries. My room, spacious and comfortable, is in the raised ground floor of the inn's several-years-old Stanley Wahab wing, named after a recent member of an island family which is descended from an Arab who was shipwrecked here in the eighteenth century and, according to Wahab legend, reached land hanging on to an oar. My room has sliding glass doors onto a porch, with a view of the swimming pool and of a good deal of asphalt shingling, lying on the coarse grass around the pool, that has been abstracted by Gloria from the Stanley

Wahab roof. I take a walk to get my bearings. On arriving in a new place, I have a need to find out how the land lies, which way is north, and where the nearest water is. It is frequently while I am setting forth on such an orientation exercise that I am stopped by people who may have just arrived by car and want to know, for instance, the way to the railway station, the fine-arts museum, or—as is the case here—the lighthouse. Since I am generally armed on these occasions with a map or, better still, intuition, and apparently possess a look of omniscience as I walk along, I don't hesitate to give directions. "Straight down that road and bear right," I say. Tourists in Bologna, Berlin, and Boston have, like these in Ocracoke, confidently accepted my help and have not, as you might think, been given pause at hearing someone speaking English or speaking with an English accent. Perhaps this particular lighthouse-seeking couple—in a car with Delaware plates—think I am a surviving example of the old Banks speech. Or, on the other hand, perhaps no such further problems bother them. How to get to where they want to go is what matters—and their question has been answered.

On this initial reconnaissance I discover that the Island Inn is several hundred yards from the south end of Silver Lake, the harbor whose exit to the sound is at its other, northern end. The lake is roughly circular, with small docks around its perimeter. The main part of the village lies along the east side of the lake, where one also finds Ocracoke Coast Guard Station and a dock from which ferries sail on two routes to the North Carolina mainland. Various lanes, generally paved with a mixture of dirt and sand, lead away from the harbor, with old houses set back behind white fences, amid tangled trees and encroaching shrubbery. There

seem to be many stagnant pools—though Gloria must
have topped them up—and a ubiquitous smell, like
that of Avon, of septic tanks that have overflowed.
Some houses are kept spruce and painted, but a large
number are tumbledown. Some residents living in
trailer homes have begun to build more permanent
structures nearby, only now both older trailer and
newer home appear to be crumbling at the same rate.
Ocracokers who aren't yet into improvement push their
abandoned cars and skiffs as far as they can from their
houses and toward the neighbors', where the boats rot
and the cars rust, half in and half out of the dividing
hedges. Bodies, like cars, remain close at hand, for
there are numerous little cemeteries—like everything
else, some cleared, some overgrown—where the late
inhabitants lie under lichen-covered and algae-
marked gravestones, in the shade of live oak, myrtle,
and oleander. In some yards and gardens close to the
harbor Gloria's waters have washed up a tide of rubbish, of eelgrass and plastic bottles. But if they aren't
all active gardeners, many of the 650 people of Ocracoke seem to be actively out and about. I pass a
number who are walking, and several cycling on solid-
looking balloon-tired bicycles. Also active are the mosquitoes; when I return from my excursion, I discover
I have six bites. I turn on the television set in my room
and find that Channel 4 displays a printout of Ocracoke news, weather, ferry schedules, and messages of
local import. Among the latter: "Jerry Midgett does
not want any more trash put in his hole at this time.
The hole may open again after the Fire Dept. burns
this load. We all thank Jerry for his help." What to do
with your garbage is evidently a long-standing Ocracoke problem.

In a place this small—and a place which is an island,

where people are stuck with one another—there are bound to be several competing focal points, seats of alleged influence or of informed opinion, where gossip is exchanged and useful news circulated, with more color and background than one gets on Channel 4. In the course of the next few days, I find myself often dropping in at one such locale, O'Neal's Dockside Store. Here you can buy snacks, cold drinks, film, fishing and hunting supplies, marine gear, bait, gas, and ice; and you can arrange to charter a fishing boat. You can stand inside the store, which is really not much more than a shed, with a snug feeling among the crowded shelves, and drink coffee from the pot which is kept on a hot plate while talking to Charlie O'Neal, who much of the time mans the tiny counter. Charlie wears a red T-shirt with white lettering on the back: *Member Ocracoke Vol. Fire Dept.* Or you can sit out on the little dock, where there are benches, a trestle table, a gas pump, and a fish-cleaning table, and where Charlie's father, William O'Neal, Sr., aged sixty, is generally to be found, maybe chatting with Dr. George Sessons, a retired G.P. from Lynchburg, Virginia, who first came to Ocracoke thirty years ago and has found himself spending more and more of the year on the island ever since. Living here most of the time, he has frequently served as unofficial island doctor during periods when Ocracoke hasn't had a proper physician of its own. What Dr. Sessons calls the unofficial town council meets on O'Neal's dock anytime after 6 a.m., and a great deal of banter and talk is exchanged while ferries and small fishing boats come and go from Silver Lake. Now and then, from inside the store, Charlie can be heard on the VHF radio, talking to fishermen: "You coming in soon, Dorsey?" A pause. "Okay, then, I'll wait around for you." Fish are a natural topic of shooting the breeze, as boat owners tie up for a can of oil and six gallons of gasoline. "How many Buddy get last night?" "Oh, four or five drum."

Out on the dock, William O'Neal tells me, "Yeah, we've had a pretty good year shrimping. The crabbing's been good. But since the storm, fishing's been a bit hit-or-miss."

In fact, fishing is one form of social cement around here. Constant reference to it is very much like saying "How are you?" or "Isn't it a lovely day?" More vital and volatile subjects of conversation are aspects of Progress (new developments, tourists, local government) and of the struggle—which affects pretty, once-sequestered places after they are discovered—between those who want to keep up with the times and make money and those who want to keep things the way they were (except, perhaps, in regard to changes they have in mind for their own properties). Often, of course, the struggle between conservative and progressive impulses exists within the same person. The O'Neals, for example, in conversation with Dr. Sessons, complain about "dingbatters" (their word for tourists who whiz through the place on the way to somewhere else) and "blowboaters" (a term—nicely suggesting hot air as well as wind power—for owners of fancy sailboats, whose sailing skills are generally exceeded by their boastfulness). And yet they remain keen to sell their wares and services to both dingbatter and blowboater. Charlie and his wife run a scenic historical tour, with accompanying commentary, in what they call the tourist trolley—an open trailer with a fringed surrey canopy pulled by a van. Time was when Ocracoke in its solitude had to put up with internal squabbles alone. This was when Silver Lake was still known as "the creek" and those who lived east of it were called Creekers;

those west of it—on the point between creek and in-let—were Pointers. Dr. Sessons, who lives on the point, says, "Pointers were the wrong side of the tracks. Creekers were the elite. I once tried to get a boy from a Creeker family to come and cut my grass, but he wouldn't."

(224)

Now, to hear them tell it, both parties pull together in the face of newcomers. With improved roads and ferry services, and the construction of an airstrip, the pressure has been mounting. William O'Neal says, "It was roads and telephones and then money—when money moves in, you can't do a damn thing about it." Three years ago, a three-story brick motel, the An-chorage, was erected down the road from O'Neal's dock, facing out over Silver Lake, and the fuss about it hasn't yet died down. In some quarters the project is thought to have got unfair or improper approval. "It looks like a big boil that's sticking out," says William O'Neal, while others maintain it would have been all right if built in Virginia Beach. The motel owner, a Midwesterner named Scott Cottrell, didn't exactly dis-arm his critics when he said that—though he had fallen in love with Ocracoke at first sight (they'd heard that before)—he thought it looked seedy. In fact, said Cot-trell, "the Ocracoke style is falling-down junk." This was in an interview with *The Charlotte Observer*, a clipping of which the O'Neals keep pinned on a wall of their store under a stuffed drum. Cottrell apparently regards the modern Sea Island, Georgia, resort de-velopment of Hilton Head as a model for Ocracoke, and he plans to add to local fury by adding to the Anchorage a fourth and fifth floor.

Next it will be condominiums is the fear on the O'Neal dock. Cable TV and pushbutton pay phones are on the way. People will have to start locking their houses. Restaurants used to shut at 6 p.m.; now they stay open until nine. An ABC state-owned liquor store has opened after long years of public dryness. Two of the village restaurants now have bars. "We still haven't got any real crime," says Charlie O'Neal, "but in the wintertime the trawlers sail in and the fishermen come ashore and drink, and now and then all hell breaks loose. Way back, they took care of lawbreakers here by just handcuffing them to a tree. More recently, we shipped them over by ferry to the jail at Swan Quarter on the mainland." Now there are two deputy sheriffs on Ocracoke and a jail is being built. Some islanders see the end of the good old days on Ocracoke in the introduction of commercially made coffins. Larry Williams, a native who is a co-owner of the Island Inn, is quoted in the same *Charlotte Observer* piece: "Everyone here used to keep their own casket boards, good wide boards, and when you died your casket got made out of them."

Ocracoke has so far got by without local government. It is unincorporated. As part of Hyde County, whose seat is Swan Quarter, Ocracoke—with only one member on the board of county commissioners—often has to follow the mainland lead on matters that might seem to require a different, island slant. In 1981 a proposal was made to control new development on the island by introducing zoning; but this was rejected by Ocracokers two to one. Some saw it as a straitjacket. Many were put off by the massive, technically phrased code that was proposed. People who had nets and crab pots and used them once in a while were afraid that, if they weren't zoned as business, they might have to give up their nets and pots. However, since the arrival of the Anchorage and a recent threat of condos, majority opinion may be shifting. A local committee is now looking into a fairly simple zoning code for a start, to control large-scale developments. But this may not be much protection against the seemingly vertical rise in value of Ocracoke property, which affects valuations, and county taxes, and consequently makes life difficult for elderly or impoverished inhabitants. "Just about every other person who comes here wants to stay here and buy a house," says Dr. Sessons, who has followed that route himself. House prices are such—and work so lacking for local young people—that only outsiders can afford to buy on Ocracoke. It is ironic that it seems to be largely tourism that creates jobs which will allow some younger islanders to stay on their own island.

One area in which most of the people of Ocracoke pull together is in supporting the fire department. This has a fire truck, an equipment truck, a portable pump, and two ambulances. There is no tax to fund it, and to bolster a county maintenance grant of five thousand dollars a year, donations are sought and cash-raising events such as fish fries are held. The fire department building is also a community hall where groups like Alcoholics Anonymous hold weekly meetings. The department is served by twenty-seven volunteers, who need a minimum of thirty-six hours of training to qualify as firemen. "We don't have that many fires," says Charlie O'Neal, who is the assistant fire chief. "The last big one was three years ago at Noah's deli. The lady there put a pot of cooking oil on the stove and then went into her house, which is attached to the deli, to answer the phone. Luckily, she shut the door behind her. We managed to save the house and most of the deli. It takes at least an hour and a half for more equipment to drive down here from Hatteras, so it's important that we don't let anything get out of hand. We have to go in and put a fire out—not just stay outside and surround it. Every one of our full-time members has a paging-system receiver, and the officers have transmitters. This setup cost twenty thousand bucks, but it has cut our response time down to nothing."

A man in a full suit of yellow foul-weather gear lands at the dock, carrying a plastic box full of fish, and says something to the O'Neals as he heads for the street. "Hear that Old English brogue?" Charlie says to me. "Some of them talk that way here—you can hardly understand them." In truth, I did not comprehend a word the fisherman said and am grateful when Charlie interprets his remark to mean that he was taking the fish up to the Pony Island restaurant. What Charlie calls a brogue is probably derived from the English West Country way of speaking, which has persisted here, like the vocabulary recorded by the Cape Hatteras students. But though Vernon Davis, the elderly merchant in Manteo, had a touch of it in his talk, I can't say that I have until now heard the broad Aussie-like accents that were once common on the Banks, even forty years ago. Then, according to *The North Carolina Guide*, old-timers—who called tourists comers'n'goers—talked of unusual hoigh toids in Hyde County waters. Some old maps spell the "Island" in Roanoke Island "Oisland." Ocracoke may well be the final bastion of Banks speech—unless the fisherman with the "brogue" was taking advantage of the credulity of a newly arrived comer'n'goer.

The name of Ocracoke is sometimes provided with an etymology that also seems concocted for the can't-stop-too-long tourist. One account is that Edward Teach, the pirate known as Blackbeard, dropped anchor here on one occasion to unload some booty and, "viewing the vast expanse of sand and water, shook his fist and yelled into the calm breeze, 'Oh, crow cock!' " For anyone who isn't satisfied with this explanation—and to fall into that category you don't have to try to yell those words into a calm breeze—another version takes place on the night before Blackbeard's fatal fight off the island with a naval crew sent to capture him. In this, Blackbeard, impatient for the dawn and battle, cries out, "O crow cock! O crow cock!" An even less farfetched derivation is from the Indian name of the island—variously spelled Wokokon, Woccocon, or Woccocock. By 1715 it was called Occocock.

The names of the island's residents are a reminder of insularity. One reference book that suggests this is the phone directory for the Atlantic–Beaufort–Morehead City area of North Carolina, which has two and a quarter pages devoted to Ocracoke listings. Among the most prevalent Ocracoke names are Austin, Ballance, Burrus, Fulcher, Gaskill, Gaskins, Howard, O'Neal, Wahab, and Wilks; other names, by comparison, seem sparsely represented. These Ocracoke names are of course found on other parts of the Banks and—according to Dr. Sessons—on other isolated islands on the Eastern Seaboard, from Tangier Island in Chesapeake Bay down to the Florida Keys. It is as if certain families were genetically disposed to settle on islands.

These names are also to be seen or traced with one's fingertip on the weathered gravestones and markers in the miniature cemeteries scattered throughout Ocracoke village. There are said to be eighty such graveyards, and in one, on a side street, I find some Fulchers, Gaskills, and O'Neals. The latter are Susan F. O'Neal and Isaac F. O'Neal and Missouri V. O'Neal, who I take to have been Susan and Isaac's daughter, and whose sad birth date and death date are inscribed under her lovely name:

A little further on along the same road, past Teeter's Campground, there is a community of three separate small graveyards. They are bizarrely prefaced by a giant red, white, and imitation wood-paneling Coke machine, which stands out in the open like a tin megalith, humming quietly. I imagine the campers are its intended customers, and that—coins having been fed in—the clatter its cans make was not judged any disrespect to the Wahabs who lie unhearing in one of the nearby plots, or the Williamses and Gaskinses in another. The third burial patch is what Ocracokers proudly call "the British cemetery." It is about twenty feet square and, according to a sign fastened to its neat, white picket fence, is maintained by the Coast Guard. Two small British red, white, and blue Union flags are planted in the sandy ground, while a larger one flies from a flagpole. There are four simple gravestones. Here lie four British crewmen from H.M.S. *Bedfordshire*, a deep-sea trawler converted for anti-submarine work, which from its base in Morehead City was patrolling the shipping lanes off the Carolina coast when it was sunk on May 11, 1942, by a German U-boat. There were no survivors. The bodies of two of the *Bedfordshire*'s crew, Sub-Lieutenant Thomas Cunningham and Ordinary Telegraphist Stanley Craig, washed ashore on Ocracoke three days later. Because the wartime lumber shortage had put a crimp in the Ocracoke coffin-board situation, they were buried in two unused sinkboxes. Two other bodies were found a week later by an Ocracoke Coast Guard patrol boat, four miles or so out to sea; they couldn't be identified, but were assumed to be ratings from the torpedoed trawler. This time, the people of Ocracoke found wood for the coffins. A memorial service for the four men was held later in 1942, U.S. naval forces and Coast Guard attending, and the burial plot has ever since served as one of Ocracoke's notable sites—the O'Neal tourist trolley halts here, for photographs to be snapped and poignant reflections to be made about the death of men at sea in wartime. If these aren't at the ready, they may be prompted by a brass plaque, also fastened to the fence, which quotes from Rupert Brooke's poem "The Soldier" the lines:

> *If I should die, think only this of me:*
> *That there's some corner of a foreign field*
> *That is for ever England.*

The engraver has in fact done a slightly sloppy job, producing his own line arrangement, leaving out the comma in line 1, and not helping the sense by putting two "thats," one after another, in line 2. But these mistakes don't detract overmuch from the gesture; they may even give it a homely touch; and the dead sailors, whose dust is concealed in this foreign, sandy spot, certainly don't care.

Apart from O'Neal's dock, the two Ocracoke landmarks where I spend most of my indoor time are the Island Inn and the Pony Island restaurant. The inn is owned by two men, Larry Williams, who was born on Ocracoke, and Foy Shaw, who is originally from Durham, North Carolina. Both are in their mid-fifties. They bought the inn nearly ten years ago and have expanded and improved it. The main building, just across the road from the Stanley Wahab wing, in which I am happily ensconced, was sturdily built at the beginning of this century, with a number of ships' timbers and entire tree trunks used in the construction. The ground floor housed the island school for some years, while upstairs was an Oddfellows Lodge—later providing room for an officers' club for the amphibious unit based on the island during the Second World War. Now the porch alongside the ground-floor restaurant has been enclosed as an aviary, with windows through which restaurant customers can watch parakeets and parrots—their plumage the most vivid tropical yellows, oranges, and greens—set an example of dainty and decorous eating, or rather, nibbling. The manager of the restaurant is a burly, red-bearded Englishman who sailed into Ocracoke with his family a year or so ago on their forty-six-foot ketch. They came in meaning to refit after a stormy Atlantic crossing, and have stayed on, apparently to repair their finances; the manager's wife and two sons have also been working on the island (his wife in another restaurant, the boys at odd jobs), and the family income, he says, generally amounts to a thousand dollars a week. "People complain there's no work around here, but there is if you want it," he tells me, after a day or so of seeming a little suspicious of me—another Englishman!—and of my interest in the place. He worked for an electronics company, Plessey, back in the mother country, before wanderlust hit him. During Gloria he stayed on board the ketch, which is called *Gentle Stranger*, tending the mooring lines he had rigged to several docks in Silver Lake. I get the impression he would rather be on the boat all the time, and at sea rather than in harbor. Behind the cash desk he looks over the head of a paying customer as if at a distant marine horizon. In a few months they will be setting off on their travels again, he says—the gloomy ocean-brooding look alleviated by what might be a smile as he cheers up at the thought. "We're heading for Brazil."

The slim girl who often looks after the front desk in the lobby tells me she is from the mainland, but married to an Ocracoker, and that one condition she placed on the betrothal was that, if ever a hurricane came this way, her husband would take her off the island. He kept his word for Gloria. She says, "I got back here to find a foot of water had covered the ground floor of the inn, the lobby carpet was ruined, and otherwise there hadn't been much real damage. But it hasn't changed my mind to want to stay if another one comes along."

One evening I have a drink with Foy Shaw—Larry is out fishing—in their quarters behind the lobby. Shaw tells me that he and his partner met in Virginia Beach, where they were both involved in amateur theater. Foy was teaching psychology at a community college and Williams taught high-school drama. Foy once appeared as Tom in a production of *The Glass Menagerie*, and his conviction that Tennessee Williams is *the* modern American playwright has been carried to the extent of naming his Angora cat Miss Amanda and his golden cocker spaniel Miss Blanche. He and Larry Williams were among the eighty or so islanders who stayed through Gloria. "We dithered," says Foy. "We thought about leaving, but by the time we'd made up our minds to go, the last ferry to Hatteras had sailed." He seems less upset about the loss of lobby carpet and Wahab roof shingling than that the Ocracoke lighthouse went dark during the hurricane and the local Coast Guard allowed it to stay off all night.

I ask if business at the inn has changed much since he and Williams bought it.

"I suppose because of our theater connections, we get a lot of actors and actresses coming to stay, and they pass the word along," he says. "And the better connections of road, bridge, and ferry bring more tourists all the time. So our trade is up in terms of numbers, though not necessarily in terms of quality. There seem to be more people who say they've come here to get away from it all and then are furious to find they haven't got a telephone in their room. Many want all the amenities of a top Manhattan hotel while not having to pay top prices. Of course, in some ways we aren't as away from it all as we were. Ocracoke now has a bank. And a full-time doctor—I was never sick when we hadn't one. Though the nearest vet is on Hatteras. This is still very much an island, and if you're fairly self-reliant, or can enjoy the company of the person you're with, and if you don't need to be bombarded by external artificial stimuli, Ocracoke is a wonderful place to be. There are no neon signs. You can see the stars and hear the birds. The sunsets are splendid. Some city people come here and can't handle it. They need phones ringing, things impinging. But I tell them, 'If you can get through the first day, you're okay.' "

Most evenings, after a long afternoon walk on the ocean beach, I have been assuaging my hunger at the Pony Island restaurant. According to Charlie O'Neal, who says he isn't related to the owners and isn't financially involved, the Pony Island has the best food on Ocracoke. By now I have had in various Outer Banks eateries my fill of grits, which are small, round, unground grains of steamed oatmeal; served with melted butter poured over them, they remind me of the hot cereals which I particularly disliked as a child in wartime Ohio and which I would sullenly stir around in the breakfast bowl, hoping they would ooze magically away. The hot "biscuits" which are often proffered and which—since decent bread seems unobtainable—I occasionally order are invariably soft, underbaked, tasteless little rolls. As for the ubiquitous hush puppies—lumps of cornmeal dough dropped by the spoonful into hot cooking oil—I no longer say yes when asked if I want them.

On my first visit to the Pony Island restaurant, an immediate indication of hopeful cuisine is that twenty people are corralled in a holding area, waiting for tables in the packed dining room. I put my name on a list, take a stroll around the dark village lanes, and return with a sharpened appetite to almost immediate seating and service. Although hush puppies are on the menu, I set aside doubt by reflecting that their presence is no more intimidating than that of sauerkraut in Bavaria or papadums in India—and I don't *have* to have them. My doubts are indeed diminished by a prominent notice which says the restaurant will, for a five-dollar charge, cook my own fish for me if I bring it in already cleaned. And my doubts just about disappear when my waitress asks me if I will drink wine or beer— no brown-bagging is necessary! So I quaff a properly chilled California dry white while anticipating the dish of the day. In my recent experience—excluding of course the excellent Queen Anne's Revenge—the day's special is generally noteworthy for its unremarkableness; that is, if it isn't uncertainly fresh or insolently inedible, with spices and garnish and method of cooking all at odds with the basic material. The Banks culinary tradition is notably upheld in the old name given a fish stew, which was a "muddle." Tonight, however, the special is stir-fried chicken and vegetables accompanied by rice and an eggroll, and it is first-rate. Desserts, I know by now, are usually less of a worry on the Banks, and the pecan-and-apple pie at Pony Island is no letdown. My gratitude to the Pony Island is immense as I reach the end of dinner without being asked if I am doing okay. The waitresses are much too busy for such questions.

I can see myself falling into place here: a skiff, or perhaps a small sailing boat; a daily walk to the general store for provisions and a look-in at O'Neal's dock, which is near the store; a lengthy thrash by foot along the beach; and then a chat in the late afternoon with Dr. George Sessons. Sessons, a cherubic sixty-four, lives in contented confusion in his house in the "Point" section, with four boats in his back yard and nets and crab-pot floats hanging from the branches of a well-placed live oak. Now that Ocracoke has a regular doctor, people no longer bring their medical crises to him; instead, he says, he fixes fishing reels and dispenses advice on fiberglass-boat repair. He rides his bike on his visits to the O'Neals over on what he calls "the other side."

In many isolated communities, residents tend to distrust the local utility companies, which may take advantage of their monopolistic positions, and Ocracokers make such complaints. Sessons tells me that electricity is supplied to the island by a line that comes over the Oregon Inlet bridge, down the length of Hatteras Island, and then via submarine cable across Hatteras Inlet. The power supply is fragile; there are frequent "outages." Sessons says, "A good downpour sometimes shorts out the insulators—I reckon the power company got them from Japan on the cheap. They even set the poles on fire." As for water, Sessons used to pump his from his own well, like everyone on the island, but since the provision of a public water supply he is tapped into that. "It was a condition of hooking up to the town system that you no longer used your well. They didn't want the risk of cross-contamination of town water by tainted well water, which there might easily have been after Gloria flooded our septic tanks. The lid of my tank floated off down the street. It's amazing we haven't had a typhus epidemic. This summer the water company had to shut off the supply for several hours a day, because water was scarce, the way it is in many places on the Banks; the company isn't hooking up any new properties for the moment. I've still got a cistern for rainwater, which is useful for outdoor purposes."

Although these practical difficulties, and the added expense of certain items, are a disadvantage of life on the island, they by no means weigh heavily with Dr. Sessons. When he is asked about the advantages, he says, "This may surprise you, but there's a lot of good singing here—many people seem to have fine voices." At various community gatherings, church events or fire-department fish fries, Ocracoke voices are raised in song. Some songs are of local origin, like the Charlie Mason Pogie-boat song, about the stranding and recovery of a menhaden boat off Ocracoke, or a similar chanty, dating from Prohibition days, called "When the Booze Yacht Came Ashore," about a yacht named *Adventure* which wrecked on the Core Banks near Cape Lookout with a cargo of hooch, upsetting the routine of the fishermen on nearby Harkers Island. According to the song, they stopped fishing, "lost their religion, and backslid by the score."

Sessons says, "If I was still a practicing doctor, I might find the isolation here a bother. I'd miss conversation with colleagues and the professional backup. But as it is, Ocracoke is the most delightful place I know. If I had a choice of going to heaven or staying here, I'd say no to heaven."

Since staying in Old Nags Head, I have talked several times on the telephone with Dave McNaught, whom I met at the visitors' center of the Nags Head Woods and who expressed an interest in any plans I had for hiking and camping. So far I have managed to avoid spending any nights out-of-doors, allowing myself to be put off by the fact that I haven't yet acquired a tent by hire or purchase, that the five private campgrounds on the upper Banks were "full-service," frequented by vehicle-towed trailers, and that the more primitive, mostly Park Service–owned campgrounds on Hatteras and Ocracoke were temporarily closed in the wake of Gloria. The comforts of a proper bed under a solid roof have also had their influence. But now such comforts may finally have to be eschewed. Camping will probably be necessary on the last fifty miles or so of the Outer Banks, which stretch in a thin, now and then broken barrier from Ocracoke Inlet to Cape Lookout, near Beaufort. Here, on the Core Banks, named after the Coree Indians, who used to live in these parts, there are no regular accommodations or facilities. These Banks are all part of the Cape Lookout National Seashore, and Park Service pamphlets advise the visitor to bring everything that will be needed, including one's own shelter, food, and water. McNaught is still interested. He does a lot of hiking, climbing, and camping; he has the necessary gear. If I want a companion, he would like to come along and bring his tent. So we have worked it out that when I leave Ocracoke, I shall meet him on the mainland, a bit farther down the coast, where we will embark on our Core Banks expedition. Because of the rudimentary access arrangements for those who don't have their own boats, and because there is at least one sizable inlet, not to be forded, it may not be feasible for us to examine the entire length of the Core Banks, but we intend to walk as much of it as we can. However, the section nearest to Ocracoke, Portsmouth Island, is most easily reached by boat, making the six-mile voyage from Silver Lake, and I have told McNaught that I will tackle that from here.

O'Neal's dock is where I begin. Through Charlie, I have booked a ride to Portsmouth with the Austins, Junius and Rudy, father and son, who provide an unscheduled ferry service. It is Junius who turns up, a tall elderly man whose white motorboat is powered by a 115-horsepower Suzuki outboard. Junius has skin like brown-cream vellum and a taciturn getting-on-with-the-job manner, and in any case, the big outboard makes conversation fitful as we roar off on this bright, windy morning, spray flying, across Silver Lake and out through the channel, or "ditch," into Pamlico Sound. Then it is hard left, southwest toward the inlet and Portsmouth beyond. This first stretch of water close to the Ocracoke shore is called Teach's Hole Channel and with a depth of nine to nineteen feet provided a sheltered spot for sailing ships to anchor and an adjacent beach where they could be careened for barnacle scraping and caulking. I don't yet feel I know Charlie O'Neal well enough to put him right when he says, "I've always been told that Sir Walter Raleigh stopped here in Ocracoke on his way up to Manteo." If I did, it would be by suggesting that he probably has in mind one of Sir Walter's henchmen, Sir Richard Grenville, who might have landed on Ocracoke after the *Tiger* ran aground. And it seems to be not just a legend that Edward Teach, originally Edward Drummond, better known as Blackbeard (a name that struck profitable fear into his victims), used this anchorage as a base from which to prey on shipping. The pirate is said to have had fourteen wives in various ports in the West Indies and Carolinas. He had an equally cozy arrangement with the North Carolina authorities—on one occasion, the governor himself, Charles Eden, received sixty hogsheads of sugar from a French ship taken by Teach. So it was Governor Spotswood of Virginia who persuaded his legislature to give a reward for Blackbeard's capture and who, in November 1718, sent two sloops down from the Chesapeake to beard Teach in his Ocracoke haven. There was a bloody dawn battle, but the royal naval forces, led by Lieutenant Robert Maynard, prevailed. Teach had heard cockcrow for the last time. Maynard suspended the pirate's severed head from the bowsprit of his sloop for the victorious voyage back to Virginia.

Now Junius Austin's boat bucks over the chop of Teach's Hole Channel and the spray shoots back like small fragments of stinging glass, rainbow prismed. When we reach the low shore of Portsmouth Island, the dock built by the Park Service has waves slapping against it, and I notice that a number of its deck planks are missing. Junius Austin, after some cautious maneuvering, brings the boat alongside so that, at the right moment in its rearing and prancing, I can jump off onto a decked section of the dock. He shouts, "Back at four!" and speeds away toward Ocracoke. Here I am, a temporary Crusoe. I set off for Portsmouth's abandoned village. (241)

Portsmouth is two things: memories and mosquitoes. Heeding Junius's rather terse instructions about following some tire tracks, I start walking. The tire tracks, on what should be the inshore side of a little dune, are quickly underwater, and the water—in the direction the tracks are heading—looks increasingly deep. Where I have been landed seems to be a little island, and between it and the distant trees and somewhat firmer-looking ground of the purported village is a tidal flat. The tide, clearly, is in, is up, is covering this flat with little white wavelets. I retreat to the dune to rethink. Perhaps I should follow the tracks in the other direction. Ah yes. They curve around in a wide sweep. Now I see that there are stakes, or withies, at hundred-yard intervals marking the way, the track, which is about a foot below the surface. I carry my socks and shoes and have rolled up my trousers. In a few minutes I have got used to the queasy feeling of the mud under my soles. In fact it is pleasant paddling along, with the warm water splashing up my calves. The tidal flat is wide. Roughly a mile out to my left, an irregular line of low dunes, marking the ocean beach, stretches southwest, shimmering in the haze and seeming to hover above the horizon like what the Dutch used to call butter islands, presumably because they seem to float in pools made from their own melting.

I reach the slightly higher, firmer, and more verdant island on which Portsmouth village stands after thirty minutes of amphibious hiking. The track passes through thick shrubbery; in places, dark pools extend across the width of the track, which the shrubbery prevents one from leaving; the murky pools are not pleasant to wade through. Putrefaction is in process, and the thick smell of it rises and encompasses one, like an unwanted embrace. And now a new menace: several mosquitoes land on my head; one goes into my left ear and buzzes loudly, as if trying to sound his way into the interior. I reach for Bill Harrison's can of Deep Woods Off and apply an ample (so I think) spray to all vulnerable parts. Neck. Ears. Wrists. Ankles. But Deep Woods Off seems to be a favored aperitif on Portsmouth; the scouts' appetites stirred, the squadrons mass. The raiders zoom in. It is a matter of keeping completely alert, watching where they land—if you wait for the sensation of landing, you're too late. You've been bitten. These Portsmouth mosquitoes are not deterred by cotton or polyester or whatever mix my shirt and trousers are. They bite right through the cloth. Soon I am hastening along, in the hope of outrunning them, arms flailing like contra-rotating propellers in a not very successful attempt to keep the varmints off. It is not much consolation to recall Marcia Lyons's remark that only the female mosquitoes bite, or an Ocracoke resident's suggestion that the mosquitoes in these parts are "the saltwater kind—they don't carry malaria." How could anyone have lived in a place so pestered? Is this why Portsmouth was abandoned?

(Later, I read the account of a lady who used to spend summers and vacations here earlier this century.

She said that the islanders learned to live with the mosquitoes and "seemed to have built up an immunity to their stinging." However, she and her family never entered the house without first brushing themselves all over to rid their clothes of mosquitoes. Window screens were kept in good repair and were painted with kerosene on nights when the gnats called no-see-ums swarmed. Insect-attracting lights were seldom lit after dusk. Chores and supper were finished before nightfall, and people developed skills in finding their way around the house in the dark. Dr. Sessons told me that there may have been less undergrowth on Portsmouth when it was inhabited; it was thus more open to sea breezes which kept down the numbers of mosquitoes. He, too, thought that the natives might have become desensitized to the bites. I also heard theories that some people give off through their pores an odor or flavor that repels mosquitoes; eating garlic is said to work well in this respect, as it does on the breath in regard to people on buses and trains. At the time of my Portsmouth visit, the mosquitoes may have been encouraged to multiply by the many stagnating pools left by Gloria.)

In the course of the next hour I ramble around the deserted village. It has the air of a disused film set, with small cottages and community buildings set curiously apart, as for separate shooting locations or representing different stages of decay and preservation. It may simply be that intervening structures have disappeared. A creek angles in from the sound, spanned by a wooden footbridge. What seems to be a wide lawn, though a little rough for croquet, bears a sign: DANGER: AIRCRAFT LANDING. The danger does not appear imminent or indeed frequent, though a modern Crusoe might be cheered to think he could be rescued this way. I resist the temptation to scrawl graffiti—to delete AIRCRAFT and insert MOSQUITOES—and walk on past several small houses isolated by huge pools of water. The shingle-sided lifesaving station appears in good shape. Wooden columns painted a terra-cotta color support the porch roof. An air conditioner—looking anachronistic, even if it is an early model—pokes its rectangular snout from an upstairs window. The building was erected in 1894, closed after the Second World War, and is now in use during the summer season as the Park Service visitors' center, of whose staff there is no sign today. Elsewhere bright yellow siding and white trim is the prevalent Portsmouth color scheme, evident on four or five cottages. One unpainted collapsing structure, back wall entirely gone, reveals an iron bed, its last piece of furniture, and a mattress that looks like a geological model of earth-folding and strata formation. The church leans slightly to one side, awaiting the final push. Under the front porch of one cottage, among dried weed and entangled eelgrass left by Gloria, lies a rusty motor mower. As with the air conditioner, there is a funny sense of something modern having been warped into a framework where it appears old. Some houses have curtains pulled across their windows, and new locks and hasps, suggestions of occasional use, but this—and the fact that they are not in use now—has the effect of making them seem eerier and somehow more melancholy than those buildings that are beyond repair. One little home declares itself to be the Robert Wallace House, circa 1850, and through a front window I can make out a framed sampler and an oil lamp. Will there be a copy of a newspaper, lying on a table, reporting the death of President Zachary Taylor? In the schoolhouse, a collection of seashells mounted on a board is visible,

and some bare desks; and listening hard, I imagine
the sounds of children's voices, the adult tones of a
teacher who monitored the lessons and the play. There
are several graveyards, and in one I read the inscription
on the gravestone of Harry Needham Dixon, born September 10, 1889, died September 27, 1931. *Beloved*
husband and father, it says. *Gone Home.* So, indeed,
has Portsmouth.

It is possible to be somewhere for a time and not
have the most obvious association strike one. I was
born in Portsmouth, England, the city that for several
centuries was one of Britain's great naval ports, its
harbor and dockyard during my childhood crammed
with gray-painted warships. This Outer Banks Portsmouth was presumably named after my Hampshire
birthplace; it, too, was once a flourishing port, and in
the 1790s was actually the largest town in North Carolina. Not far from the north point of the island was
a shoal built up to form a loading and unloading place
called Shell Castle, where cargoes were transshipped
from large vessels anchored in Ocracoke Inlet to
smaller vessels that then carried the goods up the shallow sounds and rivers. During the eighteenth century,
Portsmouth was laid out in half-acre lots, which were
sold for a pound each. Most forms of urban activity
were there, and the structures for them, in warehouse,
shipyard, church, and tavern. (In 1759, one Valentine
Wade, tavernkeeper of Portsmouth, was hauled before
the Colonial Office for keeping a riotous place.) In the
mid-nineteenth century, so many vessels were using
the inlet and the facilities of Portsmouth that the federal government established on the island a hospital
especially for sick seamen. This opened in 1846, but
that was also the year in which Hatteras Inlet and

Oregon Inlet formed. It wasn't long before coastal trade was drawn to them. During the Civil War, the people of Portsmouth evacuated their island as Northern troops advanced on it, and few returned. Despite the construction of a menhaden-processing factory in 1866, Portsmouth continued to decline. The seamen's hospital burned down in 1894. The last classes were held in the schoolhouse in 1943; seven years later, the population of the island was fourteen. The post office had closed, and mail service depended on an elderly black man, Henry Pigott, who poled his skiff out daily to meet the boat which sailed between Cedar Island, on the mainland, and Ocracoke, and from this he would pick up groceries, any passengers for Portsmouth, and hand over and collect island mail. Mr. Pigott was the last male resident of Portsmouth, and when he died on January 5, 1971, and was buried in the cemetery of the Babb and Dixon families behind the church, the last two people on the island decided it was time to leave. They were Elma Dixon and Marian Gray Babb; they moved to Beaufort. Now, in 1986, no one lives on Portsmouth. The island is on the National Register of Historic Places, which recognizes districts and buildings whose protection is important to the United States. The Park Service controls the island and leases out the remaining habitable cottages for use as fishing and hunting lodges, and I assume they are used most often in those periods when the mosquitoes are on vacation elsewhere.

Today it is just about impossible to see what would have led anyone to think this was a suitable place for a town or a seaport. The so-called island is a collection of hummocks joined by marsh and swamp; any good storm would flood it or flatten it, as one did in 1765, sweeping away the warehouse. One man who was born on Portsmouth, Ben Salter, recalled an October storm which "scared the teacher so bad she left the island and did not return." Mr. Salter was residing off the island but revisiting it in November 1962, at a time its population was down to four, when a storm hit which made him feel that not only Portsmouth but the entire (247) Outer Banks were about to vanish. And yet a place can be held together almost by the strength of what has happened in it—memories of good times put up a long struggle against low ground and rising sea. People like Ben Salter who grew up on the island in the early years of this century remembered the fishing, the oystering, and the wild ponies which were to be found the length of the Core Banks. Steve Roberts, born on Portsmouth in 1901, recollected for *Sea Chest*:

When I lived there, there was just bullrushes and grass, and a lot of wild geese . . . the geese kept the grass mowed. We had cattle, horses, and sheep. The sheep dug up the roots of the grass and that caused the beach to move in. We built sand fences and the storms would wash them down. You couldn't hold it back. Sheep and cattle were eating the shrubbery, the grass, and stuff, and there wasn't anything to hold the sand. The sand on that beach is the finest there is along this coast. It blows about bad.

Mr. Roberts thought that Portsmouth had come up out of the water, and he shared Ben Salter's belief that it would sink again beneath it. Yet while it lasted, the natural benefits were many. Fish were caught in abundance, and bartered for other things.

They'd catch a red drum and side him off, take the backbone out of him, score him down the flesh, and salt him. After they'd dried him, they'd trade him for corn which they had ground into meal at one of the mills across the sound. They would trade the geese, too. You didn't have to buy anything except sugar, coffee, and flour. You had everything else you needed to eat right there.

A woman named Dorothy Bedwell, who spent holidays on Portsmouth, published a few years ago a short book in which she recalled the tranquillity and simplicity of life on the island between the two world wars: no electricity, no phones, no traffic, no indoor toilets. But everyone had gardens. And, she wrote:

Most everyone had a fig tree, and many a jar of fig preserves was boiled off in late summer. Some of the houses had kitchens apart from the main house. A few had what they called their summer kitchens with lots of windows where families cooked and ate in hot weather. Even with the kitchens attached, as ours was, the people there always referred to "going out to the kitchen."

Sometimes the island's near-self-sufficiency was sorely tested. One winter there was a great freeze, ice on the sound eighteen inches thick, all shipping and fishing halted. Portsmouth folk ate all the provisions in the three grocery stores, killed their cattle, and ate all the geese and ducks. But mutual aid was the rule. Everyone pitched in to help in such tasks as pulling up a boat. Singing and square dancing were the common entertainment, and it was a treat to ride in the horse-drawn Coast Guard wagon. There was no doctor on the island—the Ocracoke doctor was a drunk—and Portsmouth people depended largely on home remedies. One favored medicine was made from soap, sugar, fat meat, and turpentine. Steve Roberts said, "This was to draw the poison out when you stuck something in your foot. You jumped, danced, and did the cakewalk, but Mom said, 'Keep it on.' It would have drawn a tenpenny nail out of a piece of hickory."

At last, in need of a home remedy against the winged hordes, I turn back along the boggy track. A flock of egrets stands at the creek end of the erstwhile airstrip, and shows no signs of taking off. In places, the grass is red-haired, almost halfway to being a seaweed. Then I head out once more across the tidal flat. The water has withdrawn somewhat and I have no difficulty in striding ankle-deep directly south toward the ocean beach. There I walk for an hour. The surf is low, a hundred yards out at the edge of the flat sands. The dunes are small, at the most a man's height, in fragmentary clumps, and with sea oats and beach grass growing thinly on them. There are no mosquitoes. I sit in a shallow concavity for a late lunch: a sugared bun and a bottle of fruit juice bought at O'Neal's. To get back to the spot where Junius Austin landed me, and said he would pick me up, I have to do some serious wading. In numerous places between the sand hillocks which mark the outer, ocean edge of the island, the water is deep; small inlets, perhaps Gloria-created or Gloria-deepened, run between the little dunes, joining the sea to the sea-covered flat. I take my trousers off and tie them over my shoulders—the right of a Crusoe to forgo modesty for necessity in his own domain.

Junius arrives on time at the appointed place, and on the voyage back to Ocracoke he unbends slightly. He tells me that his father was in the lighthouse service, first on Hatteras, and that they lived at Ocracoke lighthouse from 1929 to 1941; he used to go out with his father to tend the small lighthouses, built on piles, that stood in Pamlico Sound. Junius is sixty-eight. For the last thirty years, latterly with the help of his son, he has been running this private ferry service. After the Second World War, while working as a guide for a hunting-and-fishing club on Portsmouth, he built the Portsmouth airstrip for the club members with the

aid of some Ocracoke youths. He says, "We cleared the shrubbery away and planted good grass seed. That was one spring, before the mosquitoes come." He gives me a rare smile, no doubt having observed me scratching my many wounds. Still, I mustn't exaggerate the distress: the bites are vivid and immediately painful, but the irritation from them is not long-lasting.

The mosquitoes are out and about early on Friday morning to give me a send-off from Ocracoke. The Alliance is in a short line of cars at the Silver Lake ferry slip, and despite the muggy morning air our windows are all rolled up, shut against the aerial nuisances. A county sanitation truck goes by, releasing a toxic cloud. The mosquitoes attempt to beat their way into the cars, seeking shelter, wings fluttering furiously against the glass, in their wild agony looking as big as wasps. I have the Alliance air conditioning turned on at full bore, but nevertheless the noxious fumes are strong, and unpleasant. With the truck gone past, and the plague dissipated, I wind the windows down. It is trying to rain. A surf fisherman in a nearby soft-top Jeep is listening to his CB radio and, with a surprising chirpiness after the poison-gas attack, calls to a friend in a nearby vehicle: "You hear that, Tommy? Another drum just jumped." Tommy, presumably drumless, gives a rueful chuckle.

The object of this ferry ride is to reach the mainland and drive to a place from which I can take another, less formal ferry to the Core Banks. To be precise, before reaching that place, I have to drive down the inner shore of Core Sound to the spot where, at the

end of our Core Banks walk, McNaught and I intend to return by yet another ferry. This spot is on Harkers Island, connected by bridge to the mainland, and there I have planned to meet McNaught this morning. There we will leave one of our cars. Then we will drive in the second vehicle back up the mainland shore to a place called Davis, from which—we hope—a boat will take us out as foot passengers to the Core Banks. Our plans to hike along them for a couple of days seem to involve logistics of almost Himalayan complexity. The Core Banks are about fifty-four miles long and look like a thin fish hook snapped in the middle. Each main section is roughly the same length; the break is at New Drum Inlet. The upper section, which may be called Core Banks North, has the vestiges of several old inlets, a few new and shallow ones, a great area of tidal flat, and Portsmouth up at the eye end of the hook. A small ferry runs for the benefit of surf fishermen from a mainland place called Atlantic to a landing near the southern end of Core Banks North, but that would put us in a position only to walk up toward Portsmouth, assuming we could cross some of the small inlets. Heading back down, more or less southwest, we would be faced by New Drum Inlet, which isn't passable unless you have your own small boat. So we have decided to take the other ferry, which runs from Davis and which will land us about a third of the way down Core Banks South—a continuous island twenty-seven miles long. At the far end of this, near Cape Lookout, we trust we will be able to return to civilization by way of the Harkers Island ferry.

For a while things proceed according to plan, as McNaught and I have concocted it by telephone. The Ocracoke ferry, named *Silver Lake*, zigzags across shallow Pamlico Sound, following an intricate, piling-marked channel. The ferry lands at Cedar Island, which is mostly a marshy wildlife refuge and is made an island—it looks like a mainland peninsula—by a narrow creek, spanned by the bridge on which Route 12 carries traffic to and from the Ocracoke ferry. I drive past shallow bays and occasional strung-out communities, like Masontown, Stacy, and Davis, none of which seems to have any reason for flourishing other than low-lying proximity to Core Sound. (One such hamlet, placed on a side road out on Mill Point, has the literal or laconic name of Sealevel.) But the weather is something McNaught and I have not talked about. By the time I reach Harkers Island and the boatyard-and-fishing center which serves as the terminus for the Cape Lookout ferry, the gray morning sky has opened and rain is bucketing down. When McNaught turns up in his small pickup truck and we have exchanged greetings, we hastily transfer the camping gear to the more spacious interior and luggage compartment of the Alliance. Having parked his truck out of the way of boatyard operations, we drive back up to Davis. Here a family named Willis have a concession from the Park Service to run a ferry to and from Core Banks—a service they provide from the beginning of April to the end of November. And here, at the end of a muddy lane in which half a dozen four-wheel-drive wagons and trucks are waiting, we present ourselves at the Willis headquarters. This is a single-story house whose enclosed front porch and adjacent side room form, respectively, the waiting room and booking office. It immediately becomes clear that non-fisherman foot passengers, traveling without being a member of a vehicle-borne party, are a rarity on the Willis ferry, and that those buying only a one-way ticket do not seem to have been encountered here in recent memory. However, after McNaught and I explain that we intend to hike down the Banks to the end, we are allowed to pay for our passage on this unusual basis. Old Mrs. Alger Willis, sitting at the mahogany table on which she conducts business, says, "All right then, darlings, I hope you have a lovely walk. Though I wish you had nicer weather for it."

(254)

We find a parking place for the Alliance in a boggy field, jammed with the cars of fishermen who have joined companions in four-wheel-drive vehicles for the Banks trip. We try to keep things dry as—swatting mosquitoes the while—we fill our two large backpacks with food, drink, and camping equipment. Then we trudge back down the lane, rain streaming down our faces, braving the amused glances of the four-wheel-drive parties who are sitting in the shelter of their vehicles drinking beer. It is 11 a.m., but the boat that was meant to leave Davis at that hour has not yet got back from an earlier trip to the Core Banks. McNaught and I take cover in the air-conditioned Willis porch. We eat the sandwiches we have brought for lunch, deal cheerfully with the attentions of an infant Willis, which toddles in and out, and of a Willis dog, which is interested in our sandwiches, and talk to Mrs. Willis and a younger woman, her daughter, or daughter-in-law, who is the child's mother. Old Mrs. Willis has a stooped, Rembrandtesque look, with the wrinkles but also the charm and dignity of age. She tells us how she and her husband came down from New Bern to Davis, pioneering. They cut down trees to make a better landing, started up the ferry service, and built cabins to rent to fishermen on the Core Banks. For a number of years Mrs. Willis ran a restaurant here which was patronized by fishermen and duck hunters. She says, "A lot of hunters were doctors. They were very well behaved." An elderly man comes in, wearing a blue peaked cap with the title *Captain* on it. This is Captain Alger Willis. He says, "Well, the sun's out."

Outside, we see that the sun has indeed made an appearance, though this may not be of long duration. And the boat is in. It, too, is named *Captain Alger*. It resembles a coastal fishing boat, built of wood, though with a very broad deck running from slightly forward of amidships to a barn-door-wide transom stern. I gather it is the newest and largest member of the four-boat Willis fleet. Three of the waiting trucks are driven aboard; like the *Captain Alger*, they have wider than usual cargo-carrying space, presently jammed with fishing gear and provisions. McNaught and I make ourselves known as foot passengers to the young captain of the craft, who looks like a junior Willis, and we squeeze ourselves and our backpacks into a sheltered area beneath the wheelhouse, where the front fender of the forward truck is pressed up against a crude bench, and some of the surf fishermen crowd in with us. Their talk is cheerfully competitive, of likes and dislikes, of the merits of Jim Beam whiskey as compared with Jack Daniel's, and the abilities of various types of balloon-tired all-terrain vehicles. "Hell, man," says one member of a fishing party who is leaning against the radiator grille of the truck, "that Honda's a good vehicle." He seems to take pride in it, as if it were an American product. The surf fishermen preface every other remark with "Hell, man," or "Sheet, man," and punctuate their conversation with long, loud gulps of beer or soda. Most of them are cigarette smokers. One tall, bald- or shaven-headed black man is wearing a bright red jacket with the names *Harv* and *Esther* embroidered on the sleeves. He says to a white companion, "Hell, man, she ain't going to be happy unless I bring home a big big drum."

The *Captain Alger* sails, an hour or so late, though no one seems to care. We are aboard. We are under way. The dock and a few houses and wharves which are the waterfront of Davis are behind us, a low, almost ostentatiously uninteresting shore. But several hundred yards out from the dock there is a sudden bump, then a loud grinding noise. The *Captain Alger* puts her bows down and the stern lifts. We are hard aground. For ten minutes or so the vessel's captain guns the powerful engine, the vertical exhaust shrieking, as he attempts to drive the *Captain Alger* over the obstruction. At last he decides on a different course of action: he manages to back the boat off, then approach the shoal again from another angle. Bump. Stop. The rain is falling again, heavily. By my rough reckoning, it is about an hour after low water in Core Sound; the tide should be rising, though that can be affected by the strength and direction of the wind. Core Banks, which have been briefly visible about three and a half miles to the east, have disappeared once more.

After another ten minutes of banging its bows against the unyielding bottom, the *Captain Alger* reverses and creeps back to the dock. One of the two aftermost trucks is disembarked. Its crew of surf fishermen stand on the dock, laughing and waving their cans of beer at those still on the boat; they seem to be used to setbacks, perhaps from their experience of many occasions of no fish. Then we set off again. This time, despite slowing as the keel goes over the shoal, the *Captain Alger* makes it. Now we must be in deep water, I think, going to the gunwale and looking over the side. The bottom is clearly visible, a few feet down. Shells and clumps of eelgrass. It would have been simpler, from what I can see, to wade across Core Sound. But with speed up and momentum, the *Captain Alger* forges ahead, waterborne clouds of mud rising off her angular quarters; she is furrowing her own channel. **(257)** And when we reach the other side of the sound, the vessel is brought up against a wooden dock in a similar manner, a process of excavation rather than berthing, backing and filling in a little harbor that provides very little room at bow and stern, engine roaring, and mud, sand, and even grass being churned up as the *Captain Alger* is turned around, stern to the dock. All this power and fuel expended to get two trucks and a dozen men to Core Banks!

But McNaught and I, stepping ashore, do not complain. The rain is once again holding off. Backpacks shouldered, marching in the direction of the sea, the adventure ahead of us—but wait, what the devil is this? Amid the raw scenery of marsh giving way to dunes, a strange conglomeration of structures appears, like an "illegal" South African shantytown or one of those barrios that burgeon outside South American cities. Huts and cabins are set higgledy-piggledy on the thinly grassed sand. Most look as if they have been assembled from flotsam and salvage, and if not the refuse of a teeming shore, then from mainland scrapyards and dumps. No one section of wall appears to match the next. No single angle seems to be a right one. The plywood tacked over windows may be a defense against storms or a covering disguising the fact of no glass behind. These, we gather, are the fishing cabins, available from the Willises, at least until the Park Service replaces them—here and in a similar encampment on the north Core Banks—with new, sturdier, and less conspicuously awful buildings. But this isn't all. In a central area amid the shanties, in an arrangement which has at least concentration and density to recommend it, but which at the same time is almost overwhelming in its deplorable mass, are roughly a hundred motor vehicles. They are parked close together. Many resemble the fishing cabins in their lack of paint. Rust is the prevalent "finish"; headlights and fenders are missing; some list this way and that, whether because of depressions in the ground or of the state of their suspensions. Some, it seems, are waiting to be put to use by their fishermen owners; many will clearly never stir under their own power again.

For a moment, the impact of these derelict and near-derelict vehicles on one who is making happy use of his ability to walk on what he has thought will be an unspoiled shore is like that which a red rag allegedly has on a bull, or like that of a lit match touched to gunpowder. I am hopping mad. The collection of vehicles seems to be a packaged demonstration of the abuse which an automotive civilization has inflicted on the land. But gradually, as I calm down, it occurs to me that by imposing some organization on the vehicles the Park Service has started to cope with the problem. I learn later that when the Cape Lookout National Seashore was established in 1976, the Park Service inherited over 2,500 junk vehicles on the Core Banks. Of these, 2,000 have so far been removed. Those on the southern half of the Banks have been taken away on barges, while on the northern Banks a surf fishermen's association has dragged the cars on winter weekends to a disposal site, from which Marine Corps helicopters have lifted the vehicles to the mainland for scrapping. Given the continuing nature of the problem of vehicles, the Park Service seems to be doing its best to tolerate but not encourage their use, warning drivers to stay out of dunes, marsh, and grassland, and to give right-of-way to people and animals. On Shackleford Banks, an island which forms a dislocated limb west of Cape Lookout (an inner rather than an outer bank, in my book), the Park Service proposes to create a wilderness zone where no vehicles will be permitted and the remaining wild cattle and horses will be allowed to roam free. Although the concession holders may build larger ferries to accommodate more vehicles on the two routes to the Core Banks, our voyage on the *Captain Alger* seems to show that the depth of Core Sound may be a splendid controlling factor.

Meanwhile, debate goes on as to whether any vehicles should be allowed on the beaches of the Outer Banks. Their right to drive there is of course long-standing; once there were cars, there were beach buggies. Model T Fords were used by 1920s surf fishermen. But opponents say that vehicles on the beaches do various sorts of damage: for instance, crushing loggerhead turtles or the eggs which the female turtles lay in nests near the bases of the dunes, or simply creating wheel ruts that impede and disorient the turtles in their instinctive course from the sea to the dunes. (The Core Banks are about as far north as the loggerheads come to nest; these turtles are regarded as a threatened species, and as recorded in recent years, their nests on the Core Banks have ranged in number from a high of sixty-six in 1979 to a low of thirty-one in 1981.) In their study of the Carolina barrier islands, the Pilkey team writes of "the explosive increase in off-road vehicles and their severe impact upon the marsh and dune systems," which has, for example, caused the Park Service to restrict ORVs on Bodie Island to a zone a hundred feet wide along the ocean and Oregon Inlet shoreline (and to prohibit them from leaving the road which passes through the Pea Island Refuge on Hatteras). There have been estimates that more than a hundred thousand ORVs a year use the thirty-nine miles of beach open to them in the Cape Hatteras Seashore. To me, it seems curious that the Beach Buggy Association has taken a stand against the proposal to build jetties at Oregon Inlet—something their confreres in commercial fishing want; apparently they fear that the jetties would restrict their access to parts of the shore. Evan Wilson, of the Oregon Inlet Users Association, is therefore no ORV fan: "The beach buggy people have a once-a-year beach clean-up to show what good guys they are. Well, who left all the beer cans there in the first place?" I found it hard to tell from Junius Austin's expression and tone of voice where he stood on the subject when, at the helm of his boat, he told me of a new four-wheel-drive pickup which had recently sunk in soft sand at the southern end of Portsmouth Island, so that only its roof was visible.

McNaught and I walk up the beach, northeastward, well past the outposts of the fishing camp, and plant our backpacks behind a small isolated hillock of sand—one of the little dunes, about five feet high, that line the ocean side of these Banks. On the dunes grow scattered grasses and sea oats, looking like clumps of hair that have been transplanted to balding pates, on which they may or may not take. Behind this frail demarcation line stretches a gravelly and sandy plain, in places a mere few hundred yards in width. Beyond this plain there are patches of scrub and then the salt marsh which borders Core Sound. We want to cover as much of the length of Core Banks South as we can, and we therefore walk for just over an hour, almost to New Drum Inlet, before turning back and retracing our steps. Having picked up our backpacks, no longer striding so blithely, we walk on down the Banks past the fishing camp. On the Park Service map this section of coast is called Raleigh Bay, but the beach is lacking any bay-like concavity and extends nearly straight before us. The afternoon gradually improves; the rain clears; the sky lifts somewhat. Offshore, the clouds and cloudy haze are various shades and densities of gray. It is now about half-tide and we find a good, slightly dampened walking surface on the sand halfway between the dunes and the water.

Here, as elsewhere on the Banks, the texture of the sand differs from one part of the beach to another. At the base of the dunes, one is likely to find dry, loose sand, often churned up by vehicles forced to travel there at high tide. In some stretches, midway between dunes and water, the beach is shingly, gritty, a nuisance to walk on, particularly when this sand, too, is loosely packed. In other places the sand has the consistency of a well-baked cake with a good crust on it; even if the crust sinks a little underfoot, it doesn't break. In some places the most enjoyable walking surface is sand which is firm but wet, like cool cement with a yielding skim of water on it. In some patches of loose sand, the passage of one's feet creates a whistling noise, like that made by wind over the open top of a bottle. In the driest, coarsest sand, where one's feet sink in an inch or two, making a heel-and-toe impression into which the surrounding sand falls in little avalanches, the forward motion of each foot produces further disturbance. The sand flicks forward from one's toes in small bursts, each salvo flying over the spot where the previous salvo has just landed.

"I'm a beach walker," says McNaught at one point, with a happy smile. I am experiencing the same pleasure. We are on an excellent stretch of beach, the surface neither too loose nor too hard. The fact of being barefoot enhances the good feeling. I recall Wayne Gray's rhapsodies on beach walking, and Robin and Roder talking of their strolls along the Nags Head beach. Presumably it is something that most attracts people to the Banks, and keeps them there.

As we walk, McNaught and I swap observations. We stoop for shells and show them to each other—rough and routed shells, smooth and shiny shells, all warm when picked up; the shine, like the warmth, soon fades. We ask questions of varying obliqueness and directness about each other; despite the common interest that has brought us here, we are almost complete strangers. McNaught, though thirty-seven, calls himself an army brat. His father died while serving as a colonel with U.S. forces stationed in Panama. McNaught says that in the 1960s, when he was a teenager, he was a major-league hippie; after graduating from university he taught sociology at East Carolina State College. Since he lost that post twelve years ago, he has been doing odd jobs, writing poetry and folk music without much success, and has recently acquired a master's degree in environmental science from the University of Montana. For this he did a research project on "The Attitudes of Park Visitors toward Wolves"—the visitors, he reports, are surprisingly pro-wolf—and he hopes that a version of this study may interest a natural-history magazine and change his writing luck. Mc-Naught is wiry; he tells me that he ran a half-marathon road race in Washington, D.C., not long ago, and spends a good deal of time mountaineering and hiking, the latter in the company of his elderly Airedale. I have not been giving much thought in the last few weeks to the Bailey family springer spaniel, Daisy, but it now occurs to me that she would enjoy this beach—though she wouldn't like the Park Service regulations which insist that pets be kept on leashes at all times. Mc-Naught and I exchange several stories about our dogs.

On the beach below the fishing camp we pass a number of fishermen standing at the water's edge, and a number of their vehicles drive past us. Most of the fishermen so encountered give us friendly salutations; they say "How are ya?" and "How ya doing?" Now and then, however, we are greeted with looks, mingling suspicion and intolerance, of the sort car drivers often direct at pedestrians in respectable suburbs; looks behind which brood such questions as "What are *you* doing here?" or "Why aren't you in a car like everyone else?"

Toward the end of the afternoon, after some four hours of walking, McNaught and I decide that it is time to pitch camp. We pick a little hollow in the residual dunes, open enough to the sea breeze to keep away mosquitoes (we hope), and protected from ORV nighttime drivers (we also hope) by three great balks of timber, gnarled and venerable remains of a wreck, though nothing indicates what ship or schooner they came from. A sandy hillock nearby has an old car almost buried in it, one of several automotive skeletons I've seen so immured. Anonymity has come to it, too: there's no telling whether it is a Ford or Chevrolet, a DeSoto or Packard. It reminds me of the bleached brown shell of a horseshoe crab, though in this case it is not the carapace that has survived but the chassis, engine block, and odd parts that have unexpectedly proved resistant to the salt air and processes of corrosion—certain hoses, parts of seats, lengths of wiring.

The south section of the Core Banks is wider here than anywhere till Cape Lookout—all of half a mile in width. On a promontory called Guthries Hammock, which pokes diagonally into Core Sound, we can see a stand of trees, a small sampling of maritime forest, including live oak, red cedar, and American holly. There are outlying thickets of wax myrtle, marsh elder, silverling, and yaupon. Between the hammock and our campsite is a flat plain of grass and scrub, traversed by a track which runs parallel with the beach, and on which grow such flowering plants as sea pink, morning glory, and goldenrod. The natural-history authorities assure me that in and among the shrubs and plants of this sandy plain are chameleons, lizards, black racers, tree frogs, toads, and terrapins, though I don't see any of them.

Putting up McNaught's orange-brown Eureka tent is a four-handed job. The breeze is now blowing in briskly from the sea. I imagine that McNaught on his own would have needed the assistance of his feet to hold the billowing fabric in place as he bent and slotted in the nylon rods; perhaps he would have had to hurl himself on the Eureka to prevent it ballooning away toward Guthries Hammock. With my inexperienced help, the task is eventually completed. The tent—a dome-shaped structure reminiscent of medieval equipage—stands shivering slightly, its doorway with a section of mosquito netting zipped in place facing into the wind. McNaught decides that the stakes he has driven in around the bottom edge of the tent are on the short side for this terrain, so we search for additional weighty material to ensure that things hold throughout the night. I find a blackened timber, and McNaught an old smooth tire, to ballast down the guy ropes. But where we are in these little dunes there is a remarkable lack of handy and useful flotsam. I have the feeling of being in a front line which has for some time been abandoned.

At 6 p.m.—high tide—the water is twenty yards away. No, closer still, I realize, as a wave foams in over the sand toward the tent. The sun is sinking beyond Guthries Hammock, and a long way up the beach a scattering of fishermen can just be seen, outlined against the white surf. McNaught gets out his little Coleman stove and fires it up. He boils water in a billycan for wild rice and beans, and while it heats up he reads the directions on the rice package. McNaught has already alluded to the fact that he is not a smoker, and does not drink alcohol, coffee, or tea. It is suddenly clear that he is well on the way to becoming a vegetarian. *I have allowed McNaught to look after the major part of our provisioning.* As this occurs to me, I take a contemplative swig from a small former apple-juice bottle I am using as a de facto whisky flask, and while this aperitif is giving me a less anxious view of the stark culinary prospect, I remember with added relief the supply of half a dozen Snickers bars I have stashed in one of the numerous compartments of the Harrison backpack—a portable canvas pueblo of pockets and pouches. I don't customarily eat chocolate, but on hikes and small-boat voyages it is certainly useful. On such excursions, afoot and afloat, any guilt I have about eating sweet things is slightly assuaged by the thought of the energy I have healthily been expending. McNaught, it later appears, shares this non-spartan view; he, too, has brought along some candy bars. Now he stirs the rice and beans in the billycan while listening to a tiny radio through headphones. He has been a Dodgers fan since boyhood, and tonight the Dodgers are going to be playing the Cardinals. If I can remember, when he takes off the headphones I mean to ask McNaught when and why Americans determined that the end-of-season championships of baseball, a sport about as universal as curling, should be called the World Series.

As it happens, food intrudes, and to this hungry beach walker the rice and beans are remarkably good. The sun goes under at 6:30, backlighting the clouds, highlighting patches of deep-blue sky. I roll down the sleeves of my shirt and button up the cuffs. I dig my toes into the sand, which retains some of the warmth of the day. A pair of pelicans cruises low over the low surf, such slow, dreamy flight, while flocks of plovers and sandpipers work busily along the beach, each minute morsel another bite in their long-drawn-out meal. You'd think they'd get hungry from the very act of collecting food. Cape Lookout lighthouse blinks, ten miles down the beach, letting us know that it is there. McNaught doffs his headset for a moment, and he and I say more or less together, "Beautiful evening."

Dark in these latitudes comes quickly. It takes a nightfall in the open air to remind me of this, a contrast to the leisurely twilights we have in England. Abruptly there are stars in bold bands of night sky. The sand is phosphorescent when disturbed with foot or hand. Some of the surf fishermen have marked their positions with green lights, presumably so that the occasional vehicle driving along the beach with bobbing, swaying headlights doesn't run into them or their gear. I have neglected to bring a flashlight, but McNaught—baseball-bound again—lends me his so that I can scan the pages of *Tom Sawyer*. But soon my eyes begin to close for longer and longer periods, and I crawl into the tent and my sleeping bag, and—with the sea sounding in my ears—fall asleep.

Getting up is not easy, despite discomfort that seems encompassing. I am aware of having woken at many moments during the night as I tried to fit hip or shoulder or elbow into a friendlier relationship with the sand. Even now, at daylight, the temptation is to lie there with drowsiness blotting out the aches, putting off the moment of movement, of getting up and the actions and decisions it entails. But at 6:30 I unzip my sleeping bag, crouch forward to unzip the mosquito flap in the doorway, through which a good deal of sand has blown during the night, and—McNaught is still asleep—ease my way out of the tent. It is shaking about in a strong northeasterly wind which beats directly at the doorway. A huge blood-orange sun is just coming up out of the sea. I take a brisk stroll along the high-tide line, wetting my feet, swinging my arms, inhaling deep lungfuls of salty air, feeling pretty splendid despite all sorts of stiffness in legs, arms, shoulders, and back. This is Saturday. The beach is as yet empty in both directions.

I appreciate a moment, for which epiphany is too grand a word but exaltation is not, when—eyes following a breakfasting tern as it dives into the waves, ankles feeling the cool wetness of an incoming surge—everything seems absolutely worthwhile. This has been a good thing to do. This is a good place to be.

McNaught is up and about when I return. He has, he says, slept like a log. He sets up the Coleman stove in the lee of the nearby miniature dune, hoping to protect its flames from the northeaster. Porridge—that is, oatmeal—for breakfast. However, the milk is off and has to be thrown away. The sugarless oatmeal, eaten neat, is consequently pretty crunchy—or could that be the sand in it? Still, there is apple juice to drink, and a piece of coffee cake which between bites I attempt to shroud with its cellophane packaging from the flying sand. This is my morning ration of sweetness and as close to coffee as I will get.

Packs on backs, we are under way at nine. Since McNaught is carrying the tent in his pack and I am carrying the water bottles in mine, I have it easier today, my load lightened by at least five pounds. We have the wind behind us—a soldier's wind, I tell the army brat. A hazy sun is shining. Our hiking today is most arduous at its beginning in the loose sand at the top of the beach; but as the tide gradually withdraws, we follow it down to the damp and firmer surface. High water has left mementos of its visit. We come across a string of red and blue balloons, almost deflated—from what children's party or fairground vendor, one wonders, and at whose ascent there followed a wail or a "Damn!" There is the occasional plastic bottle and aluminum can, and the whereabouts of yesterday's fishermen has been here and there marked if not by these relics then by the decapitated heads of small fish cut up for bait. A drowned monarch butterfly lies pressed as flat as it would be between the pages of an album, its colors already drained away.

Where the sand has begun to dry, ethereal little sand crabs scuttle in and out of their holes. There are a million shells to be regarded: conch, whelk, oyster, mother-of-pearl, scallop, sea snail, ark, jingle, tellin, clam, periwinkle, slipper, and crab, in each of which some creature has lived. The shells cluster in chance colonies on the sand, so many abandoned houses, the remains of countless Portsmouth villages. In their intricate architecture is something Arabian, with Islamic whirls, spirals, flutings, wrappings, and unfoldings; no two alike. A snail wound and swaddled in a shell garment, delicately striped in sinuous bands of brown and white that shade into one another, does he feel more of a snail for being housed in such beauty? Yet, with a laden backpack, it takes a more than usually intriguing shell to make one bend down and abstract it from its place among its fellows—to finger it, admire it by sight and touch, and judge whether to put it in a pocket or return it roughly whence it came.

As we walk along the beach, gulls and terns wheel over us; their shadows slice across our tracks. Footprints of birds mark the sand. Here, as at Cape Hatteras, dead birds seem to have been forced by the wind, current, and tide to keep company with one another, lying packed around with wads of kelp and weed at the high-water line, feathers ruffled and parted, heads, wings, and bodies rigidly distorted. Meanwhile, the beach-grazing birds run ahead of us, now and then taking off, winging out over the surf, and coming back to land thirty yards or so on. The sea keeps them alert, with some waves traveling in farther and faster than others, rushing in over the flat sand and making the plovers and sandpipers race in before it, their thin legs a flickering blur, forced to take off when they feel they can no longer stay ahead of the water. (As the wash of the wave withdraws, hundreds of small jets fountain up from crab and worm holes in which air has been compressed.) I do my best to tell one bird from another. Is that a dowitcher with a down-curved bill, that a curlew or a willet with longer legs? Ornithological guidebooks assure me that out here on the Core Banks I should be able to see such land birds as the Northern harrier and the sharp-shinned hawk, the merlin and the American kestrel, but would I know them if I did?

As we walk, the beach moves with us. Sand is blown along like stage smoke toward Cape Lookout. Otherwise the northeaster provides the cleanest and best of air. At eleven, we pause and doff our packs, sit down on the forward slope of the rudimentary dunes, and rest by watching the sea. The rollers come in in uneven ranks, spray blown diagonally from their backs and along their tumbling crests. We listen to the eternal roar and thud of water against sand. Surely great truths will now reveal themselves. But the truths either remain latent or are subsumed in the perceptions and sensations that saturate our senses. How wide is the horizon! We are subject to wonder rather than revelation.

In the course of the morning and our advance to Cape Lookout, with the checkered pattern of the lighthouse now visible, more fishermen are to be seen on the beach. McNaught halts at one four-wheel-drive fishing team, where a radio is playing, and asks for the result of the second half of a late doubleheader last night. But the fishermen—who say they aren't catching much because of the strong onshore wind—can't help him in this respect; instead, they proffer news that the American President has authorized aerial interception of an Egyptian aircraft, or, as they put it, "Reagan has sent Rambo in to get the PLO terrorists." So, while I trek the last miles of the Outer Banks, the world continues to turn. On these sandy islands we are part of the main. Walking on, McNaught and I reflect on the pros and cons of acting tough and on how what used to be called gunboat diplomacy has been remodeled in a style of Hollywood machismo, for which the name Rambo is the current token.

Lunch is sandwiches McNaught made at breakfast: peanut butter and jelly on honey whole-wheat bread, and water to drink, though our supplies of this are now getting low. We stop at a small Park Service picnic area less than a mile from the lighthouse, but though there are a few attributes of civilization here, there is none of the precious fluid, only a great deal of litter dumped alongside some garbage bins. McNaught and I are being good citizens—or exercising a proprietary feeling about the Banks—by picking up and properly disposing of this trash in the bins, when a Park Service pickup truck drives up. There is an embarrassing instant in which it seems we may have to make it clear that we are ecologically sound and not the litterbugs; but then the two young park rangers, a man and a woman, thank us. It is an unexpected reward. We leave them putting the garbage in the back of the truck. Mosquitoes are out and about—big ones, with wasplike yellow fuselages.

We march on past the lighthouse, which is set well back from the ocean, closer to the bight behind the cape than to the sea. We pitch our second camp once again in the dunes, roughly two miles from the point of the cape. It is two o'clock. Stiff shoulders, sore calves. I lie against a bank of sand and admire the lighthouse, completed in 1859, unmanned since 1950. On the map of 1590 that was drawn by John White and engraved by Theodor de Bry, this cape is named *Promontorium tremendum*, dreadful headland. However, the lighthouse marks now not only the cape and the dangerous outlying shoals but a haven for small craft, behind the hook of the cape, in what is called Lookout Bight. After we have planted the tent, McNaught and I make a foray in the direction of the lighthouse but are soon dissuaded by the boggy ground and the natural concomitant of the bogginess, mosquitoes. We have more success in reaching the Park Service ranger station, on the shore of the bight and about half a mile on toward the cape. The dunes are higher here, the ground a little drier, the mosquitoes less numerous. At the station there is a waterpipe and a tap, but nothing comes out of it. McNaught resourcefully prospects the environs and down on the Park Service dock finds a motorboat just about to depart for the mainland with a fishing party. He offers to buy any potable liquid they have to spare; he is *given* two plump twelve-ounce bottles of Diet Coke, a dark brown beverage I have never tasted and have little desire to taste—but any drink in a drought. We then chat with the two park rangers, Peggy and Paul, after they return from their litter-collecting run. They tell us that the weather forecast is for wind and rain, and offer us shelter in a nearby A-frame cabin, if we need it. Better shelter, more mosquitoes, is the likely trade-off; but the offer is generous. I recall that Frederick Law Olmsted, farmer, writer, and landscape architect, traveling in the Southern states before the Civil War, found that the legendary Southern hospitality was almost nowhere to be experienced; when he was offered shelter, he was generally asked to pay for it, and even then found that it included fleas and bedbugs. My impression on this journey has been that Southern courtesy, at least, is real: the sirs and ma'ams that people add to their questions and requests oil the social machinery in a pleasant way. The manners of most of those North Carolinians I've encountered have a considerate, contemplative element that seems to take into account the thoughts and feelings of an absolute stranger. All this, of course, may have less to do with latitude, with North and South, than with distance from the quick-fire, get-ahead-at-all-costs life of the megalopolis.

The ranger station is basic in its furnishings. Help and information for those visitors who need it take the visible form of a first-aid kit and a labeled local shell collection. Peggy says, "You'd be surprised what people ask for. One surf fisherman had his car and gear burn up not long ago and he wanted us to keep the fish he'd caught in our deep freeze. What deep freeze?" McNaught and I as walkers take the opportunity to ask about the impact of fishermen's vehicles. But Peggy and Paul put the Park Service position, which is to be reasonably neutral. A jitney service has been set up to transport fishermen from the Harkers Island ferry dock, behind the lighthouse, to the beaches near Cape Point, but Peggy thinks the heavier rig of the jitney tractor and passenger trailer may do more damage than a number of individual four-wheel-drive vehicles. There seems to be official sympathy for the desire of fishermen to be able to move fast along the beaches in pursuit of fish which they hear are biting in one spot rather than another. As for camping and hiking, Paul says that a few people come out for weekends on the Harkers Island ferry and camp in tents on the beach near the lighthouse, but he thinks that we may be the only ones in recent memory to walk down this long stretch of the Banks.

Our beachside camp has—in terms of the promised weather—a somewhat vulnerable appearance when we return to it. The tent is bouncing around like a not-too-securely tethered balloon. Since the pegs that hold it down are little bigger than meat skewers, and there is no weighty material in the vicinity, I seek and find driftwood from which we whittle larger, heftier stakes. **(274)** Moreover, given the northeaster, it seems to be a question of whether during the night the small dune on whose southwestern side the tent is planted will shield us or, grain by fast-moving grain, bury us, a final, convincing demonstration of how barrier beaches move. Dressing for dinner—unrolling my sleeves, putting on my nylon anorak—is less an attempt at emulating the sartorial conduct of British explorers in tropical forest and Arctic waste than at keeping the flying sand from all parts of my anatomy. This evening, McNaught has a culinary, non-vegetarian surprise in store. Into the last of our water (at least he is not cooking in Diet Coke), he empties in turn the contents of two packages: dehydrated turkey tetrazzini; dehydrated beef and vegetables. He cooks in the shelter of the tent doorway, tonight placed facing away from the wind. The declining sun has vanished behind a stormy-looking haze. At 6 p.m. light rain begins to patter on the fly sheet, a passing shower but intimating more. The McNaught stew is better, somehow, than first sight of its shriveled, mismatched ingredients has led me to suppose it would be—it is not too sandy, either. For dessert, Snickers bars. While we eat, McNaught tells me about his recent reading (writers I don't know named Tom McGuane and Jim Harrison) and I tell him about mine (Defoe and Smollett), but the interaction is slight, since I haven't read the works of his men and he hasn't read mine. By seven o'clock it is almost dark. McNaught goes for a stroll along the beach and then sits outside the tent listening to his radio. The sea sounds like an express train close at hand. I read by flashlight. Once every fifteen seconds the bright beam of Cape Lookout light sweeps around, briefly brightening the tent and printing the tent's shape on the sand in a fleeting, elongated burst of shadow.

Sunday comes gray, showery, the wind more in the east. Out at sea over the Gulf Stream the clouds are churned up and squally. It is nearly high tide when, a little after 7:30, McNaught and I—leaving all our gear at our campsite—set forth along the two miles to Cape Point, *sans* breakfast, complaining to one another about stiff muscles as we lift our feet out of the soft, loose sand of the upper beach. At 8:20 we reach the point. This is it: the southern end of the Outer Banks. A score of vehicles, and thirty or forty fishermen tethered to the surf. As at Cape Hatteras, the very tip of the point is a V on each side of which the waters foam in and collide in a seemingly regular demonstration, like the bow wave and quarter wave of a ship coming together and celebrating, clapping hands. McNaught and I celebrate our arrival at the terminus of our walk by sitting on an incipient dune, watching these dancing bursts of spray, and eating the last two bars of chocolate. I try to keep out of my mind thoughts of more orthodox Sunday-morning breakfasts: scrambled eggs, toast and marmalade, coffee. In the immediate future there is the walk back to our camp; the packing up of tent and gear; the portage to the ferry dock; mosquitoes; the ferry ride to Harkers Island and its mainland connection; and the drive to Davis in McNaught's pickup to retrieve the Alliance, at which point McNaught will set off for home in Winston-Salem with my thanks for his company, and I will, I think, drive down to Beaufort and for the night check into the best hotel in the old seaport town: a bath, a shave, a bed. Sand-free! But at the moment, looking out at the arrowhead of tumbling waters, turning up my face to a sprinkle of rain, I dig fingers and toes into the fine sand, anchoring myself to the Banks through this gritty contact and the memory-making power of sensation, however transient. Although the Banks end here, I don't want them to slip away.